High Sobriety

High Sobriety

CONFESSIONS OF A DRINKER

Alice King

First published in hardback in Great Britain in 2008 by
Orion Books
an imprint of the Orion Publishing Group Ltd
Orion House, 5 Upper St Martin's Lane,
London WC2H 9EA
An Hachette Livre UK Company

1 3 5 7 9 10 8 6 4 2

A CIP catalogue record for this book is available
from the British Library.

ISBN: 978 0 7528 8955 9

Printed in Great Britain by
Mackays of Chatham plc, Chatham, Kent

The Orion Publishing Group's policy is to use papers that are
natural, renewable and recyclable and made from wood grown in
sustainable forests. The logging and manufacturing processes are
expected to conform to the environmental regulations of the
country of origin.

www.orionbooks.co.uk
www.highsobriety.co.uk

CONTENTS

Foreword   13

PART ONE: THE FROTH OF DAYDREAMS   15

One: First Taste   17
Two: Too Big, Too Small   21
Three: Lunch With the Countess   28
Four: Vodka and Lime   34
Five: Smiling Angel   43
Six: Decanted   47
Seven: Learning Curve   50
Eight: Well Done, Girlie   56
Nine: Cupid's Bottle   61
Ten: Wedding Daze   68
Eleven: Liquid Sin   71
Twelve: Blind Tasting   75
Thirteen: Party at the Palace   78
Fourteen: Wine and Dandy   84

PART TWO: FALL FROM GRACE   89

Fifteen: Panic in Paradise   91
Sixteen: Concorde   95
Seventeen: Babies and Bottles   100
Eighteen: 'Great With' Wines   105
Nineteen: Whirly Pool   110
Twenty: Birth of a Magnum   115
Twenty-one: 'Only Another Tasting'   119

Twenty-two: Light-bulb Moment 128

Twenty-three: Fabulous Fizz Party 131

Twenty-four: The Morning After 141

Twenty-five: Lady by the Lake 145

Twenty-six: Even Old Wines Die 150

Twenty-seven: Life in the Fast Lane 159

Twenty-eight: Princess on the Loose 164

Twenty-nine: Nail Bomb 168

Thirty: Pick Me Up 173

Thirty-one: Sunday, Bloody Sunday 178

Thirty-two: Downsizing 182

Thirty-three: Blow Job 188

Thirty-four: Death of a King 195

Thirty-five: Cowboy Hat 199

Thirty-six: Liver Tests 203

Thirty-seven: Sting in the Tale 206

Thirty-eight: Vampire Lips 218

PART THREE: ONE DAY AT A TIME 223

Thirty-nine: Shadow Angel 225

Forty: Temptation 228

Forty-one: First AA Meeting 232

Forty-two: Mad Hatter's 240

Forty-three: High as a Kite 243

Forty-four: Crayfishing 246

Forty-five: Naked at the Book Club 249

Forty-six: Writing for the Good of My Soul 252

Forty-seven: One Step at a Time 258

Forty-eight: First Christmas 262

Forty-nine: First Anniversary 266

Fifty: Cross Words 270

Fifty-one: Sober Surfing 275

Fifty-two: Serenity Santa 278

Fifty-three: Forgiveness 281

Fifty-four: SAS   283

Fifty-five: Faulty Wiring   287

Fifty-six: Hangover From Hell   290

Fifty-seven: Snowdrops   293

Fifty-eight: Reading the Leaves   296

Fifty-nine: Three for a Girl   298

Acknowledgements   301

For my mother

THE SERENITY PRAYER

God grant me the serenity
To accept the things I cannot change;
Courage to change the things I can;
And wisdom to know the difference.

FOREWORD

When I was asked to write this, I wasn't sure quite what to say. One thing is for sure, I am proud of my mummy.

When I found out she was writing a book about alcohol and recovery, I thought it was a good idea, as it may help other people to understand what alcoholism does to you and all those around you. I know, because I was there when many of these events happened. It was bizarre when she came home some evenings, seemingly dizzy and floppy, loping around, slightly slurring from time to time – I wasn't quite sure why.

Sometimes she used to be, well, let's say 'unreliable', to put it mildly, at picking us up from our nursery. This was because we had to wait for her to find a driver (guess why *she* wasn't doing it) to come and collect us. Now, she is not as embarrassing to us in front of our friends' parents (notice the *as!*) at school. Today, she actually talks to them, instead of hanging around by the wall, trying not to fall over in her spiky red high heels, looking for her three kids.

That was a few years ago. Now, it seems like a miracle how she has changed her life. I am delighted to have our real mummy back; she spends much more time with us, her children. Now when we go out, and we do lots of the time, it's as far away from a pub as possible! She even went surfing with us – we were amazed when we saw her in the water!

I thought it was really cool when she started writing her column 'Sobering Up' for *The Times* – it made me feel very proud. Her recovery has not only made a big difference in our lives, we can see a huge improvement in her well-being and confidence. I'm very happy for her. Through watching Mummy recover, I can see she can still have fun without a drink; she will always love to taste, though, so today we blend all kinds of lush non-alcoholic cocktails.

In recovery, Mummy has become a much nicer, kinder and generous person!

Number Two son (age twelve)

PART ONE

*The Froth
of Daydreams*

FIRST TASTE

My first taste of champagne was at my christening, a golden drop from the tip of my mother's little finger. My second, frothier still, came via her milk. That was me – always up for seconds.

As far back as I can remember, I loved champagne. Those dancing bubbles are the froth of daydreams. In reality we weren't affluent enough to drink it on a regular basis, though my father conjured it up for every christening – and there were nine of us.

My father was a wine shipper. While my classmates would write lovingly of their pets, bringing photographs and bits of fluff for school projects, I was soaking the labels off wine bottles and teaching my friends how to differentiate between a Bordeaux and Burgundy bottle from its shape. I was clinking bottles in a bag on the school bus as young as seven. At Christmas, when the other children would take the teachers boxes of chocolates or flowers, I would take wine. This was in the 1960s, long before the advent of super-market wine. Wine was a luxury. That was me all over, from the very beginning – wanting to do something to be noticed, something bigger, better, more unusual. I always wanted to prove something. I don't know what.

I knew I was loved as a child, but I felt that somehow I was different, that I didn't fit in. The sixth child of nine, I felt too big to be one of the little ones and too small to be one of the big ones. In a tantrum, I once asked my mother, 'Why am I always the odd one out? Everyone else has someone to play with – what about me? I bet you didn't really want me, did you?'

She told me, 'Alice, when your father and I got married, we decided to start off with half a dozen children and see how it went from there. You were the last of the original six planned, so you are really special.'

But somehow I could never feel it.

At home, we jostled for position around a huge dining table. We often had friends over, so twenty or more for a meal was not unusual. My mother was (and still is) an extraordinary woman, not least in her capacity to turn out wholesome, delicious food from very little. We had to wait until our guests had a plateful before we started in case she had miscalculated.

Daddy was a stickler for table manners, but mealtimes were fun – instant cabaret with a full cast. Ever-taller stories were swapped and we competed to have the last laugh. Exaggeration was born out of the competition to be noticed. Towards the end of a meal, we became quiet, desperate to think up excuses as to why we didn't have to wash up – no mean feat for such a sizeable army.

There was an air of excitement when my parents had people round for dinner, often business associates of my father. Once, I pointed out to my father's boss that Daddy had a bigger car than he had. Ours was a Ford Zephyr, green with shiny chrome bumpers and a bench seat. He had a brand-new Jag. He just smiled at me.

We'd set the table with a crisp white damask tablecloth and starched napkins. I'd polish the silver candlesticks. We always had green candles, and to this day the smell of hot candle wax conjures up a feeling of anticipation. I'd pick flowers from the garden. Sweet peas were my favourite, with their intoxicating, heady aroma and vibrant colours. The house would be full of exotic scents – the rich, sweet smell of reduced red wine and garlic mingled with herbs. Sometimes I'd be the waitress. I would swell with pride, feeling wanted and important.

My mother would look so glamorous, every so often in a new homemade dress, with her cleavage on show, her hair newly set and lipstick on. I yearned to be part of this sophisticated, secret adult world. I would listen to the grown-ups from the kitchen – their conversation, the merriment, the laughter.

I loved the ritual surrounding wine. I'd watch with wonder as my father carefully opened a bottle, sniffed the cork and decanted the claret over a candle. 'Look, Daddy!' I'd exclaim. 'You've got sentiment in your wine!'

I counted the number of different-shaped glasses at every place setting. My favourites were the fine German wine glasses, made of the thinnest glass and engraved with stars. They made the most exquisite ringing if you tapped them gently with a spoon. Daddy could make them sing. We'd watch entranced as he ran his finger round the top of a glass, and listen to the beautiful note.

My first taste memory is of a wine served in one such glass. I can still picture the tall, green bottle and the indecipherable Gothic script on the label. My reward for polishing the candlesticks was the little black cat attached to the bottleneck on a loop of stretchy gold thread. I treasured my prize, but I was even more excited when my father gave me a tiny taste of Schwartz Katz, a German Riesling, in one of those singing, starry glasses. None of my siblings was around and I felt special, chosen and different.

I can recall the heady rush and the warming sensation as this oily nectar trickled down my throat. Daddy asked me to describe it. 'Pineapples, butterscotch sauce and lemons,' I pronounced. He was impressed, I could tell.

And I was smitten. One taste instantly transported me, as

if on a flying carpet, to a faraway fantasy world of princesses, castles, jewels and attendants – all a far cry from the banality of living with eight brothers and sisters.

CHAPTER TWO

TOO BIG, TOO SMALL

I was eight years old and on my first trip to France. Mummy had bought all nine of us matching red, white and blue striped towelling jumpers from Bonds in Norwich. I was on the deck of the ferry with a sister or two, duly uniformed, when two other siblings – a couple of the boys – went by.

Two old ladies walked past. 'Look! There's another one!' said one to her friend.

'No . . . we've seen that one before. But *she*'s a different one, I think,' the other replied, looking me up and down. They thought we were from a children's home.

We were staying near the village of Montfort l'Amory, north of Paris, invited there by Pascal, a French boy who had been to stay with us to learn English. He was related to one of the Little Sisters of the Assumption, the local order of nuns, who used to come and look after us when Mummy had another baby.

Pascal was tall, with dark hair and olive skin. He had a different smell about him to that of my brothers – musty, leathery, bookish somehow, like an old library. He had a kind, melancholic smile and was very quiet. I used to chat to him while he was mending my bike. He didn't interrupt me, like my brothers did. It never occurred to me that he couldn't understand me.

He had already been to our house two summer holidays running when his mother had invited us to stay at his family's summer château. We were amazed when we drew up outside. It was enormous – red brick with sixteen huge windows, all with shutters. The older boys slept there, while the little ones, our parents and I stayed in a cottage in the grounds. On our first night I found it hard to sleep. Over-excited yet tired, I wanted it to be morning. I kept complaining about the strange, damp, hay-like smell of the bed.

'It's probably just horsehair,' Mummy said. 'Now go to sleep – we've driven hundreds of miles today and we're all exhausted.'

'This pillow is hard and lumpy,' I said.

'It's not a pillow, it's a bolster, and if it's uncomfortable, throw it on the floor,' she replied wearily.

Next morning we made our first expedition into the village boulangerie. I went with my eldest (and favourite) brother in my new holiday dress – orange nylon with a kipper tie. On our way down to the village, I was amazed at how everyone we passed said '*Bonjour*', even an old man on a bicycle.

'Why do they say hello when they don't even know us?' I asked my brother.

'Because they're French,' he replied.

We arrived at the boulangerie, drawn by the scent of freshly baked bread. People walked past me clutching what looked like polished sticks of wood. We waited in the queue. I held on to my brother's hand, baffled by the incomprehensible babble around me.

'*Vingt-deux croissants, s'il vous plaît*,' my brother said. Twenty-two croissants, please.

'*Vingt-deux? Vraiment?*' asked the baker, looking incredulous. Twenty-two? Are you sure?

My brother nodded and handed over the funny-looking money. He bought me a packet of fruit-flavoured chewing gum with the change. It was French and exciting and utterly, utterly wonderful.

We returned to the cottage, where everyone was sitting

expectantly round the table. Hands grabbed at the bags and then there was silence. Within seconds all twenty-two croissants were gone, leaving a trail of flakes across the kitchen table and floor.

After breakfast Daddy announced he was taking my elder siblings exploring. 'Can I come with you?' I asked.

'No,' he said. 'You're too little, it's a long walk, and you'll get too tired. Once we've explored, we'll take you another day, when we can go part of the way in the car.'

'It's not fair!' I wailed, but he was gone. I tried to appeal to Mummy: 'It's not fair!'

'Alice,' she said, 'life is not fair. And the sooner you learn that, the better. Go and play with your other brothers and sisters. Look, they're playing football. Join in.'

'But—'

'That's enough! Now go!' She pointed to the door.

I stalked out, slamming the door behind me. I'll show them, I thought. I *will* go – I'll go somewhere and then they'll be sorry. I walked out of the gate and stomped off down the road. I wished I were one of twins – then there would always be someone on hand of my own age. Indignant tears trickled down my face. I could taste the saltiness. An old man passed by on his bike. He had gnarled, wrinkled skin, like tree bark. '*Bonjour!*' he shouted cheerily, and waved. I put my head down and ignored him. It was *not* a good morning.

I had a one-franc piece in my pocket. I resolved to go back to the boulangerie and buy myself a packet of that wonderful chewing gum. I turned round to see if anyone was following me. No, it looked as if I was alone.

As I entered the village, I saw the old man who had greeted me earlier sitting in a café chatting with another man. Each had a steaming cup of coffee and a glass. One glass I recognised as a brandy balloon – we had some at home. It was half full with an amber liquid. The other was a long, tall glass with the word 'Ricard' on the side. It was filled with ice and a cloudy, pale-yellow liquid. What a strange lot they are, drinking before lunch, I thought.

I noticed the *boucherie* on the other side of the square and crossed over to look in the window. I couldn't work out what the furry creatures hanging there were. Their eyes stared out at me blankly. I suddenly realised they were rabbits, and shuddered. Who would eat a rabbit? My friend at school had one, called Benjamin. I must send her a postcard, I thought. 'The French eat rabbits!'

I walked back across the square, past the old men, who smiled and waved. I was momentarily disorientated, but was then relieved to see the orange awning of the boulangerie. One lonely baguette was left on the shelf, alongside a single large apricot tart, shiny with glaze. I entered, chose my chewing gum, handed over the franc and left the shop, contemplating the gum's strange synthetic taste, which was reminiscent of the orange and pineapple flavoured squash back home.

I looked around me. There were two roads leading out of the square and I hesitated, unsure which to take. Had I passed the *tabac* on my way? I walked up the road. None of the shops looked familiar. There was a boutique with a lime-green wraparound dress in the window. The mannequin had a sinister leer on its face. My chest began to feel tight. What if I couldn't find my way home? Who would know where I was? Would I end up strung up like the rabbits in the butcher's shop?

Retracing my steps to the corner of the square, I started up the other road. Beads of sweat trickled down my forehead, and the palms of my hands grew clammy. I wiped them on my kipper tie and felt my heart beating faster. Nobody knows where I am, or that I've even gone, I thought. I gulped and realised with alarm I had swallowed my gum. I hoped I wouldn't choke. I opened two more pieces and stuffed them in my mouth.

The shops had petered out and I was walking past houses now. I saw a plump woman mopping a floor one-handed while balancing a blond, chubby toddler on her hip. He looked a bit like my youngest brother. I felt a tear trickle down my cheek.

I kept walking and eventually came full circle and passed the two old men at the café again. Their glasses were empty and they were standing up to leave. By this time tears were streaming down my face, their salty flavour making the chewing gum taste sour and soapy. The old men walked towards me. I knew I shouldn't talk to strangers, but in any event I couldn't speak French. They gabbled at me. One smiled and winked.

'I'm lost!' I wailed in English. 'I can't find the right road. I'm lost!'

Frowning, they started talking to the waiter. He was dressed in tight black trousers and a white short-sleeved shirt. He had dark hair and a moustache. All three started gesticulating.

'What you name?' the waiter asked in broken English.

'Alice,' I whimpered. 'Aleeze,' I tried again, in an effort to sound French.

They were pointing at a house across the square. I shook my head. Did they think I lived there?

'You come,' said one of the two elderly men.

I followed at a distance. Where were they taking me? We stopped in front of a red-brick house with a large wooden door and the word 'Gendarmerie' carved in stone above it. They disappeared inside.

I stood outside the door, unsure of myself. It opened and two younger men came out. I realised from their uniforms and peaked caps that they were policemen. One had a gun in a leather holster. I couldn't take my eyes off it. The gendarme carrying it had deep creases in his forehead when he frowned. The gendarmes beckoned me inside. I sat on a wooden chair, looked at the bars on the window, opened my mouth and howled. They stepped back, shocked, and huddled together, talking incomprehensibly.

'Do you speak English?' I finally managed to stutter.

They shook their heads. One scrabbled around in a desk drawer and drew out a small pocket dictionary. I kept looking out through the bars on the window, hoping that every shadow was Mummy or Daddy, here to rescue me.

One of the gendarmes gave me a boiled sweet. It was red and hard and cherry-flavoured, like the cough mixture I'd had the last time I had flu. The other was writing something on a piece of paper. He handed it to me. 'We you wish help,' it said. I nodded, relieved I wasn't in trouble with them. But what were Mummy and Daddy going to say about me running away?

I was handed a tissue and I wiped my eyes. They gave me another sweet, an orange one. It tasted like Mummy's marmalade. They looked at me and smiled. How strange it was that we could both speak yet not understand each other. I was really worried now. What if I was still here when it was dark? Nobody knew where I was. Mummy probably thought I was with Daddy and vice versa.

The phone rang. There was more gabbling and waving of hands. One gendarme was smiling and pointing at me. He disappeared out through the door.

A bluebottle was buzzing, trapped at the window. I watched it crash into the window again and again. I began to count the times it flew in and out of the bars. I was up to twenty-two when the door opened. The returning gendarme handed me an enormous ice cream, complete with a chocolate flake. What a treat! I licked carefully round the chocolate, smoothing out the furrows in the ice cream and thinking how envious my brothers and sisters would be when I told them.

The door opened again and I saw the curly hair of Pascal

– closely followed by Daddy. I leapt up – holding on to my ice cream – and ran towards them, laughing. My father squeezed me so hard I thought I would burst. 'Daddy, be careful of my ice cream!'

Outside, I could see one of my younger brothers sitting in the back of the car. I ran out of the door and waved my ice cream at him.

'That's not fair!' he said. 'You run away and you get an ice cream. I want one. It's not fair!'

'Life's not fair,' I told him. 'And the sooner you learn that, the better.'

CHAPTER THREE

LUNCH WITH THE COUNTESS

Many of our family holidays were spent in France, thanks to my father's job. One year, when I was about ten, a cognac supplier invited us to lunch. And not any old cognac supplier. This was a real countess.

The Ford Zephyr had gone by now and we had a Citroën DS. I loved our frog-eyed car, which would mysteriously rise up from the ground when the engine started – high suspension meant high drama to me.

That summer all eleven of us piled into our Citroën DS and set off for France. Occasionally we would turn from a junction and Daddy would set off on the left-hand side of the road. '*Roule à droite, Papa!*' we'd chorus from the back. Drive on the right, Daddy! I noticed that Mummy would often close her eyes when this happened.

After forty-five minutes we arrived at the château. The intricate, curly, gold gates looked like the entrance to Heaven.

'Are they real gold, do you think?' I asked.

'Yeah, sure, pure gold – eighteen carat, no less,' sniggered a brother.

I was never sure whether he was being serious or not. I guessed by the others' derisive laughter he was probably joking. But how was I to know? If I was a countess and money was no object, I'd have solid-gold gates. Why not?

The gates opened, seemingly of their own accord, and we drove up the gravelled drive. The château was a real fairy castle, Gothic with four turrets. I found myself holding my breath. A small woman, dressed all in black, opened the door.

'Doesn't look much like a countess to me,' muttered a brother.

I didn't know. Having never seen a countess before, I had no idea what one should look like.

'That's because she's a servant,' said another.

I nodded. Yes, that must be right. A maid. I had never seen a maid before either.

Another woman emerged from the door behind the servant. She was petite, bird-like. I squinted and pressed my nose against the window. My eyes were dazzled.

'Wow, look at those rocks!' said one of my sisters. 'They must be real diamonds in her earrings.'

The countess shook each of our hands in turn, even crouching down for the little ones.

'*Bonjour*,' I said. '*Je m'appelle Alice*.'

She smiled and answered. I didn't understand what she was saying, but I loved her sing-song voice. She sounded like my musical jewellery box at home.

We were shown into the salon, a huge room with faded velvet drapes and a large, dark, cracked oil painting of a girl and a dog. The girl in the picture looked the same age as me and was of similar colouring. Her blonde hair fell in perfect ringlets about her face. I felt the back of my own hair. It had been cut short – 'easier for summer' – only the week before. It had been my idea, but I had left the hairdresser's in tears, gazing forlornly at the six inches of my life strewn on the floor.

I wandered around the room and spotted a chaise longue, not unlike one we had at home. This one was smaller and more ornate, with a carved end. I noted with surprise that the gold brocade was faded and slightly threadbare. Ours at home was upholstered in brown Draylon – altogether much smarter. I spotted a delicate, button-back, padded leather chair, child-size, by the open French windows. I headed straight for it and got into a tussle with an equally determined younger brother. 'I saw it first,' I hissed at him.

'Alice,' Mummy said, 'come here.' I walked over and sat down sulkily on the tatty chaise longue. It was extraordinarily uncomfortable.

Another servant appeared, a dark-haired man, even older than Daddy, with a sunken, lined face like a walnut whip. He wore a white jacket, a black bow tie and white gloves. He was carrying an ornate silver salver with a magnum of champagne and several small, engraved champagne flutes.

I was surprised and delighted when he handed me the most exquisite glass I'd ever held, etched with a coat of arms bearing what looked like a fleur-de-lis and a crescent moon. I watched the dancing bubbles catching the sunlight. I felt like Princess Alice. I wondered if the countess drank champagne every day.

My tiny taste of fizz disappeared almost immediately. There was something thrilling about the tingle I felt throughout my whole body as the prickly bubbles hit the top of my mouth and the back of my throat – quite different from the orange Corona I was used to. I realised I was holding out my empty glass at right angles. Mummy shot me a warning look.

'Why don't you go off and explore with the boys?' she suggested. 'And help yourself to water. There's a bottle and some tumblers over there.'

Fancy being rich enough to buy water in a bottle rather than simply get it from the tap!

Reluctantly, I acted out draining my already-empty champagne flute in exaggerated fashion, helped myself to a glass of water and skipped off through the French windows on to the lawn. I felt curiously light-headed, as if sparklers were going off in my brain. I nearly missed my step as I followed the boys' shrieks. I sat down on the grass and began to make a daisy chain. Marrying a count was obviously the thing to do. I could drink champagne, have water from a bottle and drip with diamonds every day.

Daddy wandered out into the garden. '*A table!*' he announced. Dinner's ready! We traipsed in through the salon into the dining room. I noticed that Mummy had relaxed. Her cheeks were glowing like two ripe peaches.

The enormous round table was dressed in crisp white damask, like we had at home for best, with two ornate silver candelabras and pale-pink candles the colour of the foxgloves at the bottom of our garden. In the centre was a posy of roses, streaked pink and white like raspberry-ripple ice cream, with an exquisite aroma that reminded me of Fry's Turkish delight. Each place setting not only had four glasses but a bewildering array of cutlery, including something that looked like a spoon someone had jumped on and flattened. We each had individual name cards. This was truly impressive. 'Alice' was written out in swirly calligraphy with a curly flourish underneath. I altered my title in my head. 'Countess Alice' sounded more unusual, more arresting somehow, than my previous aspiration of 'Princess Alice'.

We held our breath before the starter arrived. What would we do if it was snails, or frog's legs, or even that liver pâté the French seemed so fond of? We needn't have fretted. The manservant walked in with a platter piled high with asparagus. We were familiar with this, as we had two asparagus patches in the garden at home. Every June saw us eating asparagus hot with melted butter – we used the sticks to write our names in dripping butter across our plates – or cold in salads and sandwiches. I distinctly remember eating an asparagus sandwich with Branston pickle.

This asparagus was different, though. It was white and juicy and quite the bigger, plumper brother to the pencil-thin green sticks at home. And we were all surprised that it was served cold. Was the kitchen so far away? Mummy always managed to put our food hot on the table, however many people were round. Not only was today's asparagus cold, it was served with a creamy sort of salad cream I had never tasted before, something called 'mayonnaise'. The combination was delicious.

The next course looked less familiar – '*canard*', whatever that was.

'Don't worry, Alice, it's just like chicken,' Mummy said.

'Yes, but what *is* it?' I pestered. 'Tell me!'

'It's duck. Now just eat it and stop causing a fuss.'

The meat was much darker than chicken, a red-brown colour. I waited for the potatoes, but after five minutes, when nothing had appeared, I tentatively put a tiny bit in my mouth and swallowed it quickly. It was stringy with a slightly bitter flavour. Picking up a piece of bread from the table – I thought it odd they had no side plates – I covered the remains of the meat up with it and put my knife and fork together.

The manservant was solemnly circling the table, pouring red wine from a decanter. Daddy was gesturing to him to pour us each an inch or so. I could see that this wine was not in fact red, more an orangey colour, like the colour of the bricks on our new extension at home.

'Ah, Château Montrose 1893,' murmured the countess, sounding out the years in that sing-song voice. '*Une bonne année, je crois.*' A good vintage, I believe.

I knew this was amazingly special, to be served such an old wine, but it was difficult not to giggle as, round the table, I could see my elder brothers and sisters mimicking my father's wine-tasting antics just as we did back home at Sunday lunch. I closed my eyes, composed myself, pursed my lips and took a big sniff. The smell was curiously sweet, like strawberries melted in Bourneville.

The taste gave me a stab of guilt – I had once eaten a bar

of Bourneville someone had bought for my mother. She didn't find out, but I never felt the same about plain chocolate again. I looked over at Mummy and saw her in animated conversation. She glanced across at me and smiled. I hoped she couldn't read my mind.

When I tasted the wine, the flavour exploded on my tongue. It was like a velvety, liquid jam – a mixture of black cherry, raspberry and strawberry – mingled with cinnamon and cocoa. I retrieved the bit of duck on my plate from beneath the bread and washed it down with the wine. The meat didn't taste so bitter now – it was delicious, in fact, leaving me with a tangy, sweet-sour taste in my mouth. I wanted more.

I drained my glass and looked around in triumph. Wait until I told them at school that not only had I been invited to lunch with a real-life countess, but I had drunk a seventy-eight-year-old wine! I realised that the countess was looking in my direction and speaking.

'She's asking what you think of the wine,' Daddy said.

What should I say?

'*Encore une bouteille!*' I blurted out. Another bottle!

There was total silence. Mummy's eyes had widened in horror. I held my breath.

Madame La Comtesse laughed. She raised her hand and signalled to her manservant. 'Henri, *vous avez entendu la gamine – encore une bouteille!*' she said. Henry, you heard the little one – another bottle!

CHAPTER FOUR

VODKA AND LIME

Green-gold glycerine coats the inside of my glass, making it opaque, like oil on water. My mouth puckers and my tongue curls as my brain registers the flavour in my mouth – like Rose's lime marmalade with a kick, I decide. This luscious liquid slips down my throat and I experience an instant, breath-snatching sensation in my chest.

I like it. My eyes water. I take another gulp to see if the sensation is the same. It is, only intensified, and suddenly I feel an important part of the secret adult world. I feel grown-up. Each further gulp drowns the butterflies in my stomach. My confidence soars and I feel taller.

'I see you like vodka and lime,' says my friend Gina. 'That's what I drink too.'

I nod, trying to look nonchalant, and crunch an ice cube. I don't admit that I'd no clue what to ask for at the bar and only ordered vodka and lime because I heard her doing so. I'd simply nodded when the barman had asked, 'Large one?' It didn't look that large to me: the vodka barely covered the ice.

Gina goes to gymnastics. She has a tumbling routine ending in a graceful, high back flip. She is petite, with naturally corkscrew-curled dark hair – everything I am not. Try as I might, I can't get my liquid eyeliner to flick up at the corner of my eyes like hers does. We get on well, even though, at eighteen, she is four years older than me.

34

I hear a shout. Another friend – Nicci. 'Hey, Al, want another drink? Same again?' I nod.

I have been badgering my mother for ages to be allowed to come to a Young Farmers' Dance. Finally she has relented, providing I come with one of my elder brothers. My major concern has been what to wear. After changing outfits several times, I settled on my new stack-heel, over-the-knee, tan leather boots – a fourteenth-birthday present – checked shirt and a string of amber beads I have slung jauntily over one shoulder. One look at Nicci fills me with dismay. She is dressed in fitted straight-leg jeans with a thin blue belt and a striped red and white linen shirt with the collar turned up. She has straight brown hair cut like a beret – short on one side, long on the other. She gets it done free every month by the trainees at Spears, the trendy hairdressing salon in Oxford. We had recently all moved from Norfolk to Chipping Norton in the Cotswolds.

Nicci, too, is older than me, by two years, and goes to school in Woodstock, making her more exotic than my classmates. She lives alone with her mother, an architect, who is often away, so her home is a welcome refuge from all the chaos at mine. Nicci, however, seems to prefer coming over to my house.

'You are so lucky to have all those brothers and sisters,' she always says.

'I doubt you would think that if you lived here,' I reply every time. 'And the washing-up is awful. You are so lucky, having a dishwasher.'

She is confident and seems to attract boys with no effort. As she hands me a drink, a tall guy with dark-blond curly hair taps her on the shoulder. 'Hey, Nicci, how are you? Want a drink?'

She throws her head back and drains her glass. Only then does she smile, apparently coyly, and reply, 'I'd love one – large whisky and lemonade, please.'

Whisky. I shudder. I cannot bear the smell or the taste. I once helped myself to my father's Glenfiddich. The sour, malt flavour made me gag and I nearly spat the mouthful straight back into the bottle.

I shift from foot to foot, uncomfortable. Nicci whispers something into the boy's ear. He turns to a smaller guy standing next to him at the bar. 'Hey, Noddy, why don't you buy Nicci's friend a drink?'

'OK. What do you want? Aren't you Edmund's sister? Alice, isn't it?'

'Yes, that's right. Thanks. I'll have a large vodka and lime, please.' I follow Nicci's example and down the drink in my hand. My eyes water. I smile and cough to cover up the tightening in my chest.

We take our drinks and stand by the dance floor. Strobe lights flicker and the disco is playing 'Le Freak' thuddingly loud. Two girls I vaguely know from school, fifth-formers, are dancing.

'That's what I'll be doing – freaking out,' I tell Nicci. 'I can't imagine dancing in front of all these people.'

'Don't worry – you'll be fine, especially after a few more of those,' she says, pointing at my glass. 'Look, you give me the money and I'll go and get two more. They mightn't serve you.'

She disappears and after a while I notice Noddy at my side. 'Do you want a cigarette?' he asks, holding out a packet of Benson & Hedges.

'No, thanks. I don't smoke.' My experiment with a packet of Piccadilly at the end of the garden with a friend had not been successful. 'But I do drink!' I laugh and empty the glass Nicci has just handed me, which seems to be the way it's done.

The two fifth-formers on the dance floor have stopped dancing and are looking at me. Being seen talking to Noddy gives me cred – he's in the band that's playing later.

'You want to be careful – we like people dancing when we're playing, not falling over,' he says. 'Don't you get a headache when you drink like that?'

'Oh, no,' I say dismissively, 'though I do need to find the loo.'

I am hot, queasy and my head feels foggy. I haven't eaten much tea – too excited – so I can't understand why I feel sick and disorientated. Nicci has disappeared, but I spy Gina.

'Hey, Gina, where's the loo?' I ask.

'Are you all right?' she asks. 'You look white. Here, come with me. You look like you're having difficulty walking.'

'Yeah, it's my new boots – they're quite high, you know.'

She raises a finely plucked eyebrow. 'I think you're a bit drunk. You want to take it steady.'

Gratefully, I open the loo door and plonk myself down on the seat. The fluorescent overhead light seems to be moving. I close my eyes and feel like I'm spinning. I open my eyes again and cling on to the toilet-roll holder, staring at the back of the door. The graffiti seems to be alive, moving. Closing one eye, I focus. 'Shaz luvs Steve.'

'You all right in there?' comes Gina's voice.

'Yes,' I reply, struggling with my tights. I open the door.

'You're just a bit tipsy,' says Gina.

'I can't be – I've only had a few drinks.'

'How many?'

'Only three or four, I think.'

'You twit. They were large ones. You're doing well to be standing. Come on, let's go dancing – the band's started playing. That'll sober you up.'

I follow her to the dance floor. I have practised my moves many times in my bedroom mirror. I look around for my drink, forgetting that I had already downed it, and pick up a glass. I've swallowed most of it when I realise it tastes completely different – flowery, almost soapy, perfumed. It must be someone else's, but it gives me a boost and after a few minutes I feel good. I can't believe I'm doing this. The two fifth-formers are watching. I wonder what they think of my dancing. I reckon I'm pretty cool, jiving and mouthing the words to the Eagles song. Noddy waves at me from the stage. More cred. I nearly slip over and just manage to steady myself on a chair.

'Someone must have spilt their drink,' I mumble to no one in particular, as I sit down and empty the glass in front of me.

My brother walks across the dance floor. 'We're going in a minute. John is going to give us a lift. Best if you come with me, then we don't have to ring home. See you outside.'

I looked around for Nicci. She's nowhere to be seen. I feel thirsty and I need some air. I stand up, stagger and grab on to my brother's arm.

'You OK? How much did you have to drink? You better not let Mummy see you falling around – she'll go mad.'

I sit in the back of the car and several of my brother's friends pile in. John has borrowed his mother's blue Morris Traveller. Leaning my head against the cold, wet window, I feel tired and ill. Maybe I'm sickening for something. I can't be drunk. Surely you had to drink more than this to be drunk? Besides, the vodka didn't taste very strong.

It is only five miles home but it seems to be taking for ever. I close my eyes and open them again as it makes me feel more giddy still. Please, God, don't let me be sick in the car, I pray silently. I swallow hard.

The car suddenly swerves to the left, then to the right. Everything shudders into slow motion. I hear a screech of brakes. The car is turning over. My face is pressed against the window, harder and harder. This isn't happening. This can't be happening. The car finally comes to a halt and I am wedged in my seat upside down. There's an eerie silence and a strange acrid smell.

My brother is at the window now. 'Hurry up! Get out of

the car before it sets alight!' He yanks open the door and pulls me out. The others in the car pile out after me.

I'm confused. 'How come you were outside?' I ask my brother.

'I was thrown out of the back doors before the car turned over.'

I feel my stomach cramp. The next thing I know I'm leaning over, vomiting in the road, acid bile rising from my stomach. Rose's lime marmalade with diced carrots. How do they get into everything? I heave again. Definitely too much lime in my drink – too much bloody lime.

A car stops and someone wraps me in a blanket. I am still retching. 'Must be the shock, poor thing,' someone says.

The police arrive, blue lights flashing. Rather like the disco, I think. I wonder if Noddy has got off with anyone. John's mother arrives, takes one look at her crumpled upside-down car and throws up. Has she been drinking vodka too?

Sometime later I open my eyes and see my mother looking at me. My head is throbbing and my throat is sore.

'How are you?' she asks.

'Awful. How did I get home? I don't remember getting home. Did I bang my head?'

She pokes around in my hair. 'I can't see anything. You were all incredibly lucky. All eight of you could have been killed. It's no wonder you feel dazed and shaky. Perhaps you blacked out.'

'Was I talking when I got home?'

'Nineteen to the dozen – mainly slurred gibberish. I held your toes to calm you down, like I used to when you were a baby. You don't remember, do you?'

'No. Must have been the shock, like you said.'

But my mind tells me something different.

When we had first moved from Norfolk to Chipping Norton, we were the source of much curiosity – a family of nine children who had moved into a former convent, Mary-croft, on the edge of town. My parents couldn't initially afford the asking price of this rambling, run-down house, but after my mother had talked to the nuns, and they had seen her traipsing in and out with all of us, I think they felt sorry for her and sold it to us at a knock-down price. No doubt it helped that we were Roman Catholics.

Much of my early summers were spent at the open-air swimming pool. Various local girls would say, 'I likes your brother' – whichever one happened to be around – and were even more impressed to discover I had five of them.

Up to this stage I wasn't that comfortable at school. I was clever enough, but somehow uneasy. We didn't have accents, on account of my mother being a speech and drama teacher, so without the broad local burr were seen to be posh. Fortunately, such potential for bullying evaporated when my three elder brothers appeared. The fact that they were all at boarding school made them more of a novelty to those at the local comprehensive, which is where I went. It is difficult to appreciate (or even acknowledge) good looks in your own brothers, but the number of comments and phone calls from giggling girls made me realise what an asset they were. I had a steady stream of girlfriends, including some, like Gina and Nicci, a good bit older than me, who were eager not only to get a look inside our house but to spend time in such hallowed male company.

We had no TV – a source of great embarrassment for me, but rarely commented on or even noticed by my friends. They marvelled at the size of our dining table and loved to be part of our chaotic, fun family meals. An old croquet set my mother had bought at an auction brought out the competitiveness in us all, though I was never sure whether it was the croquet that attracted my friends or the chance of getting close to the boys.

Life changed for me when at fifteen I was voted 'best bum

of 1976' by the boys in my year. Suddenly I had a choice of suitors. My first real boyfriend – 'Mr Boyfriend', my brothers nicknamed him – was older then me, old enough to drive. He had a silver Ford Escort. At the weekends we would go shopping in Oxford or even Cheltenham. He lavished gifts on me – expensive grey culottes for school, an emerald-chip ring and a silver puzzle ring. The kudos of going out with someone older meant respect from the rougher girls at school.

Mr Boyfriend was kind, gentle and neat. He wore Levi's with creases down the front, and expensive shirts with the collars turned up. Every month he had his spiky hair trimmed at Spears. He was interested in me, and I had his undivided attention – not something I was used to. I was intoxicated.

We often went out for meals, where I would browse confidently through the wine list, choose and order the wine. I saw nothing unusual in this, having been around wine since childhood.

In one restaurant – the Shaven Crown at Shipton-under-Wychwood – I sent the Sancerre back because it smelt mouldy. 'This wine is corked,' I told the waiter.

He looked at me, hesitated and disappeared. A few moments later he reappeared with the restaurant owner. I held my glass out defiantly. Mr Boyfriend was squirming in his chair. The owner took the glass from me, sniffed at it pretentiously, then sniffed again. 'You are absolutely right, madam,' he said. 'I'll bring you another bottle straight away.'

This recognition of my prowess delighted and amazed me. Perhaps I had a super-sensitive sense of smell. I knew there weren't many fifteen-year-olds who would recognise a corked wine. I loved this feeling of superiority, of possessing a knowledge that was out of the ordinary, an inbuilt talent that made me special. I couldn't wait to get home to tell my father.

From then on Mr Boyfriend would jokingly call me 'Madam'. That was until, unkindly, I decided he was too boring for me – too nice, too kind, too reliable. I wanted someone more exciting, more dynamic. I didn't want to play safe. I dumped him. He cried.

Yes, 'Madam' was a fine description.

CHAPTER FIVE

SMILING ANGEL

Occasionally I used to accompany my father on business trips to France, ostensibly to practise for my French A level. One particularly memorable trip was to Heidsieck Monopole's cellars in Reims, the heart of the Champagne region.

We had lunch at the Moulin de Verzenay, the company-owned windmill majestically set among the acres of vines of the Montagne de Reims. Our hostess was Lucy, an Englishwoman with pale, almost white skin. Her eyelashes were invisible under a head of auburn hair, cut in a bob. She was striking-looking – she had presence and dressed with the precision and flair of the French in a fitted pencil-line skirt, silk blouse and high-heeled court shoes. I wore a lilac linen shift dress I'd made for the trip – I was good at dressmaking – teamed with maroon strappy suede sandals. I was mesmerised by Lucy's ability to flick between languages, and in awe of the easy confidence with which she talked.

Taken aback by the number of glasses at each place setting, I watched her to determine whether I was meant simply to taste the champagnes or drink them. Judging by her empty glasses, I concluded that drinking them was the answer.

Initially I was tongue-tied, hesitating to practise my faltering French, but after the first two glasses of vintage rosé I found the words flowing, able to join in with the conversation, even joke in French. I began to enjoy myself. Lucy asked me what I would like to do when I left school. 'The same as you, if you get to drink wines like this every day,' I said.

We had been served a mystery champagne with a pudding of *tarte aux pommes*. Lucy asked us to guess which vintage it was. My father had warned me this might happen but reassured me it was just for fun, not to be taken too seriously. He had also briefed me on vintage champagne, explaining that vintages were only declared in the best years; 1970, 1971 and 1973 being the top recent vintages. The only decent harvests in the 1960s were 1961, 1964 and 1966.

The sun had caught the champagne in my glass, casting a hypnotic shadow of dancing bubbles across the table. By this stage I had drunk at least four glasses and my mind was buzzing, high on adrenaline and the drama of the occasion. I mused how lucky I was to be sitting drinking wines like this on a Monday when I should have been at school. I couldn't wait to tell my friends back home. Eavesdropping on the conversation around the table, I deduced that this was a wine from the *les soixantes* – the 1960s.

'So, Alice,' said Lucy, 'which vintage do you think it is?'

I looked at the wine and tasted it again. It had a delicious bitter-sweet, hazelnut and pear flavour. What years had Daddy said they declared vintages in the 1960s? My brain was beginning to feel a bit fuzzy. The only one I could remember for sure was 1961, the year I was born. Looking Lucy in the eye, I replied, '*Soixante-et-une, je crois.*' I think it's 1961.

She looked at me and smiled. 'It is indeed. Well done. That definitely calls for another bottle,' she said, clicking her fingers at the waiter.

Daddy looked across the table and beamed at me.

I had been joking (or half joking) when I told Lucy I wanted her job, but in the strange way these things go, little more than a year later I had it, or close to it. At eighteen, on leaving school, I was escorting visitors and tourists around Heid-siek Monopole's cellars, which were hidden deep in the rock below Reims.

There are thousands of kilometres of Gallo-Roman cellars hewn out of the chalk seam that underlies the Champagne region of northern France – Heidsieck Monopole alone had twelve kilometres of tunnels. I traipsed around all of them, trying to commit the route to memory. Every passageway looked identical, with thousands upon thousands of prone champagne bottles. My predecessor had devised a system of arrows for me to follow, but the walls were so damp and crumbly that the arrows all but disappeared in a day or so. I have never had any sense of direction and I experienced a few scary moments, stuck in the dark with only a torch. Still, I wouldn't die of thirst, I reflected.

At first I was a little lonely and missed my brothers and sisters, but as I settled into the job and was able to find my way around and answer visitors' questions with growing confidence, my homesickness abated. I began to appreciate my incredible luck.

Most mornings at eight o'clock saw me in the tasting room with the chief winemaker, Monsieur Simon, tasting the fifty different wines, or *crus*, that would be blended to make that year's vintage. '*Tu goûtes comme un roi*, Alice, *comme un roi, vraiment!*' he would say. Truly, you taste like a king, Alice, like a king! Although I realised he was making a play on my surname, there was a part of my normally self-doubting brain that believed him.

I took to visiting the Gothic cathedral most days after work – or, more accurately, the bar opposite. There is some-thing deliciously wicked about drinking in the shadow of a cathedral, both calming and naughty. I would sit writing my journal, a glass to hand, glancing up at the famous *Sourire de Reims*, the smiling angel that adorns the cathedral entrance. She is no ordinary angel. Her smile is anything but angelic –

more a mischievous grin. It is impossible to look at her face and not smile. She is raising her right hand, as if calling for another glass of champagne, I decided. 'Just the kind of guardian angel I need,' I wrote in my journal.

One afternoon a tall, blond man interrupted my writing. It was one of the Dutch tourists I had been showing around the cellars that afternoon. 'Excuse me,' he said, 'you remind me of the *Sourire de Reims*. Do you always smile like that when drinking champagne?'

'Always.'

CHAPTER SIX

Decanted

Drinking champagne for a living was a decadent way to spend my summer holidays, but all too soon it was time to return to take up my college course. Disappointing A-level results meant I didn't secure a place at university – instead I returned to the UK to study at the London College of Fashion. I was fascinated by textiles and loved to write, so I decided to pursue a career in fashion journalism.

I was not eligible for a grant, so, taking advantage of my mother's sewing machine, I set up a business making cotton sweatshirts. I would buy roll-ends of fabric for 50p from the market. Each sweatshirt took thirty minutes to make and I sold them for £5. In my usual all-or-nothing way, I worked night and day. In four months I had accumulated enough to pay my fees and live in London for a year. My mother's sewing machine was never the same again.

Having literally sweated to go to college, I worked hard at my studies, came top of the year and was earnest that I should succeed in fashion journalism. There was, however, a problem – watching fashion shows bored me. Moreover, this was 1981 and jobs were difficult to find. Two of my brothers had good degrees, were bright and personable and had found themselves jobless. Several of us on the course realised there weren't enough openings in fashion journalism or fashion PR for all of us. I went round the class asking people what else they were interested in, aside from fashion.

What were their hobbies? Together we brainstormed, calling out relevant magazines, newspapers or companies to contact for jobs depending on our interests.

Arabella, one of my fellow students, was rich, short and snooty. She looked like a character out of *Dallas* and was always impeccably made up with bouffant, Barbie-blonde hair. Her claim to fame was that she had slept with one of the actors in the TV series *Minder*. I can picture her now standing at the back of the class, hands on hips. 'So,' she said to me, 'what do *you* know anything about?'

While delivered sarcastically, this was a good question, and one that – in my concern to motivate everyone else – I hadn't considered. I thought about it. 'Um . . . I know about wine. Especially champagne,' I replied. 'And I certainly know how to drink it.'

'Well, write to a wine magazine and ask for a job,' said Arabella. It was one of those chance remarks that change your life.

I wrote to three wine magazines. 'My name is Alice King, I am nineteen, and I think you should give me a job.' Two days later I received a reply from *Decanter*. 'The world's finest wine magazine,' it said on the letterhead. They were interviewing for an editorial assistant and had already shortlisted a few people, but invited me to come in 'for a chat'.

I panicked. What would I wear? Finally I settled on a Lady Diana-style white polka-dot blouse I had made. My friend Harriet, who later went on to become fashion editor of *Harpers & Queen*, lent me a striped Daniel Hechter pencil skirt and high-heeled navy court shoes. I had recently written a piece for the college magazine on a stonemason who had retrained as a hairdresser with Vidal Sassoon and so went straight to his Avery Row salon, where he gave me a free haircut. I emerged with a sleek bob and golden highlights.

I went to the interview looking confident on the outside.

Inside, I was quivering. I wished I had taken more notice of my father when he had talked about wine, instead of imitating him to entertain my brothers and sisters.

The interview seemed to be going well until Colin Parnell, the editor-in-chief and proprietor, asked me if I had ever actually written anything about wine.

'No,' I gulped. 'Well, not yet, but I could write you a piece about the trials, tribulations and triumphs of being a guide in the champagne cellars of Reims.'

He looked at me over his glasses. 'And what would the headline be?'

My stomach hit the floor. I grabbed for my mother's favourite line: 'Champagne makes you sing!' Well, it does, doesn't it?

A week later I was offered the job of editorial assistant on a starting salary of £4,500 a year. I was ecstatic.

Years later I asked Colin why he had employed me.

'Because I rang your course tutor, who told me I would be mad not to,' he replied.

CHAPTER SEVEN

LEARNING CURVE

Taste has always been the ultimate sensation for me. I am electrified by instant oral gratification. I need only the tiniest drop to wet my tongue and my mind races back through the bottle banks of time, searching for the memories evoked and the perfect, salivating adjective.

Fate had dealt me a trump card with the *Decanter* job. I loved watching people's faces as I told them, 'I'm a wine writer.' Everyone was interested, especially men. I was precocious with my newfound passion. My inexperience didn't faze me. I was determined to taste as many wines as possible, and I simply couldn't pull the corks fast enough. I relished the prospect of such a steep learning curve and was delighted that at last I had found something I was really good at.

In my early days in the trade I marvelled at how far and accurately people could spit. My father laughed when I told him I was losing sleep over my spitting prowess. What if I were to miss the spittoon at a big trade tasting? 'Practise in the bath,' he said. 'You'll soon sharpen your aim.'

Bathtime was never the same again. I knew I was on target when I could accurately deposit a slurp of tepid bathwater on to the floor beyond the end of the bath.

Decanter's monthly tasting was an event I looked forward to as much as payday. It was part of my job to contact the wine trade for specific samples of wines. I would catalogue and number the wines, and decide on a tasting order, generally youngest to oldest, driest to sweetest. Wines were always tasted blind, meaning that their identity was kept secret to ensure tasters weren't influenced by the label.

I learnt not to fill the glasses right up – about a sixth of a glass was ideal. This allowed tasters to tilt the glass, look at the colour of the wine and swirl it round without spillage. This releases the wine's aroma, dispelling the inch or so of stale air trapped between the wine and the cork.

I noted that the majority of our tasting panel swirled the wine in an anticlockwise direction. They would take a good sniff before tasting it, swill the wine round in the mouth, then spit it out into a bucket filled with sawdust, like the lucky dip at a fair. While some tasters were relatively silent spitters, others sounded like gagging cats. Tasters made notes – C, N, P, for colour, nose and palate – and rated the wines out of a possible twenty. I collated the results, quizzed the panel and wrote a report on their findings.

At first, as I analysed the tasting results, I was surprised at the disparity that occasionally occurred. If the experts couldn't agree, what hope was there for a trainee like me? I was delighted if any of my descriptions tallied with the panel's and congratulated myself if I awarded a wine the same or similar marks.

I quickly identified the tasters who seemed to have similar palates to mine. I would pore over their notes for hours, noting the adjectives and descriptions they came up with. Some I was familiar with – 'sweaty saddles' for French Syrah, and 'cat's pee' for the textbook aroma of the Sauvignon Blanc grape. Others could be more flowery and obscure – 'wheelbarrows full of ugly fruit . . . mimosa . . . kumquats' had me re-tasting in an effort to lock these aromas and flavours into my memory. It would irritate me if I couldn't instantly conjure up a certain aroma or flavour memory. I would return to the tasting room again and again, trying to recall an elusive taste.

After a tasting of the top Rhône Syrah wine Hermitage, I puzzled all day to recall what the aroma had triggered in my brain. I knew it was an early memory but I couldn't pin it down. Finally, after smelling the wine literally hundreds of times, it came to me – it was the smell of the hard, white rubber from my pram, an old-fashioned Silver Cross. Instantly I could picture myself sitting on the little folding seat that clipped on to the pram. This became a direct trigger in my aroma memory that said, 'Hermitage', or 'Syrah', to me thereafter, a handy, failsafe marker in blind tastings.

I was tasting more than a hundred wines a week in the office. In addition I started to be invited to trade tastings. When the first formal invitation – to a Louis Latour Burgundy tasting – arrived with my name on it, a stiff white card with curly gold script, I thought I had arrived. Soon I was receiving a dozen or so invitations every week.

The trade was generous with its knowledge, and I quickly identified my tasting heroes. Fellow *Decanter* panel tasters were happy to help me, or mark my tasting card, as there would often be as many as two hundred wines at a time. Mark Savage, a Master of Wine who owned a company called Windrush Wines in Cirencester, was to become one of my tasting heroes, as was fellow Master Julian Brind, then the buyer for Waitrose. 'Always happy to help a pretty – and intelligent – blonde,' he would say. And I have never forgotten Terry Horton, the modest yet passionate Marks & Spencer buyer. On one occasion, after an arduous blind tasting of fifty or so Liebfraumilch, he silenced us all by correctly identifying his own M&S brand as well as those of rivals Sainsbury's, Tesco and Waitrose – and then picked out Blue Nun. This impressive performance made me more determined than ever that I too would become such a magician. It seemed the ultimate party trick.

I always dressed carefully for tastings. The majority were held in smart London hotels I had never been to, such as the

Dorchester, Inn on the Park and the Intercontinental. I favoured fitted skirts and striped shirts with the collars turned up, or tailored dresses. I had one favourite, a black crêpe Jean Muir I had paid £150 for – three times the amount I had ever spent on any item of clothing. I decided it was money well spent, as it helped me feel grown-up, powerful even – a proper journalist. I teamed it with a pair of Zandra Rhodes black suede court shoes with silver lacy bows. Sometimes I put my hair up, Lois Lane-style. I convinced myself that the outfit made me look older. Perhaps I could pass for late twenties, rather than late teens. At home, I would pose in the mirror with a wineglass, practising swilling water round to ensure I didn't show myself up by spilling wine on the floor at a tasting.

I was always the youngest at these tastings, sometimes by as much as ten years. Often I would be one of only a handful of women in a sea of suited, middle-aged former public schoolboys. I was taken aback when one chinless wonder commented, 'I say, aren't you lucky? I wouldn't let my secretary go to a tasting.'

Looking down my nose at him, I replied, 'I am not a secretary, I am a journalist. And what's *your* name and who do *you* work for?' I regretted it immediately, softened my voice and added, 'Perhaps you'd like to tell me how you think the wines are showing today, and how they compare with the last vintage?' but he had scuttled off.

Once or twice I found myself being introduced to my father: 'Alice, have you met Dominic King?' We would laugh and one of us would reply, 'Yes, we've met a few times, actually,' then shake hands or kiss each other French-style on both cheeks. I was determined to go this one alone, however. I wanted acceptance in the trade; I wanted to be known for my own skill as a taster and a journalist. Asked how I had developed an interest in wine, I rarely confessed to the family connection, concocting instead evasive stories around working as a student for a champagne company – which was, of course, true.

My first Sauternes tasting was memorable. I had never encountered such intensely sweet wines before. I found the concept of their production tricky to fathom – the wines were made from shrivelled grapes that had been infected with a desirable type of 'noble rot', *Botrytis cinerea*. It sounded like a nasty disease to me, but the resulting golden, honeyed wines were sensational. Adjectives flew around at the tasting – 'freesias ... peaches ... pears ... caramel ... lychee ... citrus'. The secret of a top sweet wine is in the balance between luscious, sweet fruit and the citrus-like tang of acidity. I decided these wines were extraordinarily 'moreish', a word I was never quite sure how to spell but one that became not only part of my tasting notes but a mantra for me – I loved moreish wines, moreish people, moreish places.

On the day of the Sauternes tasting, the bosses left the office early and the rest of us set about a spot of intensive research among the leftovers, including the legendary Château d'Yquem 1967. Even then it retailed for over £50 a bottle. We calculated that this worked out at more than £1 a sip.

At six o'clock, the last drop of Château d'Yquem long gone, we divided the remainder of the spoils and left the office. I was teetering down the stairs to Blackfriars Station when I realised that, in my rush to swipe the best bottles, I had left my purse on my desk. As my Tube pass was in my coat pocket and I only had to get to my father's London flat, where I was now living, I decided not to bother returning to the office. I had already struggled to make it this far with two carrier bags of wine. As I walked through the underpass, a tramp with matted ginger hair and bloodshot green eyes asked me for the price of a cup of tea.

'I haven't got any money on me,' I mumbled, hesitating and feeling guilty. I had just been drinking a £50-a-bottle wine but had nothing for a tramp. I opened one of the bags. Which should I give him, the delicately elegant, coconutty Château Lafaurie-Peraguey, or the majestic, deep-orange, apricot and cream Château Rieussec 1976? I handed over the Rieussec.

The tramp smiled. 'God bless you,' he said.

CHAPTER EIGHT

WELL DONE, GIRLIE

After less than a year on *Decant*er I was promoted to assistant editor. There was my name – *there* – on the masthead of 'the world's finest wine magazine'. I stared and stared at it.

By way of recognition for my promotion, Colin, the editor-in-chief, sent me to a Muscadet tasting in the Loire Valley. I was the only woman among the bevy of wine merchants and restaurateurs on the trip, and the youngest there by a good fifteen years.

I was nervous. On the plane to Paris – club class, no less – we drank quarter-bottles of stylishly elegant Pol Roger champagne. I felt more relaxed after the second. You have nothing to be afraid of, I told myself. As we clambered off the coach at the vineyard, a big guy with wild, black, curly hair and mischievous, twinkling eyes introduced himself.

'What's a young lass like you doing here?' he asked.

'I'm the assistant editor of *Decanter*,' I replied. 'Like you, I'm here to taste the new Muscadets.'

He looked at me and laughed. 'OK, girlie, and I'm Black Jack – John Milroy from Milroy's of Soho. You been to one of these before?' I shook my head. 'Stick with me and you'll be fine,' he said. 'Nice legs, by the way.'

I wasn't sure how to reply to this. I followed him into a marquee, next to the winery. We were greeted with a large glass of Muscadet. Black Jack virtually downed his in one.

'Always get the leaky glass, that's me. Come on, lass, drink up. Shall I get you another?'

I looked at my glass – there must have been at least a third of a bottle in it. 'No, I'm fine. What are they doing over there?' I said, pointing towards a long table laden with bottles covered in foil.

'Ah, that's the grand tasting – blind tasting – that's what we're here for, girlie. Taste the wines and score them, rate them. All the growers taste their wines and the marks are added up to determine which grower's wine will be the co-operative's top wine – the Coupe d'Or. You have to sing for your supper. No such thing as a free lunch, girlie.'

Several tasters were already handing in their completed tasting sheets to Louis Metaireau, the film-star-handsome vigneron who headed up this unusual Muscadet cooperative. Someone was playing an accordion, and several of the winegrowers were standing around smoking. Oh, no. It was one thing blind-tasting wines at home, but in public? Now I was panicking. What if people realised I was no good?

I picked up the first of seven wines the growers had pre-selected as the best cuvées. I had only drunk Muscadet once before, in a fish restaurant. What should I be looking for?

I tasted along the line of wines, dutifully spitting them out on to the earth floor of the marquee. I felt like the new girl at school again, the odd one out. Everyone was laughing and chatting. Several of the growers were swallowing rather than spitting.

I re-tasted what I thought to be the best wine. It was crisp, dry and had an attractive, distinctive yeasty aroma and a tangy, citrus, almost pineapple-like finish. This one definitely seemed to have the most complexity. There were layers of flavour. Some of the others were all mouth-searing acidity and no fruit, leaving a nasty, astringent taste in my mouth. No, this was the one. Every time I re-tasted it I detected new flavours. I just needed to pinpoint them. I swallowed another mouthful and noted that the aftertaste lingered on – apple and pear fruit salad. I had just taken another mouthful to check on this description when I felt a tap on my back. I turned round to see Louis Metaireau. Had he seen me swallow the wine?

'Aleeze, *vous avez choisi?*' he asked. Have you chosen?

I nodded, not knowing whether to spit out my mouthful in front of him or swallow it. It would be more professional to spit it out, I thought and, turning my head to one side in an exaggerated fashion, spat to my left.

He was smiling and holding out his hand. I handed him my empty glass. He laughed, shook his head and wagged a Gallic finger – '*Non, non, tes notes,*' he said, pointing to my tasting notes. I handed them over.

Black Jack approached. 'Done the tasting? Right, come with me, girlie. Now the party really begins.'

I followed him to a table and we sat down with five or six others. There were two huge silver platters piled high with oysters. I had never tasted oysters before. I looked around to see if there was anything else to eat. Aside from baskets of bread and bowls of red-wine vinegar and chopped shallots, the rest of the table was covered with bottles and glasses – six at each place setting.

'Let's get started on the shucking,' said Black Jack. I glanced sharply at him. Had I misheard him? He carried on, oblivious. 'Hope you like oysters, girlie. I'll open you a dozen to start with, eh? They do great things, you know.'

I watched as he skilfully opened the oysters, sticking the stubby knife between the shells and prising them open. I remembered watching my father doing this when I was a little girl, which is exactly how I felt at that moment – small and out of my depth.

'Actually,' I said in what I hoped was a conspiratorial air, 'I've never eaten them before.'

Black Jack laughed, selected one, doused it with the shallot and wine vinegar and handed it to me. I looked at it with horror. Milky-white, globby-looking – I couldn't imagine putting it in my mouth.

'Down it in one,' he said. 'Don't try to chew it, just slurp it – like you would a wine.'

I closed my eyes and did exactly that – trying not to gag as the oyster slithered down my throat. I swallowed and picked up my glass, taking a large gulp of wine to drown the flavour of seawater and vinegar. The combination was . . . interesting. I was trying to work out in what way the flavour of the wine changed the taste of the oyster when I heard someone chinking on a glass.

'*Silence, silence,*' said a voice.

Louis Metaireau was welcoming us to the tasting. Every so often I would jot something down in my notebook. I wrote in shorthand because I thought it appeared more professional, and it meant that my neighbours couldn't read what I'd written. The downside was that after the event, and certainly after a few glasses, I usually couldn't read it either.

I was considering the shorthand outline for 'Muscadet' when I heard my name. I looked up, alarmed. Metaireau was holding up my tasting sheet. My heart started to race. What was he saying? His French was too fast for me. He was gabbling and smiling. I felt sick.

Black Jack slapped me on the back so hard I nearly dropped the empty glass I was cradling. 'Good for you, girlie!' he said. 'Good for you!'

'What have I done?' I whispered, terrified.

'You're the only one who placed the wines in the same order as the growers. Well done, girlie! Go on, up you get – he wants you at the front.'

The marquee had gone silent. I stood up, my stilettos sinking into the grass. I felt light-headed and queasy. Everyone started applauding as I made my way up. Metaireau shook my hand and kissed me on both cheeks. My prize –

once bottled – was a case of each of the top three wines.

Blushing, I mumbled, '*Merci*,' and returned to my table.

'Top girlie,' said Black Jack. 'Here, let's have a celebration drink. Cheers!'

Everyone at the table chinked glasses as I sat there letting all this approval wash over me. I might not have gone to university, but I could taste! It felt good. My face was glowing. I felt special, clever, recognised.

I wasn't quite sure what to do, so after a giant slug of wine I simply beamed at people. A sea of faces was talking to me, asking me what I did, how long I had been working at *Decanter*, how I had learnt to taste. I felt as if I had just won an Oscar. Meanwhile, a little voice somewhere at the back of my mind was sneering, 'It's just chance – a fluke.' For a few seconds I pondered the probability. Then I shrugged, dismissed it, reached for another oyster and recharged my glass.

CHAPTER NINE

CUPID'S BOTTLE

As an ambitious journalist, I wanted to see my name in print as often as possible, so, in 1982, I suggested we run a series of articles on country wine merchants. *Decanter*'s August edition was dedicated to New World wines – then still a novelty in the UK – so I asked my editor, Tony Lord, which merchant I could interview who sold Australian and Californian wines.

'Go and see Naughty Niall over in Hungerford,' he said, drawing on a Silk Cut. 'He's good for a laugh.'

'Why "Naughty"?'

'You'll see.'

I dressed in a striped linen suit and pointy, tan heels. I was still living in my father's London flat, above his office in Ebury Street, and Daddy said, 'You look smart. Where are you off to today?'

'I'm going to interview a wine merchant in Berkshire,' I said. 'But I'm nervous I won't know what to say – that I'll say the wrong thing.'

'I've never seen you at a loss for words. You'll be fine.'

'But what if he asks me what I think about a wine I've never tasted, or even heard of?'

'Just be honest. No one has tasted everything. Anyway, remember you're interviewing him. If in doubt, turn the question round and ask him what he thinks. Flatter him. That's the salesman's trick – works every time.'

I stepped off the train in Newbury and looked around. Niall was meant to be meeting me. At first I couldn't see anyone waiting for me, but then a slim young man in tight red cotton trousers, a striped shirt and bow tie came bounding towards me. He had narrow, drooping eyes surrounded by laughter lines, a big nose and enormous, full lips. 'You must be Alice – I'm Niall,' he said, shaking my hand. 'I'm late because the car wouldn't start. I've had to leave it running.'

I followed him to a grubby VW estate. I flicked cigarette ash off the passenger seat, sat down and crossed my legs, trying to appear nonchalant. There was a loud crack and something exploded under my shoe. I nearly jumped out of my skin. He burst into loud, raucous laughter. 'Oh, sorry,' he said, 'that was left over from last night. I play bass in a band called Haze and we had a gig in London. We use those little fire crackers onstage.'

As we pulled away, he told me how he had got a job as a van driver for a wine merchant so he could use the firm's van to transport the band's equipment. 'Then I realised how much I loved wine, so – as they say in the ad – I bought the company.'

He talked non-stop in a public-school accent. Wines were 'amazing'; wine producers were 'amazing'; his mail shots and special offers were 'amazing'; even my suit was 'amazing'. I had the impression he thought he was amazing. Even so, I was struck by his confidence. I had never met anyone quite like him before. I didn't know what to make of him or how to respond.

In Hungerford, the town hall clock struck twelve as we walked into Niall's shop on the Georgian high street. It was crammed with hundreds of wine bottles. I noticed a rubber hand sticking out of a pot plant. A smallish chap with glasses and pockmarked skin, Niall's assistant and housemate, was sitting hunched over invoices in the back office. A whoopee cushion lurked on a nearby chair.

We went out on to a lawn at the back of the shop, where Niall handed me a glass of his house champagne and busied himself with a barbecue, cooking lunch.

'So, Niall,' I said, 'what makes you sell Californian wines in a town like this?'

'Fuck knows. Nobody much buys them.' It was the first of many unprintable remarks.

I asked him what he thought of the New World wines and began to note down his comments, which became increasingly eccentric as the afternoon wore on. I tasted all the wines he opened, conscientiously spitting them out on to the lawn, and scribbled down my own tasting notes.

At four o'clock I closed my notebook and decided I may as well indulge in a glass of champagne. At least with fizz I was on familiar ground. Niall opened a bottle of Bollinger NV. I drank the first glass quickly. The excitement of the day pushed the creamy, toasty fizz into my bloodstream. I stopped worrying about what I was going to write. I had always been able to come up with something. It began to rain, and there was a fine mist in the air.

It was Friday and that weekend feeling began to envelop me. I confessed to Niall how champagne fired me up and gave me inspiration. He listened to my stories about working in the champagne cellars. 'Amazing, amazing,' he said, as he refilled my glass.

Three glasses into the Bollinger I felt bolder but still curiously thirsty. I was mesmerised by Niall's flamboyant and exaggerated eccentricity. I felt elated. Rather than come out and ask him how old he was, I used the old wine-trade trick of asking him if he was born in a good vintage.

'Would that be claret or port?' he asked.

He's got me, I thought – I wasn't really up on port vintages. 'Either or, indeed, both,' I replied.

'Actually it was an amazing year for both – 1955,' he said. That made him twenty-seven, six years older than me.

He seemed to have achieved a lot – he had his own company, was his own boss and also a would-be pop star. He had a degree in music, played the cello and had been a Queen's chorister at age eight. He knew about wine – could taste it, buy it, sell it – and had a shop full of it. And by the looks of things, he knew how to drink it.

'I was born in possibly one of the greatest claret vintages of the century,' I said, trying to match him.

'Well, it wasn't 1928 or 1945,' he said, looking me up and down. 'So 1961, then, was it?'

'Yes. I understand it was a great vintage for champagne too. Have you ever tasted a 1961 champagne?'

'Oh, yah,' he replied. 'I think so.'

'Which house?'

He hesitated. 'Actually the best champagne I've tasted recently is Bollinger RD 1973. What do you think of that?'

I went to stand up, but my heels sank into the wet grass of the lawn and I nearly toppled over. He caught my elbow.

'Do you know,' I said, 'I don't think I've ever tasted it. Tell me about it.'

'I can do better than that,' he said. 'Let's have a glass.'

I was beginning to feel light-headed. Time to go. 'I'll need to find out about trains back to London,' I said. 'Can I use the phone?'

'Oh, don't worry about that. I'll get my housemate to check in a minute. In fact, why don't you stay for supper? I'll cook and we can drink a few really good bottles.'

I opened my mouth to decline but found myself uncharacteristically mute. My stomach lurched and I caught myself smiling coyly.

'OK. That sounds like fun. I can get a train later. Thanks for the invite.'

An hour later I was sitting in the kitchen of Niall's cottage, glass of fizz in hand. The three of us – Niall, his housemate and me – had demolished the best part of a magnum of champagne and I was watching Niall cook. Was there no end to this man's talents?

'Is there anything I can do to help?' I asked.

'Yah, chop these mushrooms.'

I set to, making sure to use the safety bridge I had been taught in school cookery classes. These knives were sharp, I thought. 'Fizzed-up wine critic bleeds to death chopping mushrooms,' ran the headline in my head. I looked at the higgledy-piggledy chopped mushrooms and laid down the knife. 'I need to call my dad,' I said. 'He'll be waiting to know if I need a lift from the station.'

'You can always stay here. We have a small spare room. Then we can have dinner at a more leisurely pace. I have some friends popping round later I'd like you to meet.'

Was this man flirting with me? 'OK,' I said.

I called my father, trying to sound more sober than I felt. 'I'm staying on for supper – I'll get a train back tomorrow.'

'Well,' came my father's voice down the line, 'if you're staying for supper, it has obviously gone well. I told you you'd be fine. So, what is he like?'

'What do you mean?'

'The wine merchant – young, old, middle-aged?'

'Oh, definitely middle-aged.'

It was midnight and Niall and I were still sitting at the dining table, alone now. His friends had been and gone, and his housemate had long retired to bed. There were empty glasses, bottles and decanters all over the table. We had eaten well – lamb chops, Jersey royals, courgettes with coriander and mushrooms sautéed in garlic. There were a few stray mushrooms left on my plate, finely chopped into regular, wafer-thin slivers.

'I didn't chop those,' I said.

'No. Yours were such weird shapes I threw them away and chopped some more.'

'Oh,' I said, feeling deflated by this put-down. 'What's that smell? It smells like something's burning.'

'Stock. I've thrown the lamb bones into the stockpot. It's the only way to make decent sauce, you know. Fancy an Armagnac?'

'Oh, I don't really drink spirits, but as I'm here, why not?'

He poured an inch or so into a large brandy balloon.

'Whoa!' I said. 'Are you trying to get me drunk? Anyway, on a more technical note, tell me about this Armagnac.'

'Amazing company, amazing aroma . . .' Off he went again, 'amazing' this, 'amazing' that, but I wasn't listening. I was watching his mouth, fascinated, trying to work out how I would describe his lips in my article. He had a caricatural mouth – his lips looked like rubber, rather like those red plastic ones from a joke shop, the kind you operate with your fingers. Yes, that was it – 'finger-puppet lips'. They were stained nearly black from the Californian wine we had been drinking, Alicante Bouschet 1975, from Angelo Papagni.

I realised he had stopped talking and was staring at me. 'What are you looking at?' he asked. He sounded faintly unsure of himself for the first time that day.

'Um . . . your lips.'

He roared with laughter. 'I sell wine to Roald Dahl,' he said. 'He's always talking about my lips. He writes to me as "Ruby Lips".'

Charlie and the Chocolate Factory popped into my head, with all those sweets. I looked at the bottles on the table. That's what Niall was like – a kid in a sweetshop. There was something magnetic about this man. I wished I had his confidence. I lived in constant fear that I was going to be found out, exposed as a fraud and not a real wine critic at all.

'I need to go to bed,' I said.

'Good idea. I'll show you your room.'

I staggered up the stairs. 'Which way?'

'Straight on.'

I opened a door and sat on an unmade double bed. He sat down beside me. 'This is large for a small spare room,' I said, recalling what he'd told me earlier.

He laughed. 'Actually, it's my room. You could always stay here.'

He leaned over and kissed me with those enormous lips – a wet, squishy kiss. I could taste the caramel residue of Armagnac.

I drew back. 'I don't sleep with people I interview.'

That laugh again. 'Best show you the spare room, then.'

The following morning we set off to walk along the canal into the town. My head was hazy, but the sun was shining and I felt curiously uplifted, as if I had left my body and was looking down at myself from above.

We chatted like old friends. He grabbed my hand as I teetered along in my high heels, laughing at the ducks and marvelling at the water lilies. Something had happened overnight. Cupid had hit me over the head with a bottle. Then it came to me – I was going to marry this man; of that I had no doubt. No matter that I had planned to make a career and get married at around thirty. I was just twenty-one, but I could have a career anyway – what could be a more perfect combination than a wine writer and a wine merchant?

Rather than let me get the train home, Niall drove me to my parents' house in Chipping Norton. 'Hi!' I said, bouncing in. 'Meet Niall.'

Ah, yes,' said my father. 'The middle-aged wine merchant.'

CHAPTER TEN

WEDDING DAZE

Six months later Niall and I bought a cottage together in a village outside Hungerford, and six months after that we were married. My father did us proud and from his bottom-less cellar produced scores of bottles of Heidsieck Monopole – the Deluxe Cuvée, Diamant Bleu 1961. 'The wine has immense style and charm and all the staying power of a good marriage,' he joked in his speech.

I wore a calf-length 1920s guipure lace dress, nipped in at the waist. I had vintage Swiss lace court shoes and tiny pink roses in my hair. I look about fourteen in the photographs. Niall and I drove from the reception in a yellow open-topped 1919 Citroën. We spent our wedding night at Brown's Hotel in London, where I fell asleep over dinner – tired, happy and full of fizz. We honeymooned on the Isle of Mull. I packed two cases of champagne with my trousseau.

Back home and settling into married life, not a day passed without us sharing a good bottle or two over supper or stop-ping at the pub on the way home from work. I was Alice in Wonderland, with Niall as the zany March Hare for com-pany. It was perfectly normal to talk, write, taste and drink wine all day at work, then come home and carry on. Our social life, inevitably, revolved around wine. There was only one thing to do with the hundreds of nearly full bottles left over from big tastings – invite friends round to drink them. We were the golden couple. Everyone wanted to know us.

Boozy dinner parties were the norm – we surrounded ourselves with other passionate wine-lovers and heavy drinkers, who were only too happy to help us dispose of the leftovers.

I worked hard, adored my work and began to travel extensively. I enjoyed the life of a cosseted journalist, treated to the best of everything – first-class travel, the best wines, restaurants and hotels. I worked out that if I paid attention carefully, tasting and making notes on the wines at the start of dinner, I could relax and indulge myself towards the end of the evening. I rarely had far to go to fall into bed.

Generally Niall and I kept our working lives separate, but in an effort to comprehend the intricacies of Bordeaux – his area of expertise – I joined him on a week-long tour of the leading classed-growth châteaux. His knowledge of claret was impressive and he was fast building a reputation in the *en primeur* market – the practice of buying and selling clarets at advantageous prices before the wine is bottled.

My thirst for tasting was only matched – indeed, surpassed – by Niall, whom I nicknamed Billy Whizz for the speed at which he tasted and tore around the châteaux of the Médoc. In that one week alone we sampled more than a thousand young clarets, which, to my palate, tasted simply tart, bitter and tannic. I marvelled at Niall's ability to predict how theses wines would taste when mature in ten to twenty years' time. To secure the best prices he had to put his money where his mouth was. He would order thousands of cases of wine – tens of thousands of pounds' worth – based on what his palate told him.

During that week I drank more fine vintage clarets at legendary châteaux such as Margaux, Latour, Palmer, Gruaud-Larose, La Lagune than I had drunk in my life. The Bordelais were generous hosts, especially when they could see the order books filling up.

On the last day of the trip we spent the day with Alan Johnson-Hill, the English owner of Château Méaume, an up-and-coming Bordeaux *supérieur* property I had met while writing a feature for *Decanter*. It was a hot, airless day and we sat around the swimming pool as Alan's three young daughters splashed around. I watched Alan with his wife, Sue, and noted their gentleness with each other. It made me strangely sad. Our marriage was fiery, passionate. Fireworks were commonplace in such a volatile, wine-fuelled environment. I loved Niall with an intensity I didn't understand.

Sue served Pimm's mixed with sparkling wine and packed with red fruits – raspberries, strawberries and redcurrants. I have a hazy recollection of the barbecued quail that followed, and of eating raspberries while lying drunkenly on a lilo floating in the swimming pool.

Next morning Niall and I were due on the 6 a.m. flight back to Heathrow. Hung-over, we only just made the plane. I had an 11 a.m. tasting appointment – for the fifty top white Burgundies. Kill or cure, I thought. I noticed that my left hand was shaking. How bizarre. Jet lag, maybe.

On the Tube into London, I fell asleep. I dreamt of claret rivers, suitcases overflowing with wine and a man who stood like a fountain, red wine pouring out of his eyes, nose, ears and mouth.

CHAPTER ELEVEN

Liquid Sin

The stretch Mercedes was waiting at Bordeaux's Mérignac Airport to take Jane McQuitty and me to the Médoc first-growth claret property Château Lafite. Jane was a respected, serious journalist from *The Times*. I was twenty-two and still feeling like the kid who got lucky, though I had at least learnt to *appear* as nonchalant as my colleagues. I was like my black monogrammed Samsonite suitcase: hard on the outside, soft on the inside. Secretly I wanted to whoop with joy. People dream of drinking Lafite – I was actually going to stay there.

As we drew up at the château, Jane and I were greeted by a scruffy man in his forties. He was barefoot and wore a torn corduroy jacket. There was a huge pink rose in his lapel. I thought he was the gardener.

'*Bonjour*,' he said. 'I am Baron Eric de Rothschild. Welcome to Château Lafite.'

I giggled as I shook his hand. I had never met a baron before.

'Come join us in the salon,' he said. 'We have just finished lunch with friends and we're enjoying some of our special cognac, which we have bottled for the château.'

'Oh, I'd like to taste some,' I replied, rather too enthusiastically.

He laughed. 'I'm sure we can arrange that.'

In the salon Jane and I were served tea on a silver salver,

and the baron handed me a generous slug of cognac in a brandy balloon.

Jane declined the cognac. 'Too early in the day for me,' she said. Was that a look of disapproval she shot at me?

'I have to write something on cognac soon,' I said, taking a large slurp. It was delicious – rich, with a honeyed, caramel flavour and a taste reminiscent of . . . What was it? Marzipan? As the spirit warmed its way down my throat, my anxiety began to dissipate. I felt more confident.

To business. I had done my homework by reading up on the château and talking in depth to Niall about its recent 1982 vintage and its pricing structure.

'So, putting up the opening price of Château Lafite 1982 by seventy per cent over the 1981 price was a bold move, wasn't it?' I put to the baron.

Jane's eyebrows shot up. 'More to the point, what do you think about all the *négociants* putting a massive mark-up on the price overnight?' she asked.

There followed a heated discussion about what was a reasonable profit margin. The baron insisted that reputable wine merchants – or *négociants* – would merely apply their standard mark-up rather than reflect the market price, which was rising daily. Jane and I knew this not to be the case – as I'm sure he did – and carried on trying to point this out.

After half an hour I noticed my brandy balloon was empty, and so was Eric's. I could hear frogs croaking in the garden and the high-pitched zing of the cicadas. I reflected that I could do with a siesta – it had been a long day, and the combination of the cognac and the afternoon sun was making me sleepy. I noticed the baron swallowing a yawn.

He asked, 'Thinking of dinner, what vintages were you two born in?'

Stony-faced, Jane replied, 'In 1953.'

I added, 'I'm 1961.'

'Aha, so you know the good vintages! What years were you *really* born in?'

We repeated our birth years.

'Well, I'll look in the cellar and see what I can do. See you for dinner at seven.' Before leaving, he winked at me. 'More cognac?'

I found myself shaking my head. If I wasn't careful, I was going to be drunk before dinner even started.

Later that day I hesitated over dressing for dinner. Both the baron and his wife had been quite casual – shabby, even – during the afternoon, but I didn't want to get it wrong. Better to be too smart than too scruffy, I reasoned, putting on a navy drop-waisted angora Louis Féraud dress.

I was glad I had because when I entered the candlelit dining room, the baron was resplendent in a velvet smoking jacket and matching velvet winkle-pickers bearing the Lafite crest, and his wife, while barefoot, had on a full-length green silk dress, her dark hair dropping in ringlets around her shoulders. What a lifestyle, I thought with a stab of envy darker than the baroness's dress. The table glittered with glasses, which twinkled in the candlelight. Down its centre stood six identical decanters arranged in precise formation. Six decanters – we were in for some dinner!

'In honour of my two guests, I present the 1961 and the 1953 vintages,' the baron announced. 'Two vintages with immense class and charm, if I may say,' he added.

Lafite 1961 was already then a legendary wine, trading at more than £200 a bottle. I couldn't wait to try it. I hardly gave my food a glance, concentrating instead on the notebook on my lap. The room seemed to be enveloped in a rich, spicy glow that spread quickly to my cheeks. The wine in my glass was the colour of smoky rubies, and had such an intense aroma you hardly needed to taste it. But taste it – or rather, drink it – I did, marvelling at its richness and spicy, plum-like, fruit-cake flavour.

'Would there be much bottle variation?' I asked the baron, cheekily.

'Only one way to find out.' He smiled. 'Let's try the second decanter, and the third, and taste all three side by side. But before we do that, let's try Jane's wine, the 1953.'

This was equally stunning, though a sweeter wine, and showed more brown in its colour. It had an oaky, plain-chocolate flavour. This was a moment meant for legend – six glasses of vintage Lafite lined up in front of me, calling to be drunk.

So, was there much bottle variation? My notes became more indecipherable with each glass. Eventually I gave up trying to write. I was past caring, amazed and privileged to be drinking such incredible clarets.

It transpired that the baroness was also born in 1961, and we spent the rest of the evening reminiscing about favourite pop stars and songs. 'Did *you* lose your heart to a Starship Trooper?' I asked her.

It was long past midnight when I climbed up the winding stairs of the tower to my bedroom. Giggling to myself, I kicked off my shoes. Someone had turned the sheets down, and beside the high bed was what looked like a horse's mounting block. I climbed up, swaying, and fell on to the bed.

Drunk on Lafite, I thought. It didn't come much better than this. I felt like a princess in a fairytale. So much hedonism in one night. The ultimate liquid sin!

Speaking of sin, I couldn't wait to tell Niall about this one. He often grumbled, rightly so, that we journalists were treated more regally than the merchants who shelled out the money. He'd be as jealous as sin.

CHAPTER TWELVE

Blind Tasting

Decanter's hundredth edition and our biggest ever. It fell to me to pass the final pages. I was determined the magazine would go to the printers on schedule, so I stayed late at the typesetters every night. The edition was finally signed off on time and I caught the train home. It was Friday night. Niall picked me up at the station at seven o'clock, reminding me we had friends coming round for dinner at eight.

'I'm not going to be good for much tonight – I'm shattered,' I said. 'I didn't get much help from the typesetters and then the train was late. I'm a bit wound up, actually.'

'Don't worry,' he said. 'I've been home and prepped the food. I've even set the table. You get into a bath and I'll bring you up a drink.'

Relieved, I lay back in the bath, full to overflowing with white bubbles. I was pleased to have got such a big edition off to the printers on time. No mean feat. I took my job – and myself – very seriously.

Niall walked into the bathroom and handed me a brimful champagne flute. 'I expect you could do with this, Queenie, after the kind of week you've had,' he said, ruffling my hair. 'What do you think it is?'

I squinted at the fine bead of bubbles racing up the glass, sniffed the wine and took a gulp. Aaaah, nothing like a glass of champagne to pick you up, liven the taste buds, make you feel alert and alive again.

'It's champagne.'

'Yah,' said Niall. 'Vintage or non-vintage?'

I took another drink. 'Non-vintage.'

'Right again. Which one is it, then? Come on, Queenie, let's see how good you are at this blind-tasting lark.'

I looked at the pale-gold colour, took another large mouthful and let the delicate bubbles trickle over my tongue and down my throat. It reminded me of apple pie with a tangy kick of acidity on the finish. Cox's apples. What had I tasted before that was like this? I thought of the fizzes Niall stocked in his shop. He could be pulling a fast one, but this seemed like a good place to start. It wasn't rich enough to be Veuve Clicquot or Bollinger – more likely Taittinger or Joseph Perrier. I tasted it again. The apple flavour seemed to be more pronounced, and the finish was honeyed with a hint of honeysuckle that triggered my taste memory. That gave me the clue I needed.

'Joseph Perrier.'

'Wow! Yes, it is. Well done.'

I laughed. 'More, please!'

He disappeared with my glass. I felt better, refreshed by the fizz and glowing with a sense of achievement. Was it fluke or skill? I wondered, not for the first time.

Niall reappeared with a new flute. 'What's this, then, Queenie?'

This was clearly champagne, but much deeper in colour with very fine bubbles, much less fizzy than the first wine.

'Champagne, but vintage this time,' I said before tasting it.

'Yep, but what type and what vintage?'

I sniffed it and took a gulp. This was seriously classy stuff, with a biscuity aroma and honeycomb-like fruit on the palate. The flavour lingered in my mouth, reminding me of dried apricots. 'Bollinger RD 1973,' I pronounced. The champagne Niall had served me the day we met.

'Christ, impressive or what,' he laughed. 'Well done. You'd better get a move on – our guests will be here in fifteen minutes.'

I lay looking at the glass in my hand, resting the stem on my belly button. I was happier now, buoyed up with confidence. It couldn't be a fluke; I really must be good at blind tasting, exceptionally talented, even gifted. I must have a fantastic, super-sensitive palate! I had cracked it – the ultimate dinner-party trick.

I dressed and went down to meet our friends. We had two vintage clarets with supper, both served blind. I was, respectively, fifteen and twenty years out with my estimates. So much for being a blind-tasting star.

CHAPTER THIRTEEN

PARTY AT THE PALACE

Niall and I were the archetypal 'dinkies' – Dual Income, No Kids Yet – in the middle of Margaret Thatcher's more, more, more 1980s. With the money washing around, we bought a larger property in Hungerford, Avon House, a majestic, four-storey, nineteen-room Victorian townhouse, even though our cottage hadn't yet sold. We dressed in designer clothes, ate and drank in expensive restaurants and enjoyed ever more exotic holidays. Weekends in country-house hotels were the norm. For my twenty-fourth birthday, in 1985, we took over Hintlesham Hall in Suffolk, along with twenty friends. There were three black-tie dinners, culminating in the opening and drinking of a jeroboam – the equivalent of six bottles – of Château Canon 1955, Niall's birth year. Great wines need to be drunk with friends and there was no doubt as to the greatness of this Saint-Emilion Premier Grand Cru Classé. Few of our friends had seen a jeroboam, let alone drunk one.

We chipped off the wax and carefully extracted the giant cork. The room was enveloped in an enticing, sweet aroma so pungent it seemed to me you could see it. Rich with violets, mingled with cigar-box and chestnut flavours, this wine conjured up the taste of stolen chocolate digestives. It had the same addictive effect.

Pudding was accompanied by the top Sauternes, Château Rieussec 1970, an intensely concentrated, tangy, marmalade-like sweet wine. The evening ended with wild games of table tennis, accompanied by brandy balloons full of old Green Chartreuse.

I loved these occasions. I never knew when to stop. I couldn't understand why some people went to bed at midnight when there were still bottles on the table. Life was for partying, and with so much good wine around I liked to party until I dropped. I began to become blasé, continually seeking perfection – a better hotel, finer cooking, rarer wines.

But even I, with my growing delusions of grandeur, was not prepared for the magnificence of the party Niall and I attended in the orangery and grounds of the Palace of Versailles. It was held to celebrate champagne Piper-Heidsieck's bicentenary. As luck would have it, Niall and I were already in France. A strike by airport personnel had stranded the other British guests on the wrong side of the Channel.

We stayed in the Trianon Palace. Even the bathroom seemed the size of a ballroom. Lying in the bath, marvelling at my surroundings, I sipped my fifth, or perhaps sixth, glass of champagne of the day – I'd had lunch with a winemaker. Life was sweet. Niall and I had had a good holiday in the Dordogne with friends, and tonight's party was a suitable finale before going back to work. Not that work was so bad, I mused. After all, this party was work, wasn't it?

My hair was piled on top of my head, cascading in a shock of Marie Antoinette ringlets. Stepping out of the bath, champagne flute in hand, I slipped on the wet marble and slid a good ten feet before completely losing my balance and crashing to the floor. There was a split second in which I surveyed my nearly full glass, bubbling furiously in my hand, and wondered if I should drop it; but I held on tight and landed on my shoulder, clipping the back of my head on the porcelain sink.

'You OK in there, Queenie?' called Niall, hearing the crash.

He came in. 'Ah, well held!' he laughed. 'Glad to see you didn't drop your glass.'

'I think I bumped my head,' I lamented. 'Thirsty work, this skidding around the bathroom. You'd better pour me another glass.' I drained the flute dry.

I dressed in a fitted black velvet ball gown. It was an off-the-shoulder, Terence Nolder 1950s-style and had flashes of turquoise silk round the plunging neckline. I turned to Niall. 'Wonder who will be at this bash,' I said. 'I believe more than fifteen hundred people have been invited, including all the A-list French film stars. How do I look? Can you see where I bashed my head? Is there a dent in my hairdo?'

'You look fine,' said Niall. 'I doubt there will be anyone we know at the party, with all the Brits stranded. We'll just have to drink their fizz for them, I suppose.'

Once at Versailles, we strolled through the grounds. I tried to avoid the cracks in the cobblestones in my strappy black Gina heels. We saw the queue for the party, stretching in front of us like a giant serpent. I quickly surveyed the women's dresses, long and short, a myriad of colours and fabrics, all worn with that impeccable style French women seem born with.

'God, we're going to have to queue for hours,' said Niall.

'Maybe not,' I said, watching two men alight from a taxi. 'Look, there's the winemaker I had lunch with. Let's go and say *bonsoir*.'

We crossed the courtyard and the winemaker greeted me like an old friend, kissing me three times on the cheeks. After shaking Niall's hand, he linked arms with me and signalled to Niall to follow. It was one of my finest moments. We bypassed the queuing film stars and went right to the front. I felt like royalty. I realised, and relished, that we were the subject of much scrutiny.

As we entered the gate, dusk was falling. Dramatic blazing torches lit up the palace and its gardens. White-coated, white-gloved waiters stood in formation holding up silver salvers with magnums of Piper-Heidsieck. The champagne flutes twinkled. The sky was a curious crimson, streaked with amber, the sun hanging as if waiting for a signal to set behind the lake. As I stared, mesmerised, the fountains lit up and an orchestra struck up Handel's *Water Music*.

We moved with the crowd towards the orangery for dinner. Chefs in crisp, starched whites were lined up along either side of the room as far as the eye could see. I lost count somewhere over a hundred.

After a deliciously subtle consommé laced with gold leaf, the chefs really set to work. There was every cold delicacy you could imagine – roast quail, caviar, crayfish, crab, lobster. There were sizzling giant prawns cooked in woks with ginger and garlic, and delicious stir-fried *magret de canard*. Exotic aromas filled the air, mingling with an excited buzz in many languages as a new Fabergé egg, commissioned for the bicentenary, was unveiled.

We drank bottle after bottle of Piper-Heidsieck's new *deluxe cuvée*, the aptly named Rare 1976. This was a curious wine: crisp yet steely, like a tight-fitting glove, with a youthful and complex taste even though it was already ten years old. I took delight in explaining to those at my table why this wine was so tightly structured. 'It's on account of it not going through malolactic fermentation,' I said to the Belgian importer on my right.

'Are you sure?' questioned Niall.

The colour rose in my cheeks. 'Quite sure. The winemaker told me himself just this afternoon.'

The Belgian asked, 'Do you help your husband in his business?'

I saw red. 'No. I'm a wine journalist, the assistant editor of *Decanter* magazine. I was the one invited to this party. And *he*' – I jabbed a finger at Niall – 'came as *my* guest.' Suddenly I felt tired and deflated. I was sick of continually having to argue my case, defend myself, make myself heard. Why did men always assume I was a dumb blonde? I scowled and got up from my chair. I skulked around for a while, eventually spying Justin Llewellyn, the UK agent for Piper-Heidsieck.

'Come and join us for pudding,' he said. 'What do you think of the party? How do you think the wines are showing? Come and tell these Dutchmen about your tasting today.'

I joined the table, relishing the attention, and launched into my spiel. By the looks of things, these guys had enjoyed a liquid lunch too. They were drinking even faster than those on my table. We took it in turns to propose toasts. When it was my turn, I was at a loss, so adapted Marie-Antoinette's famous line: 'Never mind cake – let them, and us, drink champagne!' I raised my glass in the air. At that precise moment, almost as if I had given the signal, a rocket whooshed overhead, heralding the start of a stupendous firework display. I stood with the Dutchmen and we watched the *feu d'artifice*. Giant Catherine wheels spun so fast they moulded into crowns of burning fire, and oversized Roman candles poured golden lava into the lake.

The smoke from the last rockets cleared. It was a bright night and the stars shone like diamonds against black velvet. The almost-full moon passed behind a cloud. I left the Dutchmen and began walking. In the distance I could hear dance music. As I walked past a bench, I spied a bottle of Rare on the ground. My glass was empty so I picked up the bottle and discovered it was half full.

My feet were beginning to ache, so I took off my shoes and in a moment of defiance decided to take off my hold-ups. Irritatingly, the left one had kept falling down. I realised I had too much to carry, so jettisoned the stockings into a piece of topiary shaped like a hen. Or was it a cockerel? 'Cock with stockings,' I said aloud to the night. Yes, an apt name for this piece of garden art.

I had no idea which way to walk towards the hotel. There

were people milling around, but everyone seemed to be engaged in intimate conversations. I passed a couple locked in a passionate embrace. I felt totally alone. This is ridiculous, I told myself. How can you feel alone at a party with fifteen hundred people?

Changing direction, I headed towards a wooden gate. As I opened it, I had a split-second memory of an illustration from *Alice in Wonderland* in which Alice's hand was on a similar gate. I opened it and stepped through into a small, cobbled courtyard. Sitting on a bench was a dishevelled man with blond hair, his bow tie undone. He was about my age. Without a word he held an empty glass out towards me. I filled it, topped up mine and sat down beside him.

'*Santé*,' he said.

'I'm lost,' I responded.

'Are you alone?' he asked.

I nodded.

'We are all alone. And many of us are lost,' he said, and drained his glass.

CHAPTER FOURTEEN

WINE AND DANDY

I open my eyes. My left leg dangles out of a single bed. I gaze at it, my eyes gradually focusing on the pearly-pink nail varnish. Where am I? I try to sit up. My head feels like an unsecured suitcase on a roof rack. I lower myself gingerly back down. I can taste something strong, alcoholic and vaguely coffee-flavoured. Tia Maria. I smell the sweet, yeasty aroma of fresh bread.

On the floor next to the bed lies my Daniel Hechter navy gabardine dress, one arm bent up at an unnatural-looking angle. My black lace La Perla bra points skywards as if still nursing its owner. I can't see my knickers anywhere. My eyes dart around this strange room. Everywhere there are piles of children's comics – *Dandy*, *Beano*, *Eagle*, *Whizzer* and *Chips*, all neatly piled and tied with string. From my pillow, Desperate Dan's prickly chin stares at me. I look down and read the word '*Dandy*' on the duvet cover. I appear to be lying under a giant copy of the comic. I do not feel fine and dandy. Where am I? Is this a child's bedroom?

A cold shadow of fear passes over my heart. My chest contracts, and sweat breaks out on my forehead. My head pounds. I breathe out quickly, several times, and lever myself out of the bed. I quickly retrieve my dress from the floor. I find my lacy black knickers. As I am buttoning up my dress and looking around for my shoes, there is a knock at the door.

'I've baked fresh bread and made coffee. Would you like some?' asks a deep voice – an actor's voice, gravelly and cultured.

What the hell? I search my memory of the previous evening. There are gaps, but scenes begin to flicker through my mind, like stills from a film . . . I'd flown back from Portugal following a press trip – Taylor's port – and had gone straight to a Hermitage tasting in London hosted by Liz and Mike Berry, owners of fine-wine specialist La Vigneronne. Nice people – unassuming, knowledgeable and quietly good fun. I knew Liz, a Master of Wine, from my early days at *Decanter*, where she was a regular tasting-panel member. After the Hermitage tasting they had invited me back to their Kensington flat for supper. Liz had cooked pheasant. We had finished off the best bottles from the tasting as well as guzzling a few others.

What exactly had we drunk? I had already been tipsy when leaving the plane from Portugal, so the evening was a little fuzzy. A magnum of rich, creamy, biscuity Krug Grande Cuvée while she was cooking. Then what? The Chave Hermitage 1978, followed by Jaboulet's Hermitage. I couldn't remember the vintage. Was it 1982?

Somewhere along the line, Mike and I had shared a Montecristo No. 4 cigar and had done a spot of Armagnac tasting. Well, Armagnac drinking. They had invited me to stay, but I'd already arranged a bed at a friend's mews house near Baker Street. I vaguely remembered a cab, the driver opening the door for me. I hadn't been able to get the key to turn in the lock of my friend's house. The cabbie had also tried and failed. I'd thrown stones up at the bedroom window. Nothing. Eventually I had given up and taken the same cab back to the Berrys'.

Once back at Liz and Mike's house, I had thought that if I went round the back of their apartment and climbed over the fence, I would be able to knock on their bedroom window.

This had seemed perfectly logical to me. Unfortunately, the fence was too high. I could only just see over it in my high heels. I had asked the cabbie to give me a leg-up. He had told me not to be silly, snarling something about it being four in the morning and him needing to get to bed. 'Well, that's what I'm trying to do!' I snapped, throwing his £30 fare at him.

Then . . . Then what? Wandering around the streets, trying to find my way back to the front door. All the houses in the crescent looked the same. When I found their house again, I had rung the bell for ages, but there had been no reply. I had tried all the bells of the flats above theirs. Then the light on the entryphone had lit up and a male voice had said, 'Yes?'

'I'm Alice King.'

'Ye-e-e-s?' rising in inflection, questioning.

'I've been having dinner with your neighbours – Liz and Mike Berry. And, um, I can't get into my friend's where I was going to stay so I need to try and get back into Liz and Mike's. They'd invited me to stay, you see, but they must be asleep now. Perhaps if I knock on their inside door they will hear me. Could you let me in? Please?'

Moments later the door opened. A man with tousled red hair stood there in a short, brown towelling dressing gown. The hairs on his legs were ginger, interspersed with freckles. We shook hands. I stepped inside and rang the Berrys' internal bell. No answer.

'Come up to mine and you can try ringing them,' the man suggested.

There were four or so flights of stairs to his flat. I traipsed up behind him, able to see the bottom curve of his buttocks. It was a *very* short dressing gown.

Brown velvet drapes tied with gold organza bows lent a bohemian, theatrical feel to his apartment. Twisted gold candles burned in a crystal candelabra. Louis Armstrong sang in the background. I tried telephoning the Berrys, but the phone just rang and rang.

'What are you going to do?' he'd asked.

'I don't know,' I'd replied. 'I live miles away, and the first train back isn't for a few hours yet.'

'Well, come and sit down and we'll work something out,' he said. 'Would you like a drink of tea or coffee?'

'That's kind. I must admit I wouldn't mind a real drink. It's been a long day. Are you here on your own?'

'Yes. My wife has left me. She thinks I'm gay. She's trying to divorce me. Now, let me see what I've got . . . Whisky, gin, Tia Maria?'

I relaxed. If his wife thinks he's gay, he probably is, I thought. I'm safe.

'Tia Maria would be good,' I said. 'I went there once – to Jamaica, I mean – to the Blue Mountain coffee plantations where they make Tia Maria. I'm a wine writer. That's how I know Liz and Mike.'

He worked in the theatre, something to do with sound. He had been working late on a new show and had not been home long.

In a lull in the conversation he stood up and said, 'Why don't you stay here? Then you can rouse Liz and Mike in the morning – well, in a few hours. It's five thirty now. Don't worry. I've got a spare room.'

'Good idea,' I said. 'That's really kind of you.'

I followed him to this little room. 'I've got the second biggest collection of cartoon comics in Europe,' he said.

'Wow,' seemed the only response. I'd gone to bed.

And woken up not realising how I had ended up here, not at first.

I walked into the kitchen. The nine o'clock news was just starting on Radio 4. The man, whose name I still didn't know, was standing at the wooden kitchen table with a bread knife in his hand, still in his short dressing gown. The table was set with white and gold china plates. I stood sheep-ishly in my bare feet and he handed me a white damask napkin.

'Sit down,' he said. 'Freshly baked bread with honey for the lady. Coffee?'

Sober now, my imagination went into overdrive. What had I been thinking, going into a stranger's flat? Scenes from *Silence of the Lambs* flashed in front of me as he reached over to pick up the bread board, knife still in hand. Am I mad? I thought. No one in the world knows where I am. Anything could have happened to me. He could have raped me, killed me – no one would have been any the wiser. I stuffed the bread into my mouth and drank the coffee so quickly I scalded my tongue. I couldn't taste anything for three weeks.

'Thanks, thanks, thanks so much. I've got to dash – I'm going to be late for a tasting,' I said, spotting my shoes neatly paired by the front door.

He kissed me on both cheeks. 'Come again!' he called, as I scurried out of the flat and down the stairs.

My head was swimming. The coffee threatened to come back up. I hailed a cab back to the Baker Street mews. The key opened the door straight away and I realised that I must have been trying to get into the wrong house.

I vowed I would never drink so much again.

PART TWO

Fall From Grace

CHAPTER FIFTEEN

PANIC IN PARADISE

Nothing beats the thrill of your first book, of seeing your name on the cover. 'Drink what you want, when you want, where you want – it's called being winewise!' rang the opening line of mine. I followed my own advice.

Winewise was published in 1987, when I was just twenty-six, and generated huge publicity, with newspaper and magazine reviews, plus radio and TV interviews and appearances. It was all heady stuff, and on the surface I was coping but underneath I was terrified. I would throw up from nerves before going in front of the television cameras, rewarding myself with a large drink or six when I returned home exhausted from a live studio appearance on *Good Morning, Britain* at the Pebble Mill studios in Birmingham.

All this publicity resulted in a telephone call from the *Daily Mail*. The newspaper invited me to become their wine correspondent and write a weekly wine column. I believed that the way forward in the UK wine trade would be via the supermarkets and the mass market. The *Mail* was the first tabloid to promote wine on a regular basis. I was thrilled and flattered to be billed as 'Britain's youngest nationally read wine writer . . . the brightest writer on wining and dining'. I reasoned it was down to luck – I was in the right place at the right time.

As soon as my column appeared in the *Mail*, the phone started ringing off the hook. *Marie Claire, Living, Best, House*

Beautiful, *FHM* – all wanted regular columns. I had gone free-lance in 1985, retaining my connection with *Decanter* as a contributing editor, and now, less than two years later, I seemed to be flavour of the month. Each week I was asked to more tastings and lunches than it was possible to find time for and was increasingly invited on more exotic press trips – to California, Australia, the Caribbean, even India, where, yes, they do make wine. I was abroad about 50 per cent of the time.

Several magazines ran profiles on my lifestyle. Sometimes they interviewed Niall and me together. *Company* interviewed us for a feature on modern marriage.

'Doesn't he mind you being away all the time?' the interviewer asked.

'I don't know. I never thought to ask him,' I replied honestly.

'What about the competition between you?'

'He's more knowledgeable about Bordeaux than I am, whereas I know more about the rest of the world's wine, I think.'

Asked for my recipe for a successful marriage, I answered, 'To love, honour and laugh.'

Increasingly, though, I wasn't laughing. There were rows at home. I didn't really understand why this was happening, though I consoled myself that the making-up was fun. I had stopped phoning home so frequently from press trips, as it always seemed to end in one of us slamming down the phone. I became guarded about the fun I had while away.

I would wake up most mornings with my heart racing, in addition to the usual hangover. Wine was the only thing that seemed to calm my nerves, especially when I was scared or felt out of my depth, which was much of the time. The alcohol and my insecurities combined to produce a terrifying, drowning, suffocating feeling.

I decided I needed a holiday. I borrowed a villa from Don

Hewitson, a friend in the trade, in the tiny village of La Croix Valmer on the French Riviera with friends Jenny and Bill, my hairdresser, Julie, and her partner, Mark. Niall would join us later. The routine was bloody Marys at ten, followed by half a lobster and a carafe or three of the local rosé in the super-market café or lunch with a Cahors red. Sometimes we would have more wine in a beach café during the afternoon or a siesta. In the evenings came dinner with, naturally, more wine, followed by cognac, Armagnac or the French eau de vie made from pears, Poire William.

En route to Nice Airport with Jenny and Bill to pick up Niall, I suffered some sort of panic attack. A pain struck me in the sternum, my heart raced, and I became breathless. White dots danced before my eyes. As I gasped for breath, doubled over, by the side of the *autoroute*, I wondered what was happening to me. Was it a heart attack?

I recovered sufficiently to carry on and we met Niall at the airport. He seemed jovial and quite merry, fresh from a cognac tasting in London. When we had a moment alone, I told him I hadn't been sleeping well. Because our cottage hadn't sold before we'd bought Avon House, we'd borrowed money from my parents and I was concerned about paying it back.

'It'll sell, eventually,' he said. 'Anyway, it's only money.'

'Yes, but it's my parents' money, and it's worrying me.'

His merriment evaporated. 'Oh, get over it. You're always worried these days – I don't know why.'

I opened my mouth to explain, but didn't bother. He wasn't listening.

Back at the villa, we settled ourselves on the balcony with drinks. We were all topless, men and women alike. Julie started cutting Niall's hair. It was a sybaritic scene, but I was wondering what was happening to my life.

Julie finished cutting Niall's hair. 'Where's my T-shirt?' she said. 'I'm feeling a bit exposed now.'

'I know what you mean,' I said. 'I always feel like that when I'm on telly. It's weird how my mind goes totally blank when they say, "On air." There's a split second when I'm asked a question and all I can see is black in front of my eyes. It's difficult to explain, it's like—'

'It's like it's time for a beer,' interjected Niall. 'Come on, Bill, Mark, let's go to the café.'

'Why do you always interrupt me?' I asked.

'Because you're always talking about yourself,' he snapped, storming off and slamming the villa door behind him.

My lips quivered. I felt my heart beating fast, as it had before the panic attack. Tears dripped down my face into my glass. I took a gulp. The taste of my tears soured the wine. I nearly gagged, but emptied the glass anyway.

'More supplies?' asked Jenny, trying to cheer me up.

'Oh, I think so,' said Julie. 'What shall we drink to?'

'Fun, prosperity and happiness,' suggested Jenny.

I sniffed into my empty glass. 'Happiness. I've forgotten what that is. Why is Niall always so stroppy with me these days? Is it me? Do I always talk about myself?'

Nobody answered. The only sound was the sing-song buzzing of the cicadas.

'Has it ever occurred to you that Niall might be jealous?' said Jenny, refilling my glass.

'Jealous? Of what?' I replied, my voice rising incredulously.

'Your success, the publicity surrounding your book.'

'I thought he was proud of me,' I replied.

'Oh, underneath I think he is. Anyway, let's not waste time talking about him. Get showered, you two. Let's go to that bouillabaisse restaurant in Gassin. Do you know the Marseille myth behind bouillabaisse? Venus, goddess of love, is said to have first served it to her husband, Vulcan, to lull him to sleep while she cheated on him with Mars.'

'Mars,' I said, 'the god of war! Sounds appropriate to me.'

CHAPTER SIXTEEN

CONCORDE

It is a grey November day and the last envelope I open in a pile of post is sent from Heaven. How would my partner and I like to take part in a supersonic wine tasting on Concorde on its way to Barbados? This has to be the Holy Grail of freebies. I have always wanted to fly on Concorde, and what a rare treat to be invited on a press trip with one's other half. The jaunt is the idea of Peter Nixon, the then British Airways wine buyer. The West Indies in December seems like the perfect destination.

Niall and I arrive at Heathrow, hung-over from a standard Friday night in Just William's, our local bar. I look around at my colleagues. Many of the good and the great of the wine-writing world are here. Michael Broadbent, the doyen of Christie's wine department, looks dapper alongside his wife. Fellow freelance journalist Roger Voss has come alone: his wife is too pregnant to fly. 'You should have brought a friend,' I say. 'I had hundreds of people clamouring to come with me – several of my brothers and sisters for starters.' Joanna Simon is here with her art critic husband, Robin. She has been in the game about the same time as me, only she seems much more grown-up. I feel childlike beside her, though we both write for national newspapers and have each had books published. She is pencil-thin and has long, beautifully coiffed straight hair.

We go to the first-class lounge and it is Krug all round. I cannot keep the grin from my face as we mount the steps to the plane. I glance at the other fliers and wonder if they assume we are proper paying passengers. Concorde is quite cramped, compared with flying first class, but it seems pretty good to me as we relax in our plush cream leather seats. Anyway, with three hours and fifty minutes' journey time, who cares about leg room?

Niall and I are laughing. Many of my colleagues are casually reading their newspapers, behaving as if they fly Concorde every day of the week. Over the years I have learnt to contain my excitement, but that always leaves me flat and wanting more, so I tend to drink instead – must be nerves – and today the champagne is flowing. No need to wait for take-off before quaffing a few glasses when you fly Concorde. This Mumm Prestige Cuvée Réné Lalou is superb, a hazelnut in every sip.

We roll down the runway at 175 miles per hour, and as Concorde takes off, the ascent is so steep I feel as if I am on a fairground ride, pinned to the back of my seat. Adrenaline mixed with champagne – fizz to give me whizz – and all before breakfast.

'Ladies and gentlemen, the speed of sound,' announces the pilot. As we pass through the sound barrier, it feels like a car changing gear. My ears experience a supersonic pop. 'Ladies and gentlemen, twice the speed of sound.'

There is lobster on my plate and I have a glass of Leflaive's Puligny Montrachet 1983. I want to get up and dance around the plane, but everyone else is studiously eating or drinking or looking out of the window as if this is no big deal. I am too excited to eat the fillet steak that follows, but not too excited for the velvet-like claret, les Forts de Latour 1982.

So, do the wines actually taste different in the sky? Who cares? However, surprising as it sounds, they do. They taste more mature, especially the clarets. The pressure and restricted oxygen add about ten years to a wine. It softens out the hard tannins that distinguished the wines earlier that morning when we tasted them on the ground. I had thought that if I were paying over £3,000 to fly, I would expect wines with more age. Thank goodness I could detect a difference, otherwise, I wondered – as happened many times in my career – what I could write to justify this incredible freebie?

'Wouldn't it be fun to join the Mile-High Club?' I whisper to Niall. Whenever I suppress my excitement it seems to come out in another way. Once I have a few drinks, I feel reckless, wanting to do something to shock. Niall laughs, but seems more interested in his claret as he chats to Michael Broadbent across the aisle. Typical, talking shop. I feel as if I am his guest rather than the other way round.

'I'll do a reccie,' I reply, wandering off down the plane, bottle in hand. There are only two loos, both at the back. What would Michael Broadbent think if I disappeared into the loo with my husband? I sit down with the claret bottle, pour another glass and stare out of the window. Now I am just as po-faced as my colleagues.

We stay on in Barbados for a week. British Airways pick up the tab for the weekend, and then we spend more on hotels, food and drink in five days than we have ever spent on a holiday, flights included.

On the Saturday morning, lying on the beach at Glitter Bay, Concorde comes across the sky. 'Look! Niall, Alice, there's your plane!' screeches the American on the sun lounger next to me. We have achieved quasi celebrity status on the beach, both for travelling by Concorde and for our capacity for drinking rum cocktails and Red Stripe at the beach bar.

Homeward bound, boarding Concorde for the second time in seven days, we are sun-kissed and laughing. On the outward journey, I had tried to look the part of the wine writer in a linen dress, subtle make-up and styled hair, but now I've gone native and am dressed Caribbean-style in T-shirt and striped shorts, with no make-up and my wind-blown, matted hair not brushed for a week.

Once on board, glass of Krug in hand, I am passed a copy of the *Daily Mail*. I am flicking through it to see the article I phoned through earlier in the week when I overhear the woman sitting behind me.

'Seasoned jet-setters will know there is only one possible setting for this supersonic wine tasting – Concorde,' she says, reading out loud from my piece.

I experience a moment of pure joy. It's rare in a writer's life to see anyone reading your work, let alone be a secret audience when it's being read aloud.

'"Seasoned jet-setters" – that's us, darling!' she chortles to her partner.

It has made her day, and hearing my words repeated makes mine. I am cock-a-hoop. All writers secretly wonder if anyone ever reads their words.

But there is more to come.

Niall asks one of the cabin crew if they have any of the Puligny we had enjoyed on the way out. 'Actually, today we are serving a Chablis from Laroche,' says the hostess. She returns with a glass and another copy of the *Daily Mail*. 'You may like to know there is a very interesting article about our wines in today's *Daily Mail*.'

'I know. My wife here wrote it,' he replies, like the cat that got the cream.

The hostess glances at me, then back at him and laughs, unsure whether to take him seriously.

'I'm not always this scruffy,' I tell her. 'The wines are amazing, don't you think?'

'Oh, I thought he was joking,' she laughs. 'You look about fourteen.'

I smile as she fills up my glass. Recognition from her, the people sitting behind us and Niall. It really does hit the spot. Better than the Mile-High Club.

CHAPTER SEVENTEEN

BABIES AND BOTTLES

In 1992 I discovered I was pregnant while in Sydney, on the last day of a three-week tour of Australian vineyards with a hundred members of the wine trade. We'd made the headlines by drinking the plane dry en route. It was this trip that opened the floodgates for Aussie wine into Britain.

Every vineyard we visited was anxious to outdo the previous one. Jacob's Creek, at huge expense, filled up its eponymous creek with water and took us up in a hot-air balloon to see it. Another producer transported us to lunch in a seaplane. Wolf Blass took us 'yabbie' – cray – fishing. The tastings, parties and beach barbies became ever wilder and more raucous. I tasted and tasted, clocking up over three thousand wines in the three weeks. It was a surprise at the end of it all when the blue line appeared on my pregnancy test – I certainly wouldn't have partied so hard had I known. I had always planned on having children, I just hadn't quite decided when. But after we had got over the initial shock, Niall and I were delighted.

I had an easy pregnancy, not sick once, which was fortunate as I was tasting most days and filming a BBC series with Delia Smith. I also spent weeks in France researching my latest book, *A Bootful of Wine*, written to coincide with the change in the duty-free laws that allowed consumers to bring up to ninety litres of wine into the UK. *GMTV* gave me a weekly slot, the camera angled so as not to show my swelling tummy.

Giving birth was a monumental shock. I had a difficult twenty-eight-hour labour. When my son was finally born naturally, with no drugs or pain relief, everyone in the delivery suite cheered. After I had cuddled him for a few moments, the midwife took him away to 'give him more oxygen'. One of my sisters – a midwife by training – and Niall were there. A bottle of champagne was popped, but I was too weak, exhausted and shocked to drink it.

An hour later, when I had been helped into and out of a bath, I was sitting in a wheelchair when the paediatrician came flying through the swing doors. She was wearing a Spider Man jumper. 'Your baby has just clinically died,' she said. 'We've successfully resuscitated him, but you'd better come and see him now. He might not make the night.'

I had an out-of-body experience. I floated up out of the wheelchair and saw the scene – in black and white, bizarrely – from the ceiling. Niall burst into tears. I saw the woman in the wheelchair comfort him: 'Don't worry, he'll be fine – you'll see.'

At times like this the brain needs no drugs. Survival took over and my mind went into denial, refusing to accept that this situation had anything to do with me. Things like this did not happen to me. These people were not talking to me. They couldn't be. I had never even been in a hospital before.

A day or so later my firstborn spat out his ventilator and began to breathe on his own, giving the first sign of the determined, independent boy he was to become. A real fighter.

Still weak from the effects of the birth, I threw myself into work, determined to prove I could and would be a high-flying, do-it-all mother. At eleven weeks old, my son went part-time to Norland Nursery, conveniently just down the road. For months I would express my milk into bottles for him before hurtling off to London for the allure of other, more potent bottles. Each month for a year I had to take him back to the hospital. They would never tell me what they were checking for, saying such checks were routine for any baby that had been in a special-care unit.

Normally Niall and I went together to the hospital, but unusually I was alone at our son's first-year check. The same Spider Man consultant, in a white coat this time, said, 'I'm glad to report there was no brain damage.' I was so shocked by this that on the way home I had to stop the car and weep. I realised that since the birth I had been holding my breath. Now I could heave a huge sigh of relief – it was safe to love this beautiful child.

That night Niall and I had a special dinner party to celebrate the fact that we had all survived the year. It had been a tough one.

Niall's wine company was having problems. At trade tastings I would overhear members of the trade speculating about his business. I could only stand by and listen and try to be as supportive of him as possible. Once or twice angry suppliers knocked on our door demanding money. I reacted by pouring myself another glass of wine.

Drunken rows between the two of us became the norm. I found myself drinking more, and my tolerance for alcohol became unpredictable. I would be drunk when I didn't think I should be.

Around this time, in 1993, I started writing a twice-yearly supermarket wine guide, *Check It Out*, which involved tasting 2,000 wines and deciding on the top 500 for under £5 a bottle. Pregnant again (my second child was conceived on my first-born's first birthday), I restricted my intake to two glasses a day and things calmed down at home. When I was pregnant, Niall became softer, less competitive and more supportive of my work. Or was it simply that I became gentler, less strident and more cooperative?

My second son was born in early August 1994. Expecting another drawn-out labour, I was almost caught short – I had to cross my legs to stop myself giving birth in the car on the A34! As soon as I put a foot inside Oxford's John Radcliffe Hospital, the midwife took one look at my face and showed me directly to a delivery suite. Reminding her I had planned a water birth, she eyeballed me and enunciated in school-teacher fashion, 'No time to turn the taps on, dear. No time!' I didn't believe her and was amazed when my second son arrived ten minutes later to the strains of Johann Pachelbel's 'Canon in D Major'. We had barely turned the tape player on. I was even more surprised by my son's shock of red hair, a throwback to the Irish side of my father's family. I didn't dare tempt fate by taking champagne with us to the hospital and so enjoyed the more standard fare – a cup of tea and a slice of toast and Marmite. Four hours later I was bemused to be back at home in my own bed, wetting the baby's head with Krug. Born on a Sunday, this child was indeed 'bonny and blithe'– a joyous bundle, full of gaiety.

I took a few days off, but was soon back at my desk. With a book launch looming, I decided to stop breastfeeding my second son at three months – I couldn't face the thought of leaking breasts at the launch party – and he joined his brother at Norland Nursery.

Soon after the birth of our second son, Niall's company stuttered to a stop. He wouldn't let me accompany him to the fateful meeting, where he faced customers who claimed they had paid in advance for *en primeur* clarets. His too-successful PR hype and huge press coverage meant he attracted a high amount of critical publicity across the national and local press. It seemed that customers feared they wouldn't receive their wine. I wasn't involved, but I think there had been an offer of some sort whereby customers could have wine allocated to them by paying an additional amount to the company. Not surprisingly, this created a hostile atmosphere both among customers and the trade. As a result, it was embarrassing for me at trade tastings, but I couldn't avoid them – one of us had to generate some income. Now the major breadwinner, the pressure was on me to earn even more money. My drinking stepped up a notch.

Disillusioned with the wine trade, Niall stayed at home trying to think up some money-making venture. He spent endless hours at the computer. I suggested selling the house to reduce our immediate overheads – we didn't actually need all those rooms, surely – but he was adamant that we shouldn't. He had lost his company and wanted to hold on to his castle. He wouldn't discuss his feelings on finding himself unemployed. I urged him to talk to someone about how he felt – anyone, a professional or a friend – but he refused.

One night, returning home late from London, I found him in front of the Wurlitzer jukebox I had bought him one birthday. His head was in his hands, a glass by his side and 'Don't Give Up' by Peter Gabriel and Kate Bush was blaring out. There were tears streaming down his face.

I took hold of his hand and reassured him: 'It'll be OK, darling. We'll work something out. I'll earn some more money. It will be all right, I promise you.' I picked up his glass and drank it down in one gulp.

CHAPTER EIGHTEEN

'GREAT WITH' WINES

Matching food and wine was a great love of mine and something I was instinctively good at. When I had people round for dinner, I loved to try out combinations, fascinated at how the flavour of the food could alter the wine and vice versa.

A favourite trick was to give guests a glass of a lusciously sweet, sticky dessert wine such as the Rhône beauty Muscat de Beaumes-de-Venise. Sweet wines evoke strange reactions in people. If they have just started to become interested in wine and are moving away from the usual safe medium dries, they turn their noses up at all sweet wines, regarding them as a bit naff. Often I would have to cajole friends to taste a sweet wine at all. Many would politely agree that, yes, it was indeed sweet. Next I would ask them to take a mouthful of an intensely sweet pudding such as chocolate mousse and then re-taste the wine. Amazement all round – the sweetness of the chocolate would cancel out the sweetness of the wine, leaving a delightful, almost bitter-sweet, rich, yet tangy wine that complemented the mousse.

Successful food and wine matching, especially involving trickier foods like asparagus, eggs or anything spicy, is not an intellectual exercise. It requires a hands-on approach. It was music to my professional ears therefore when Tesco asked me to help them with their 'Great With' wines. I can't take the credit for this brilliant and simple concept. That

105

must go to Bibendum's Dan Jargo. His argument was that few people had confidence matching food and wine, so why not do the job for them? The first four wines were labelled simply 'Great With Chicken', 'Great With Steak', 'Great With Fish' and 'Great With Pasta'. Supermarkets were beginning to cross-merchandise and put bottles next to the appropriate foods, making life a good deal simpler for their customers.

It was a fantastic marketing idea, but I was not so impressed with the taste of their chosen wines. Tesco wanted me to write tasting notes for the bottles' back labels and add my endorsement and signature. Already a consultant, I expressed my disappointment at the wines' lacklustre flavour and suggested I take part in the blending and selection process.

They agreed and, as a result, one rainy day I made the long journey from Hungerford to their offices in Cheshunt, Hertfordshire. I went by train because the M25 is best avoided, and besides, I always anticipated drinking at some stage in the day.

Tesco wanted me to find a wine they could label 'Great With Chinese'. When I arrived, the tasting table was piled high with Chinese food – sweet and sour chicken, Singapore noodles, beef in black bean sauce, chicken and cashew nuts, prawn chow mein and the like. We had around twenty or so white wines to try from producers the world over.

Ideally we needed a wine that could deal with the aromatic flavours of Chinese food as well as the chilli used in many dishes. Gewürztraminer from Alsace would be a natural partner, an over-the-top grape that smells and tastes like tropical fruit salad, but the idea behind the 'Great With' wines was to keep them good value, as we planned to retail them at £3.99. This meant Alsace Gewürztraminer was out of reach.

Eventually we narrowed the choice down to a handful of wines, including a sample of another aromatic grape, Muscat. This, together with a crisp, gooseberry-like Sauvignon Blanc seemed the favourites. Both were from the Val d'Orbieu winery in the south of France. Back and forth we went between the food and the wine. I had to drink, not spit, since it's tricky to spit out food. Dan Jargo was happy to settle on either and seemed anxious to conclude the tasting, but I felt that as my name was to appear on the label, the wine needed to be good, something classy that people would taste and remember.

'It needs to be "Great With" – not just "OK With",' I said. 'How about we try blending these two grapes, so we get the floral flavour of the Muscat and acidity of the Sauvignon?'

'Nobody blends those two grapes together,' Dan protested.

'Well, why don't we try? Who says we can't blend the two? Perhaps this will be something new.'

He tipped the two samples into one glass and we tasted it, along with another mouthful of sweet and sour sauce. Anne-Marie Bostock, then head of Tesco's wine team, had now joined us.

Just occasionally in life, I know when to shut up. I didn't say a word.

'This blend is by far and away the best combination,' said Anne-Marie.

Job done. I was delighted and shot a triumphant look at Dan, who scowled, but had to agree.

On the journey home, I reflected that it felt good to have been involved in the creation of something new, to be valued for my expertise, credited for my skill. On reaching Hungerford, I toyed with the idea of going home and telling Niall about my day. Then I pictured him absorbed in his computer.

The lights of Just William's loomed in front of me. I thought I'd pop in for a quick drink and tell Sarah, the landlady, my news. I would be welcomed, visible and – with a captive audience – listened to as well.

*

A month or two later it was Chinese New Year, and friends Jenny and Bill were hosting a Chinese banquet. Jenny, laid-back and generous to a fault, was an inspired cook, while Bill, a white-haired scientist with a mischievous twinkle in his eye, was the perfect host. There were a dozen or so guests, including some people I didn't know. As was my way, I took along several sample bottles from my tasting room – mainly spicy, full-bodied Rhône and Aussie reds, the perfect foil for more robust dishes such as chilli beef and spare ribs.

I thought I'd have a bit of fun so I also took two empty decanters and some bottles of my newly blended 'Great With Chinese' wine. I wondered what the guests would make of the blend, but I wanted them to taste it blind. I knew some would be sniffy about drinking super-market wine, their growing knowledge having made wine snobs of them.

Next to me at dinner was a man I'd never met before who supplied sauces for supermarkets. He'd been to a lunch party beforehand and was already the worse for wear. It was entertaining – and novel – to see someone ahead of me in the drinking stakes. But his attitude and snooty accent annoyed me. I asked him as sweetly as I could what kind of wines he particularly liked.

'The one in the glass in front of me,' he joked, draining his glass and reaching for the bottle of Pol Roger down the table. 'Seriously, though, I only drink wine from reputable merchants – none of your supermarket crap for me.'

'Don't you sell your sauces to supermarkets?'

'Yes, but that doesn't mean I'd drink their wines.'

I went into the kitchen, poured my 'Great With Chinese' wine into the classy, salmon-pink 1920s decanters I had brought along with me and returned to the table with them.

'What's this, then?' he asked.

'That's for me to know and you to guess.'

Turning to the other diners, I announced, 'This is a mystery wine. I'm interested in what you think it is, if you like it, if you feel it complements the food and how much you think it costs.'

Sound of slurping all round.

'I think it's French, maybe from Alsace, and at least ten or fifteen pounds a bottle,' ventured the sauce seller. I smiled encouragingly. 'I can always recognise pedigree in a wine,' he added.

Others round the table offered, 'Australian?' 'German?' 'Spanish?' The rate at which they emptied the decanters suggested they liked it.

Everyone guessed it to be at least £10 a bottle. 'Alice only brings us decent wines,' said Bill, 'she's that kind of gal.'

I went back into the kitchen, grabbed the empty bottles and strode back into the dining room.

'Here – a present for you,' I said to the sauce seller. 'This is the wine. It's three ninety-nine and you can buy it at Tesco. I blended it. Not bad for supermarket crap, eh?'

It works every time. Serve something in a stylish decanter and people think they are drinking an expensive wine. Or could it be that this was a genuinely skilfully blended wine?

'Come on, Bill, what did you really think of the wine?' I asked. 'I know I can rely on an honest answer from you.'

Picking up his glass, Bill swirled it, sniffed it ostentatiously and slurped heartily in a wicked parody of wine tasters like me.

'It's *grrrreat* for getting pissed on,' he pronounced.

CHAPTER NINETEEN

Whirly Pool

It was unbearably hot. Number Two son was in his pram in the garden without a nappy. He was asleep and smiling, helpless but happy. I frowned as I looked down at him. I was helpless and deeply unhappy. My head was throbbing. Perhaps it had been a mistake to down that pint of Stowford Press cider in Just William's at lunchtime. But I had finished my writing for the day and had felt I deserved a break. Anything to escape from the house – and the atmosphere following yet another row last night. Ever since the demise of Niall's company, screaming arguments had become the norm. He wouldn't stop criticising me.

'You can't even put a nappy on properly,' he'd sneered the night before. He wouldn't listen when I tried to explain I had put it on loosely because it was so hot.

'Anyone would think you'd given birth to those boys, the way you carry on!' I'd screeched at him.

Now, a butterfly alighted on the hood of the pram. For a second it flittered around the baby's nose, dusting him with its wings as if kissing him. My second son didn't wake. He just wrinkled his nose and sighed contentedly. The butterfly fluttered off. I wished I could escape so easily. I rubbed my eyes under my Ray-Bans. I felt trapped. The more work I did, and the more money I earned, the more irritable Niall seemed to become.

It wasn't as if I spent the money on myself. Once the

mortgage and the household bills and the – alarmingly high – credit cards were paid, there was little left. We were arguing all the time. The latest cardinal sin had been to put the dishwasher on at night. What was wrong with that?

'Are you completely stupid?' Niall had spat at me. 'It's a fire risk.'

'Don't be ridiculous. Why don't you just bugger off?' I'd responded.

Such was the nature of our exchanges.

The door opened and Niall came into the garden. I tensed. Not more confrontation, please. But he ruffled my hair and smiled. 'Queenie, you haven't forgotten, have you? We're meeting Venice and Steve for a picnic. We're going to have supper in the whirly pool. We'll take the wine in the pram.'

The honeyed, caramel-like aroma of Armagnac hung on his breath. His friendly tone surprised me. Was I supposed to have forgotten last night's row?

The doorbell rang and the babysitter arrived. I lifted the baby out of the pram and handed him to her. 'I expect he'll be ready for his tea now. There's some rhubarb crumble I made last night he can have. Then maybe you can give him a cool bath. It's so hot we're going to sit in the river – it's the only way to cool down.'

Niall began to pack the bottles into the pram crossways, cork to punt. The mattress cover was still warm and wet from the baby's sweat. I stood, hand on hip, counting – two bottles of Ruinart champagne, two bottles of Wairau Rivers Sauvignon Blanc, two bottles of Dujac Morey-Saint-Denis 1978, one bottle of golden-orange Château Rieussec 1976 and a half-bottle of Hine Early Landed cognac.

'Do you think that will be enough?' he asked.

'I thought we were taking the pink fizz.'

'All gone – anyway, this Ruinart is much better,' he replied.

'No, the whole idea was the rosé was to go with the salmon. I think I've got some bottles in my office. Oeil de Pedrix – you know, that very pale, eye-of-the-partridge rosé champagne – will be best.'

I found two bottles in my office wine rack and placed them on top of the Ruinart. Better to have too much than too little.

Opening the front door, we manoeuvred the pram down the steps on to the pavement, bottles clanking. I pushed the pram down the hill towards the marsh. Niall walked in front clutching a candelabra.

As we passed the doctor's surgery, the local midwife came out. 'Ah, taking the baby for a stroll?' she said, peering into the pram.

Niall roared with laughter. 'No, he's at home, asleep. Just going for dinner with friends in the whirly pool.'

'Well, it's a different use for a pram,' she said, shaking her head and smiling.

We walked through the churchyard, the church spire looking like a cardboard cut-out against the cloudless sky. Crossing the swing bridge over the canal, I stopped to catch my breath, sweat trickling down my face. I looked across the fields and saw the river in the distance. A train passed along the Great Western line. This could be a tapestry scene – the quintessential English day. Life wasn't so bad, I told myself. Even Niall seemed in good humour. We arrived at the stile.

'We'll have to lift the pram over,' I said. 'I'll go round the other side and you pass me the bottles. It will be easier then – not so heavy.'

'No, I'll manage,' said Niall, attempting to lift up the pram. 'Christ, you're right, it is heavy. You'll have to help.'

'Just take some bottles out – it's quite simple.'

He glared at me. He was opening his mouth to reply when a man appeared on the bridge with two Dalmatians. 'Need a hand?' He peered into the pram and raised his eyebrows.

Was that a disapproving look? 'Looks like some picnic you're going on. It might be easier if we take these bottles out, don't you think?'

'No!' insisted Niall. 'We can manage it like this.'

After much huffing and puffing, with the pram finally manoeuvred over the stile, bottles intact, we set off again. There were hundreds of yellow flag irises and tiny speckled marsh orchids, but I didn't stop to examine them. I was walking ahead waving the candelabra, thirsty after the trek and definitely in need of a drink.

A white plastic table and chairs stood in the river. The whirly pool was a local beauty spot where the River Kennet gathered in a dip, swirling and bubbling to form a large, natural jacuzzi on its way to the Thames. All the local children used to swim in it during summer. Venice and Steve were already there with Venice's friend Carrie. I grabbed one of the bottles of Ruinart and opened it as I walked along. The fizz spurted out into the river. Venice held out glasses and I filled them up. I kicked off my shoes and sat dangling my legs in the river. My glass was empty within seconds. The fizz was deliciously cold, as cold as the river that came up to my shins. I felt exhilarated.

'You see, champagne *is* the elixir of life,' I said to Venice.

Carrie started doing headstands on the riverbank. 'Ooh, I'm not sure I have any knickers on,' she simpered – not that it mattered, as she couldn't manage to get her legs to stay up.

Buoyed up with fizz, I couldn't resist the challenge. 'Make a triangle with your head and hands, like this,' I told her, as I executed a perfect headstand. I taught her how to cartwheel right-handed, left-handed and finally one-handed, and we cartwheeled along the riverbank until we were giddy. I felt like a child again.

I stopped in midair when I heard a champagne cork pop. 'Come on, back to the serious business. If we're not careful, there'll be nothing left!'

We sat with our feet in the clear water, eating salmon trout with new potatoes, cold asparagus and mayonnaise.

The local mayor passed by with her dog, stopping to accept a glass of Sauvignon Blanc. 'What a good idea,' she said. 'It's wonderful to see people enjoying the marsh.'

Pudding was raspberries served in a bowl made of ice with flowers and rosemary frozen inside it.

'This Ree— Reu— Rieussec is fantastic,' I told Venice. 'Well, *you* try saying that after a few glasses. Look at its glorious colour.' I held my glass up to the sinking summer sun. 'I know – let's float the raspberry bowl, Ophelia-style, down the river!'

I jumped up, knocking an empty bottle into the water, and dropped the bowl into the deepest part of the whirly pool. It caught in the current and bobbed up and down for a few seconds, making a dramatic swirling motion as it was swept away.

'It's out of control! An escaped ex-raspberry bowl being swished this way and that by the current. It's no idea where it's going and we can't do anything to stop it drowning,' I giggled.

'It's not the only thing out of control,' said Steve to no one in particular.

CHAPTER TWENTY

BIRTH OF A MAGNUM

April 1994 and I am lying in the bath, a flute of Krug Grande Cuvée in one hand and my brand-new baby – my third son – cradled in the other. It has always been a dream of mine to give birth at home in my own bed, and now I've achieved it. I am overcome with gratitude and can't stop gazing at him. Just ten minutes old, this baby looks like a fragile bird, with hungry, pouting, thick lips like his father's. The baby is thirsty, gently sucking on my left nipple.

Never has champagne tasted so good. After months of indigestion, when I couldn't even enjoy fizz, the Krug in my glass is the ultimate reward. I am high on adrenaline and can't wait to share my good news with my friends. Catherine, my midwife, pops her head round the bathroom door to check I'm OK.

'My only problem is an empty glass,' I joke. 'Such a shame you are teetotal – this really is delicious. Is there any left, or has the thirsty father drunk it all?'

Niall arrives and drains the remains of the bottle into my glass. 'Sheets in the washing machine,' he says. 'How efficient is that, Queenie?' He ruffles my hair.

'Amazing. I must ring Sarah and cancel our table at Just William's tonight.'

'I'll do it.'

'No, I want to do it – I want to tell her about the baby. Here, you take him.'

He prises the baby from my nipple and our new son looks puzzled as Niall gently wraps him in a soft, fluffy, white towel, complete with hood and little rabbit ears.

I stand up, glass in hand, feeling wobbly. Catherine appears with a huge bath towel, which she wraps round me. When I was a little girl, my mother would cloak us in our towels as if we were royalty. I used to love admiring my 'train' in the mirror. I dry myself, peering at my stretched stomach in the mirror. I hastily cover it up with an old, orange-striped poplin Paul Smith shirt. I climb into bed, lying back on the crisp, laundered sheets, and pick up the phone.

'Mum, it's Alice.'

'And how is Ally Pally?'

'I'm good. And I've got another son. It was fantastic – everything I dreamt about. He's beautiful.'

'Oh, how marvellous, you clever girl. I told Dad to put some champagne in the fridge when you didn't answer the phone earlier.'

'Oh, don't worry, I've already had a glass or two of Krug.'

Next I ring the pub.

'Sarah, it's Alice. I'm afraid I'll have to cancel our table for dinner.'

'That's a shame. I was looking forward to seeing you.'

'Oh, and Sarah,' I add with mock nonchalance, 'I have another son. Come and see him – he's beautiful.'

'That's amazing! It's Al,' I hear her say away from the phone, addressing the bar at large. 'She's had another son.' I hear a boozy cheer from the regulars.

Niall comes in with the baby, hands him to me, lies down on the bed and closes his eyes. 'I'm shattered!' he says.

I wrinkle my nose and snort derisively. *He's* shattered?

The doorbell sounds. 'Get that. It might be Sarah.'

'What, already?'

A few moments later Sarah comes bounding up the stairs

waving a bottle of Krug. 'I had it ready in the fridge. Well done, you. I can't believe it – we were only chatting a few hours ago. You look fantastic.'

'Thanks. I've had a glass or two already. This giving-birth lark is thirsty work, isn't it, Niall?'

'You look exhausted, Niall,' says Sarah, laughing.

He makes no reply.

'Let's open the Krug!' I say.

'What, now?' replies Sarah.

'Churlish not to wet the baby's head, don't you think?'

We fill our glasses and clink them together.

'So how heavy was he?' asks Sarah.

'Good point. I don't know. We haven't weighed him yet, have we, Catherine? Can we do that now?'

The midwife sets up the scales. The baby seems to be asleep, though his mouth is firmly clamped round my nipple. I gently stick my little finger in his mouth and lever him off. He looks peaceful in his white smocked nightie. I recall with pride the A I got for my needlework O level.

'Six pounds, fifteen ounces,' announces the midwife.

'Ah, the smallest of my three.' A thought occurs to me. 'Catherine, leave the scales out. Niall, get that magnum of Mumm Cordon Rouge, can you, please? It's standing beside my desk in my office.' Catherine raises her eyebrows. 'Don't worry, I'm not planning to drink it. Well, not right now. I just want to weigh it. I'm writing a piece for the *Daily Express* about what wines to take to a friend who's just had a baby.'

Niall returns, clutching the magnum. 'Seven pounds exactly,' pronounces Catherine. 'Almost the same weight as the baby.'

We gaze at the magnum. Sarah, who has no children – just Great Danes – gasps, 'Christ! Glad I stuck to my dogs.'

We drain our glasses.

Another thought occurs to me. 'Catherine, can you measure the diameter of the magnum?'

She reaches into her bag and pulls out a tape measure. 'Almost ten centimetres.'

Sarah looks at me quizzically.

'That's the exact same measurement the cervix has to dilate to before you can start pushing,' I explain to her. 'Every woman who has ever given birth will be familiar with that magic number.'

'Yes, and it's the number that brings tears to the eyes of the men looking on,' puts in Niall.

There's a knock on the bedroom door. The doctor pops his head round. 'The front door was open, so I let—' He stops in mid-sentence and stares. I am in bed holding the baby and an empty champagne glass, while the midwife stands by the magnum still on the scales.

CHAPTER TWENTY-ONE

'ONLY ANOTHER TASTING'

The clock said 8.03 a.m. It was winter 1997 and I was trying to get the boys out of the house. I had Number Three son in my arms and Number One son, aged five, in front of me. 'Where's your brother?' I asked him impatiently. 'I'm in a real hurry this morning. We need to get going. You look upstairs. Perhaps he's hiding.'

I found Number Two son in the tasting room. There were some fifty bottles on the tasting table, all Australian reds. He turned as he heard me open the door. He had a deep-crimson moustache and a glass in his hand. He promptly put down the glass, knocking over another. Red wine splattered over the wall and down his dungarees.

'Grab that cloth over there and come here so I can wipe that wine off you. What were you doing?' I snapped.

'Tasting, just tasting,' he answered in his sing-song three-year-old voice.

'Get in the car and hurry up. I've got a long drive this morning,' I replied crossly, though it was difficult to remain cross with him for long – he was such a funny child with his spiky red hair and mischievous grin.

He skipped out of the door in front of me, laughing, and into the garden. I thought about finding him some clean dungarees but decided there was no time. When I reached the end of the garden, Number One son was nowhere in sight. I heard him shouting from the house. 'Mummy! You've locked me in!'

It started to rain as I fastened my two younger sons into their car seats and hurtled back down the garden to retrieve their older brother.

'Did you forget me?' he asked. 'I was looking for my brother. You told me to.'

'Of course I didn't forget you,' I said, guiltily. 'I thought you were in the garden. It's just that I'm in a hurry. I've got an important tasting.'

It looked as though it was going to be one of those days. I had thrown up earlier, but I put that down to nerves. I was throwing up with nerves a lot in the mornings these days. And to make matters worse, I had a headache. A friend, Jenny, had come round for supper the night before and we had ended up having a bit of a Calvados tasting, under the guise of writing about it. When I'd come down in the morning, there were five or six bottles of the stuff on the breakfast table among the cornflakes. I hadn't realised I'd had so many different types. I had no recollection of what any of them tasted like, let alone which was the best. The least-full bottle was probably the technical answer, I reasoned, as I plonked them in the pantry out of the way.

I still felt groggy and hoped I was all right to drive, though looking at the traffic, I wasn't going anywhere fast this morning. There were roadworks and the traffic was backed up almost to my house. If it was like this here, what would the M25 be like? I decided to drive across the common to the boys' nursery school.

Driving in through the gates, I was already thinking about the champagne tasting I had to do for a hundred of Tesco's wine sales staff that day. How long should I spend talking about each champagne? Would they be the right temperature? Had the tasting sheets been printed? Did they have enough clean glasses, properly polished? A hundred people, six glasses each – 600 glasses. I hoped there would be someone on hand to help.

'Mummy,' said Number One son, 'I've got French today. I can't do French.'

'Nonsense,' I said. 'You can do anything you like in this world.'

'You can't. I can think of at least two things you can't do.'

'Like what?'

'You can't kill God and you can't drill through to the centre of the Earth because it would be so hot the drill would melt.' Perfectly mimicking my voice, he added, 'Well, what do you say to that?'

Here I was, panicking about a champagne tasting and I had a child genius in my car! 'Good call,' I said.

The boys clambered out of the car and I took them to their respective classrooms. I was about to leave Number Two when I realised he still had red wine around his mouth. Hastily I licked my finger and rubbed it off. I had to scrub hard and he whinged. A few other parents gave me looks. What was their problem? I had to stop myself asking one what she was looking at. Some mother was having an interminable chat with one of the Norland nannies. I waited, impatient, looking at my watch. It was eight thirty-three. I needed to get a move on.

'Look, I'm in a real rush,' I told the nanny. 'Don't worry if you think he smells of wine – he does. Just as we were leaving he knocked over a glass of wine in my tasting room and I didn't have time to change him. There are some spares in his bag. Their father will pick them up later.'

I didn't wait for a reply. I simply climbed back into my car and took off down the drive. Thank heavens for nursery school, I thought. The boys were old hands here now. I could remember the first time I had left Number One son here. I was still weak from his difficult birth and frankly terrified of him. Other first-time mums had been crying, but I had felt relieved, looking forward to resuming my normal life. Work certainly seemed the easier, less frightening option to motherhood. I didn't think I had the imagination to be a full-time mother. Besides, with Niall not working since the company went down, we needed the money.

Number One son had started at nursery part-time, but as my work had increased, I had soon upped it to five days. Although we had had an au pair for a while, when Numbers Two and Three sons came along they had joined him – you could rely on Norland to provide consistent care. The extra plus was that with a team of nannies, the boys didn't form an attachment to one person. The downside was that it cost a fortune – £90 a day for three of them – though I reasoned it was money well spent.

The tasting had gone smoothly, I reflected, driving home. Once I'd got going it wasn't nearly as frightening as I'd feared. I had selected six different fizzes and they had all had shown well, neatly demonstrating the differences in taste.

As well as teaching the wine sellers how to taste champagne, I had given them a thumbnail sketch of each variety and described the types of food and occasion each would complement. Everything had gone well. The glasses had been clean and polished. I'd even had a round of applause. They had been responsive, lively and questioning, and had laughed in all the right places.

I smiled, thinking of the one difficult question I'd been asked. There's one clever clogs in every audience and over the years I had learnt how to deal with them.

'Do you think wine number three has undergone a malolactic fermentation?' he had asked.

'Good question,' I replied, groaning inside. I knew all about malolactic fermentation from my days in the champagne cellars in Reims, but hadn't done my homework on this particular wine. Why hadn't I looked up the technical information last night rather than getting smashed on Calvados? 'Off the top of my head, I'm not sure. But since you are so knowledgeable about the subject, perhaps *you* would like to tell us if you think it has.'

The questioner blushed and shrugged his shoulders.

'Tasting it alongside number four,' I went on, 'it appears an altogether softer, less tart wine, so, yes, my guess is that it probably has. Tell you what, leave me your email and I'll talk to the grower and find out,' I concluded, turning to the next person with a question.

'If you had to choose just one of these wines, which one would it be and why?'

This was a familiar question and I gave it the standard joking reply – 'Whichever one is in my glass' – before going on to select a wine. Then I turned the question on the questioner: 'What really interests me is what *your* favourite is. You're the important person here – you have to sell these wines.' Flattery – it worked every time.

Over lunch many of the staff had said how much they'd enjoyed the tasting, and how much easier it was to be enthusiastic and helpful in their recommendations to shoppers when they'd tasted the wines and knew something about them. Audiences were always far more vocal after a tasting than before. While I had conscientiously spat out my wines, I noted many of the spittoons in the room were empty.

The main thing was that the cheque-signing head office team had seemed impressed. I could tell it had gone well when one of the buyers started to discuss which wines we should feature in our next tasting.

Now, I stopped at traffic lights. A woman with short, spiky hair pulled up to my right in a black Mercedes estate. She smiled and I smiled back.

I used to have my hair like that when I was eighteen, I remembered. It wouldn't suit me now. God, those were the days – footloose and fancy-free, no kids, no mortgage, no husband. I watched her tapping her steering wheel in time to the music on the radio. She had a wedding ring on. I bet *her* husband was kind and thoughtful, I reflected.

I grimaced, thinking of the marriage-guidance counsellor Niall and I had been to see. I'd had to plead with Niall to get him there. It hadn't been a success. Both of us were hung-over – we probably still smelt of booze. The counsellor had asked us each to make two lists, one detailing our partner's assets and one our own. My list of Niall's assets was twice the length of those I attributed to myself. His was the reverse: his list of his own assets ran over the page; the list he wrote of mine did not reach half a page. That said it all, I fumed. I could be generous enough to see his assets without believing I had many of my own. Why hadn't the counsellor commented on this?

There was another curious thing. Neither Niall nor I had said anything about drinking. It was as if we had an unspoken agreement not to mention it. It wasn't discussed at all.

On the M25, the traffic was at a standstill and the rain was falling ever heavier. At this rate, the boys would be in bed before I got home. I liked to put them to bed, to be able to check they were happy, find out how their day had been. Each night they pleaded for one of my Hungry Giraffe stories – I had invented two brothers, Horatio and Horace, giraffes who were always hungry, who helped people and were invariably repaid in food. I could do with Horatio and Horace's help right now, I thought, as I stared despairingly at the stationary traffic. That was it – I'd tell the boys a story of how the Hungry Giraffes lifted me, crane-like, car and all, off the motorway and neatly home in time for bedtime stories. The boys would always dream up the giraffes' rewards, describing in detail their feasts, often falling asleep as they conjured up ever more exotic and fantastical ice-cream creations.

Home at last, I opened the back door. I could hear Niall

in his office, coughing, but there was no sound of the boys.

'Hi, there,' I said to Niall. 'Good day?'

He didn't look up and carried on at his computer keyboard. 'Yeah, fine. I put the boys to bed.'

'I'll go up and see them, then.'

'No, don't, they'll be asleep. I put them to bed about an hour ago.'

'OK.' I felt deflated. 'Aren't you going to ask me how my day was? How the tasting went?'

He looked up for a second and turned back to his keyboard. 'I expect it was fine. It's was only a tasting, wasn't it? Nothing complicated.'

'Nothing complicated that I'm paid a lot of money for,' I replied, half under my breath. I added more loudly, 'What's that awful smell? I could smell it halfway down the garden. More stock?'

He laughed and took a swig from the glass of red wine beside his desk. 'Yeah, just boiling up the carcass and giblets of the pheasant I had for lunch.'

'Well, it smells to me as if it's burning. Perhaps you better check the bones haven't flown out of the pan.'

He took another gulp of wine and walked past me out of the door. I heard his footsteps on the stairs to the basement kitchen. I picked up the large Riedel glass beside his desk and took a sniff – a good red Burgundy. I took a big gulp. Why did he always open such good wines when I wasn't here? I finished the glass in two more mouthfuls and looked around for the bottle. God, I was tired. I'd been up since 6 a.m. and driven 200 miles. It might have been 'only a tasting' but they always left me shattered, so tired sometimes I could hardly speak.

I could hear pots and pans being banged around in the kitchen. I picked up my handbag and quietly opened the front door. Just William's was ten houses down the road. I walked quickly down the street, and as I pushed open the doors, I could hear the murmur of people, smell rosemary and roast lamb. I realised how hungry I was. I had only played around with my food at lunchtime.

'Hi, Al, how are you? You look smart, all in Armani. What have you been up to? What can I get you?' said Sarah.

'I've been doing a tasting for Tesco – lots of fizz. What I'd really like is a glass of Pinot Noir. I'm gagging.'

'The Edna Valley, then? How many glasses? Is Niall coming?'

'Dunno, didn't ask him. As ever he's tap-tap-tapping on his computer. Actually, I didn't even tell him I'd gone out. Don't suppose he'll notice for a while anyway.'

The Pinot Noir was delicious, one of California's finest, and great value for money. If only I could source a wine with this intensity of flavour that Tesco could retail for about £5.99, but there was nowhere in the world that could produce this richness of fruit at that price.

I looked around the restaurant. It seemed full of laughing couples with seemingly happy lives. Sarah turned to talk to another customer and I felt that familiar feeling of being in a crowd yet alone.

'Penny for them,' said a guy I didn't know, sitting at the bar. 'You look really sad. You OK?'

'Yep, I'm fine. I was just thinking about this wine, actually. It's delicious. You should try it. Sarah, can I have another glass, please?'

It was midnight when I left the pub. The guy at the bar and I had eaten dinner together and shared a second bottle of the Edna Valley, followed by two half-bottles of a luscious, marmalade-like Orange Muscat from Brown Brothers with our crème caramels. I'd talked about my day and he'd chatted about his. He was some kind of engineer overseeing some project. Pretty boring stuff, actually, but he'd seemed very interested in wine – his hobby, he'd said.

Climbing up the steps to the front door, I had to hold tightly on to the iron railings for support. So, so tired. I tried the door handle. It was locked. Typical! How did Niall know whether I had a key?

I felt inside my handbag and grabbed what I thought to be the key. It was Number Three son's silver rattle. I emptied the contents of the bag on to the top step and sat down. I knew my house key was in there somewhere.

A car drove by and tooted its horn. I raised my hand to wave, still holding the rattle, laughing, shaking it. It had a dainty musical tinkle, like Tinkerbell.

I realised with a start that my eyes were closing. God, so tired. Ah, there was the key, stuck inside Number One son's favourite book, Dr Seuss's *Cat in the Hat*. As if on cue, one of our two cats, Lafite – we had christened them Lafite and Latour after the clarets – arrived to investigate.

Another car drove by, blinding me with its headlights. Drunken yobs, I thought. I opened the front door. The hall was in darkness. I felt my way to the stairs, the cat padding along behind me. I was desperate to use the loo and sat down gratefully on the wooden seat, kicking off my high heels, letting my trousers and knickers slide down around my ankles. I could see the moon through the window.

The bathroom started to spin. Losing my balance, I grabbed for the bath to steady myself, knocking my wrist hard. Ouch! That really hurt! The room kept spinning. I felt sick. Stepping out of my trousers, I gingerly opened the bedroom door. Loud snoring greeted me. I climbed into bed.

I awoke to hear the town hall clock striking 4 a.m. My wrist was throbbing – I had broken it, though I didn't know that yet – and I was beside myself with pain, rocking backwards and forwards just as I had during childbirth. Niall snored on. I looked down at my swollen, misshapen wrist.

Only one thing for that kind of pain. Vodka, neat.

CHAPTER TWENTY-TWO

LIGHT-BULB MOMENT

The door slammed. I stood alone in the music room. The jukebox stood slyly winking at me, one eye blue, the other red. I pressed 111. The machine clunked, the disc was selected, and the crackling sound of a kitsch Hollywood version of 'Ave Maria' came on. I savoured the berry-like taste of the Mad Fish Pinot Noir in my mouth. And then started to cry. 'Ave Maria' always made me cry. I'd told anyone who would listen that I wanted it to be played at my funeral, and right now I felt as if I would rather be dead than face the inevitable. I knew the time had come for surrender. I couldn't go on like this. Something had to change.

I looked down at my dress, an old Moschino favourite – my *Alice in Wonderland* dress, I liked to call it – soft crêpe patterned in roses, big red satin hearts, nipped into the waist, a full skirt cut on the cross, all lined with crimson chiffon. I caught sight of myself in the mirror. By some trick of the light I could see only one half of the middle heart – it was cut in two. How apt.

I was exhausted. A furry, creeping hangover did not help. The second bottle of the St Hallett's Old Block Shiraz the night before had been a mistake, I knew that now, but at the time it had been impossible to resist its spicy, plain-chocolate depths. I always felt as if it gave me strength. That was what I needed now, strength. I felt sick to the pit of my stomach. I realised I had only one course of action.

I had just told Niall that I was exhausted, that I needed a holiday, maybe just a few days away, alone.

'What have you ever done that makes you think you could possibly be exhausted?' he'd sneered.

I'd opened my mouth to reply but then closed it. What I wanted to say remained unsaid: 'Only had three children in five years, been a loyal wife, believed in you and stuck by you when your company failed and the wine trade told me to leave you, earned the odd hundred grand a year to keep us going, loved you with a vengeance.' I stood glaring at him.

And that was it. A cartoon light bulb popped into my head inside a thought bubble. It flashed and in that instant I gave up. I knew I had to leave him, that I could stand no more rows. I was beginning to doubt my every move, my every sentence. I had to get away, otherwise I was going to become madder than the Mad Fish wine in my glass.

I pressed 216 and turned up the jukebox. 'D–I–V–O–R–C–E,' sang Tammy Wynette. I wasn't going to take her earlier advice and 'stand by my man' any longer.

Decision made, I felt strangely elated, but the enormity of the decision I had been wrestling with for months made me extremely thirsty. There was only one thing to do. I went straight to my local and got drunk on dry Blackthorn cider to try to dull the pain and disappointment I felt within.

I knew that the way ahead wasn't going to be easy. The next challenge was to make the proposition attractive to Niall, to make him think that splitting up was his idea. I decided to present it as a marketing plan: neither of us was any good at saving money, we didn't like working in the same house or having an au pair living with us, so why not invest in a separate house that one of us could use as an office? We went away for a few days and I put it to him over a drunken dinner. He fell for it, and by the time we returned and set about looking for properties, he was convinced it was his brilliant idea. Although it was never discussed, I felt sure it would end up being me who moved out.

Until the famous champagne party.

CHAPTER TWENTY-THREE

FABULOUS FIZZ PARTY

Avon House was the ultimate party house. Opening the front door, you could be forgiven for thinking you were in a wine shop as wine racks flowed from floor to ceiling in the arched twenty-foot hall. Books spilled out of wooden claret boxes, and flowers drank deep in ice buckets that doubled up as wastepaper bins and spittoons. Off the hallway was my tasting room. This was originally the main sitting room of the house and it retained the original plasterwork-ceiling frieze of moulded vines.

A bay window let in north light – the perfect light in which to assess a wine's colour. The boys delighted in telling their teachers about 'Mummy's spitting room' and laughed, shaking their little heads, when asked, 'Don't you mean sitting room?'

To the far end of the hall was the music room, resplendent with grand piano, the Wurlitzer jukebox and glass doors opening on to a designer, wild yet cultivated garden. Alongside the music room was a long, narrow utility room. This housed all the usual suspects, such as a washing machine and tumble-dryer, but also a wine-bar-sized bottle fridge and ever more wine racks.

Leaning against the back wall of the four-storey house was a much-loved sculpture called *Storm Music*. Originally the trunk of a poplar tree that had crashed to the ground during the hurricane of 1987, I liked to imagine it protected me from the storms without, if not within, for many years. The end was carved to resemble the scrolled end of a cello, and I'd bought it after a solo liquid lunch in Bath as an impulsive birthday present for Niall, once a keen cellist. The sculptor's name was John Jokeas, and given its price tag of £2,000, there were those among my friends who commented that the 'joke' was definitely on me.

A half-basement below the level of the garden housed the kitchen and playroom, which were best in wintertime, when a roaring fire added warmth and colour to this otherwise chilly floor.

The best views of surrounding marshland, the River Kennet, the Avon Canal and St Lawrence's Church were from my office, which was located one flight up from the hall and directly above the spitting room. Here, on this middle floor, was my adored bathroom, which was painted sunshine yellow. It housed an original roll-top bath, which took gallons of comforting steamy water, and tiles adorned with cheery frogs on lily pads kick-started my day.

A few feet away, you stepped into the fabulous main bedroom. Two large windows flooded this room with light and glorious sunshine, which on fine days danced on the bed. Dramatic stripped vertical beams gave the illusion of a room divider where once stud walls had split this stunning space into two rooms. When the boys had been born, these were adorned with over a hundred cards from well-wishers.

The children's rooms were at the top of the house, along with another bathroom. Here, stencilled gold stars encouraged dreaming, and on the same floor, a narrow galley kitchen in the eves was a reminder that in a previous life the house had been converted into flats.

It was an easy house to get lost in. Anyone could do anything in Avon House and no one would be any the wiser.

*

A small hand clasped mine. 'Mummy,' the voice whispered in my ear, tickling my cheek like a breathy feather, 'one of the champagne bottles has exploded – the stopper has flown out.'

I turned over in bed to see Number Two son standing there, strawberry-blond hair sticking straight up like a squirrel's tail. He was looking at me with mock alarm.

'Don't worry, darling. I'll get up in a minute and sort it out. What time is it?'

It was 6 a.m. He slipped into bed beside me. He was soft and warm. 'Mummy, what time does the party start? Can I help blow up the balloons?'

'Oh, yes, the party . . . Of course you can. But it's not until tonight. Don't worry. We have plenty of time.' I looked down at him, his face spattered with freckles – God's kisses, my father use to call mine whenever I complained I didn't like them.

I had an unusually deep bond with my second son. We were almost telepathic and often went to say the same thing at the same time. We frequently knew instinctively what each other was feeling and didn't really need to talk, though we chatted endlessly.

I thought back to when I was about the same age, three or four. I could remember looking down at my red sandals and then into my mother's eyes, pleading with her, 'Promise me you love me the best?'

'I love you all, all nine of you, but in different ways, so I don't love anyone in the same way as I love you,' was her reply.

I lay for a minute, blinking. Had I come to bed late? I couldn't remember coming to bed at all. I remembered talking to someone on the phone, finishing a half-bottle of Roederer Riche demi-sec champagne and then looking for another one. After that it was a blank. What was happening to my memory? More often than not, I couldn't remember going to bed.

Best not to think of that. Guilt made me feel sick, and once I started being sick in the mornings – a regular occurrence – I couldn't stop. Besides, I needed to be on form for tasting. I couldn't afford to throw up. Just fifty more champagnes to taste, I thought to myself, lying there in the half-light. That would bring the week's total up to 300 and mark the end of the major tasting research for my latest book, *Fabulous Fizz*. The call from Anne Ryland of publishers Ryland Peters and Small asking if I would like to write a book about champagne was like asking if the Pope is a Catholic.

I might as well get up and taste them now, I thought. I never regarded tasting champagne as work, however bad my hangover. It was always a pleasure, especially since I'd left the best ones, the vintages and deluxe cuvées, until last.

I could smell the overpowering scent of white lilies long before I reached my tasting room. I had bought them for Niall as a fifteenth-anniversary present. I couldn't think of anything else – what do you buy a husband when you know it's to be the last anniversary you will have together? He had arranged them in a spectacular display with stippled pink foxgloves from the garden. I looked at them, standing up straight and defiant on top of the piano, seemingly mocking me.

Later, the tasting finished, I surveyed the last glasses on the table. The three best wines stood there, bubbling in the sparkling light, calling to me. I knew it was early in the day but what the hell, I'd done my work and it was my wedding anniversary. The least I deserved was a glass of fizz for surviving fifteen years, I told myself, settling down on the squidgy sofa with a glass of Taittinger Comtes de Champagnes Blanc de Blanc 1989 – elegant, rich and creamy. I felt curiously elated. Champagne had that effect on me. I knew I was doing the right thing leaving Niall. Just don't think about it, I told myself sternly. To drown out the chattering committee in my head, I swiftly drained my glass.

The door opened and Number One son stood there, bleary-eyed. 'Can I have some cornflakes? And then can we start blowing up the balloons? I bags the gold ones!'

Both baths in the house were filled with gold and purple balloons and bottles of champagne left over from the tasting. There were bottles of champagne everywhere, in fact – 300 of them, in three fridges and in a big cast-iron bath outside in the garden. Having a party to dispose of them seemed an obvious solution. It would have been sacrilege to tip them down the sink. I looked out from the bedroom over the candlelit garden and sipped a glass of Schramsberg Napa Valley Rosé Cuvée de Pinot 1994 – a sensational wine with a curious hint of raspberries, peaches and cinnamon. I pulled my slinky Umani Ronchi black dress over my head. Number Two son was sitting on the end of the bed. 'Mummy,' he said, sounding shocked, 'you haven't got any underwear on.'

'No,' I laughed. 'You can't with this dress – it would show.' I pushed up my breasts, which were held in place by a thin piece of silver chain, which joined up the dropped deep-cowl neck of the dress. Not bad for having fed three children, I thought. Now, which shoes? Number Two son chose a pair of gold and silver strappy Charles Jourdan sandals. The heels were so high it was tricky to stand in them. I teetered around in front of the mirror, careful not to let the narrow heels disappear between the cracks in the floorboards.

'Do I look OK?' I asked. He nodded his head.

The doorbell clanged and I set off downstairs to let in the first of the guests. The house was strangely quiet, as if awaiting some momentous occasion. When I opened the door, I noticed that the sky was a strange shade of translucent grey. There were smudgy rain clouds in the distance.

I greeted our guests. 'Help yourself to a bottle – they're all over the house and the garden. Glasses in the tasting room. Enjoy. And I shall expect a full report later on all the bottles you've tasted.'

'What style!' said Bruce, a dentist friend. 'Normally you get given a glass – here, it's a bottle.'

Next to arrive were two men from our local Chinese take-away van, bearing woks and prawn crackers and ingredients to cook Singapore noodles for a hundred. More people came streaming in through the door. The jukebox started pounding. Every few seconds or so I'd hear the pop of another champagne cork. Some of the guests I barely knew. I assumed Niall had invited them. A dozen or so handed me happy-anniversary cards that I promptly abandoned, unopened, in the hall.

One of my younger brothers, Francis, disappeared upstairs to the top kitchen in search of the best bottle I'd stashed in the fridge. I caught him on the stairs armed with Perrier-Jouët Belle Epoque 1990 in its distinctive art nouveau painted bottle.

'Ah . . . definite aroma of violets,' joked Francis.

'My tasting notes exactly. But to be sure, I'd better sample it again.' I held out my glass.

The doorbell clanged again. I adjusted my dress, yanking up my boobs. I opened the door to Maria José, one of my Spanish friends whose family produced Viña Tondonia Rioja. Her arms were full of crimson peonies, which she thrust into my hands.

'Come upstairs with me,' I told her. 'I've hidden the best wines in the top fridge, reserved for family and favourite winemakers.'

'I can't wait to taste them!'

'Oh, there's no serious tasting going on here – everyone is simply drinking.'

At the top of the house, I peeped into the boys' room. The two younger boys were there, but there was no sign of their elder brother. Roxanne, the nanny, was reading a book.

'Fancy a glass of fizz, Roxanne?' I asked, pouring out three glasses. 'This is Iron Horse 1996, one of California's finest.'

'What shall we toast?' asked Maria. 'Ah, look – it's called Wedding Cuvée, that's appropriate – isn't it your wedding anniversary?'

I looked away. 'No. Let's toast the success of my book,' I replied.

We raised our glasses and I downed the spicy, red-berry-like fizz in two neat gulps. For some reason I was left with a nasty taste in my mouth.

'Drink up and I'll find you another one, Maria. Let's try this – Veuve Clicquot's top cuvée, La Grande Dame 1990. This has to be one of the most complex fizzes I've tasted. Grab a glass of this, come down to my office and I'll show you some of the photographs for my book. It's so exciting – ten books and finally one that's going to look amazing. Peter Cassidy – the photographer – has done a fantastic job. When I saw the photos, I actually cried with joy. And I don't do that very often these days.'

On the top step, I almost lost my footing, my left heel catching on the edge of the carpet rod. As I stumbled, I kept hold of my glass, but the contents cascaded down the banisters to the ground floor. Somebody looked up and squealed.

'The best champagne and it's gone over their heads,' I shouted down the stairs, pleased with my private joke. This whole party was that – a supposedly happy occasion, champagne flowing. A sham, I thought. If only they knew. Not that any of them would truly care.

'You OK?' asked Maria. 'You look really sad.'

'I'm fine,' I lied. 'Look at this cover picture.'

I heard a kerfuffle outside and looked down from my office window into the street. Two people were having difficulty leaving, climbing into a car and straight out of the other side. Bill, my scientist friend, was wandering down the middle of the road, bottle in hand, kicking his legs up and bawling 'New York, New York' along with the jukebox. He was out of time with the music.

A strange, detached feeling washed over me once again, as if I wasn't really there – as if I were simply an observer, watching this madness going on around me.

On my desk stood more abandoned bottles. 'Pelorus 1993 – now, you need to try this one, Maria. It's a really rich, unusual, biscuity wine from New Zealand. Look, we're in luck – there's enough left for two glasses.'

Maria José was laughing. 'How do you do it? I mean, drink so fast and stay standing, especially in those shoes?'

'Years of practice. Come on, come downstairs and have some noodles and meet some other people. Niall's around somewhere – though I've not really seen him all night.'

The ground floor was buzzing. There were people everywhere – sitting on the stairs, draped around the banisters, dancing in front of the jukebox. Someone was playing the piano, and someone else lay underneath, bottle in hand, twitching in time to the music. I picked my way across the dance floor to the pulse of 'Le Freak' and picked up a few empty bottles. Through the garden door I could see the evening primroses, now open, a strangely fluorescent yellow in the candlelight. There were bodies and bottles strewn around. I stopped to chat to a group of people sitting on the *Storm Music* sculpture.

'Hey, Al, have you tried this one? It's from Lorigan, I mean Oregon, Willamette Valley. I'm having difficulties saying that,' said Tim, Niall's brother. We were drinking partners and soul mates who shared some unspoken link that led us on several occasions to telephone each other at exactly the same time.

'Of course I've tasted it, you twit, that's why we're having the party, because I've tasted them all. But, well, I had better taste it again, just to refresh my memory. Ah, yes, this is the one that tastes like liquorice fizz. It would be good with the Singapore noodles. Have you had any?'

'Two platefuls. Hey, Al, some of your friends are out-rageous – especially that Scottish girl in the green dress with her tits all on show, the one with the stud in her nose. Music teacher. She keeps offering blokes mouth-organ lessons.'

'What do you mean, mouth-organ lessons?'

'Come on, use your imagination – you're the writer. Anyway, no one, to my knowledge, has been stupid enough to take her up on it. Mind you, I don't know where she is now.'

'Come on, let's dance. Hey, Maria José, it's Madness – "One Step Beyond". I love this record!'

Some hours later I was doing my Leaning Tower of Pisa impersonation, beginning to feel weary and woozy. Not that I felt that drunk. I had taken it easy because I didn't want any scenes with Niall. I hadn't seen him all night. He seemed to be keeping out of my way. The fizz was beginning to wear off and I felt flat. Although many of the guests had left, there was a hard core of a dozen or so dancers and various bodies floating around.

'Can't find any more fizz,' moaned Bruce.

'Try the basement fridge. Or right down the garden.'

He lurched off.

I climbed the stairs up to my office, stepping over two or three people on the way. My office door was closed and the room was in darkness. I sat down at my desk and swivelled round on my chair. Looking at the window, I could see light over the church – the sun was coming up. I had been up for twenty-four hours. I needed to go to bed.

I stood up, lifted my dress over my head and opened the door. Looking straight ahead, high heels still on, I took the two steps across the hall to the bedroom. As I was about to close the door, I noticed someone sitting on the stairs.

'Sorry,' I said, 'I didn't realise anyone was there. Hope you didn't see my stretch marks.'

'I wasn't looking at your stretch marks,' came a man's slurred voice as I collapsed on to an empty bed.

CHAPTER TWENTY-FOUR

THE MORNING AFTER

The next day I was woken at eleven by snoring. I poked Niall and tried to wake him. He was out for the count.

Pulling on a short denim skirt and a spotted silk T-shirt, I opened my bedroom door. Empty champagne bottles lay around like scattered skittles. Glasses, streamers, deflated balloons and cigarette ends littered the stairs. A bowl of forgotten noodles perched precariously on the banister.

'Good party,' said Roxanne.

'Was it? I'm not sure. God, look at all this mess. What time did the boys wake up?'

'We came down about seven thirty. I made them pancakes for breakfast.'

Roxanne and I made our way down the two flights of stairs to the kitchen, the champagne battlefield becoming more treacherous with every step. Number Three son pulled at my leg. I bent down to pick him up and almost toppled over.

'You OK there?' asked Roxanne.

'Just thirsty. I could do with a can of Coke.' About to open the fridge, I spied a half-full bottle of Bollinger left on the high chair. What a waste. There were no clean champagne flutes in sight so I poured myself a tumbler. It was lukewarm and barely fizzy, but one gulp cleared the fuzziness in my head. I laughed – an alcoholic Alka-Seltzer.

Bleary-eyed guests carrying empty bottles were emerging from rooms all over the house. I saw one guy I didn't recognise at all. Where had he come from? No matter. It was time to go to the pub for brunch – the clearing-up could wait until later.

Wandering down the road, I bumped into an old friend, Wendy. People often mistook us for sisters. We settled in the pub garden, me with my customary Sunday bloody Mary in hand, to discuss last night.

'What an amazing party!' she said. 'I've never, ever seen so much fizz or so many people drinking so fast. It was a full moon – perhaps that's what drove people into such a frenzy. We didn't leave until seven. We met the paperboy!'

'You lasted longer than me,' I said. 'I went to bed about four thirty. Were there many people left at seven, then? Was Niall still up? He was fast asleep this morning. I couldn't wake him.'

Wendy looked at me and hesitated. 'I don't know how to say this . . .'

'What?'

'Well, he was still up. . .'

'There's no surprise!'

'He was in the hall when we left with that Scottish girl – the mouth-organ woman – and . . .' She stopped, blushing, her eyes wide.

'And what?'

'She was giving him a blow job. Right there in the hall, just outside his office.'

I choked on my bloody Mary. '*What?* Are you sure?'

'Alice, I couldn't miss it. I had to walk past them to the front door.'

I emptied my glass and stared in disbelief. I locked away my anger and outrage and began to laugh manically in shock. 'Ye-e-esss! There *is* a God! I've got Niall now! I told him we were splitting up and now I'll get to stay in the house. Bloody hell! Well, I'm blowed – if you'll forgive the pun. This definitely calls for another drink. Large one!'

The following morning, Monday, Niall and I overslept. We still hadn't spoken about what had happened. Our youngest son was in bed with us. I was suddenly awakened by a knock at the bedroom door. My eyes felt as if they had been massaged with grit. It was difficult to focus. It was Number Three son's nanny. She started gabbling and I had to concentrate to keep up.

'Good morning. So you survived the party, then? Wow, some party – we had a ball. Thank you so much. You sure know some wacky characters. Who was the lady with the diamond stud in her nose, the one in the green dress with her boobs spilling out – she seemed to be having a good time?'

'Well, she certainly gave me a good time,' said Niall. 'She gave me a blow job in the hall,' he continued, smirking across at me.

The nanny's eyes widened and she looked at me uncertainly. I shrugged my shoulders. I heard myself laugh, a high-pitched squeal as if I'd inhaled helium. There was a second or two of silence. The baby stirred, nuzzling his head into my breast. I could feel my heart beating fast.

'There are two bottles of milk made up for him in the drinks fridge,' I told her, handing her the baby.

I escaped to my office and busied myself with a VAT return. Nothing like numbers to concentrate the mind – a fire door against troublesome thoughts. Come lunchtime, Niall poked his head round the door. He was dressed in a double-breasted Yves St Laurent suit, his standard hangover outfit. 'I'd like to take you out to lunch to apologise for embarrassing you,' he said, looking boyish.

'You didn't embarrass me, you embarrassed yourself,' I said, raising my eyebrows and looking down my nose at him.

'I'm not sure I want to have lunch with you.'

But I knew we needed to discuss what had happened away from the kids so we went anyway, taking a taxi to a pub in the next village – in fact the first pub Niall ever took me to. He ordered a bottle of Barratt Hills Australian Pinot Noir. I ordered potted shrimps and played around with them. The tiny shrimps looked helplessly trapped, drowned in the yellow clarified butter. I knew how they felt.

After ten minutes of silence I asked, 'Why did you do it? How could you? Do you think that was acceptable behaviour, you who insisted on putting "fifteenth wedding anniversary" on the party invitations, even though I asked you not to? It was luck, not judgement, the children didn't catch you at it. They came downstairs minutes later.'

He took a large gulp of his wine. 'Just get over it,' he sneered. 'I don't really see what your problem is. We're splitting up anyway, so what's the big deal? Typical of you to make such a drama.'

I'll give you typical, I thought. I stood up, picked up my glass of wine and poured it over his head. Grabbing my handbag, I marched out of the pub and across the road to the train station. Waste of a decent glassful, I thought, as I stalked on to the London train.

Two days later I caught the train home – sober. I had been retching almost continuously, literally sick to my stomach. I felt like a fish that had been gutted but left alive, twitching on the riverbank for passers-by to gloat over. I'd had my mobile phone on voicemail, avoiding the humiliation of admitting to more friends and acquaintances that, yes, the gossip was true.

How would I hold my head up in Hungerford again? If someone had chopped off my hand the word 'hurt' would have appeared in blood, running through my wrist like letters through a stick of rock.

CHAPTER TWENTY-FIVE

LADY BY THE LAKE

A week after the party Niall and I were invited to lunch at our old friends Debbie and Steve's. We were putting on a brave face for our children while we tried to sort out the details of the separation. Debbie was petite, self-effacing and vivacious, and Steve was super-bright with a penchant for dressing up like Freddie Mercury at fancy-dress parties. We had all known each other for years, as Niall's mother had looked after their sons. Debbie and Steve had seen Niall and me at our best and worst, and we enjoyed many a good bottle with them at home and on holidays in Ireland and Spain. I envied their relationship – passionate yet tender, just how ours had been in the very early days.

On this Sunday we ate outside, lunching on barbecued chicken, tomato, basil and onion salad with balsamic vinegar and potato salad dressed with black pepper and chives from the garden. Sludgy summer pudding followed with whitecurrants and blackcurrants. We were drinking Beaumes-de-Venise.

'It's amazing how the wine seems to taste of raspberries,' said Debbie.

'Yes,' I agreed. 'Niall, do you remember we used to drink gallons of this the first summer we met? We would barbecue trout and eat it with salad and Stilton. I was so impressed – we always had champagne to start, and the odd bottle of red and white in between, and would finish with bowls of raspberries and huge glasses of this in bed. I'd never tasted Beaumes-de-Venise before I met you.'

He looked at me glassy-eyed. A chalk-blue butterfly landed on the table. 'Look, a chalk-blue,' he said.

Was that all he could say?

There was an awkward silence.

Steve stepped in. 'Niall, come and see my new car.'

Glasses in hand, they walked over to the gleaming green 7-Series BMW. I looked up as I heard Niall's familiar laugh. 'Love the registration,' he chortled. 'BJB – that's me, Blow-Job Boy! I presume you've heard how the party ended.'

A look of horror crossed Debbie's face. 'God, how can you bear it?' she hissed at me. 'How can you even speak to him? Come on, let's make some Pimm's and take it down the garden.' I followed her into the kitchen.

'I don't like to think about it,' I told her. 'It hurts so much. But I'm trying to tell myself that it's all worked out in my favour, as now I'll get to stay in Avon House. I'll have to pay him off, but I think it's settled. He appears quite chuffed that the whole town seems to know. He seems to have told everyone. Sad, isn't it? Fifteen years of marriage, only to end like this, in public humiliation.'

Debbie was furiously chopping apples. 'You have all those rooms and he chose to do it in the hall. Almost as if he wanted to be seen. It must have been a shock for those leaving, drunk or not.'

'Well, I was going to leave him anyway. This just served to sharpen my resolve.'

I suggested we strengthen the Pimm's with a slug of vodka. I found a bottle of Stolichnaya and poured about a third of the bottle into the jug. Adding ice cubes with raspberries frozen inside them, I realised I had overfilled it.

'We'll have to sample it – just to make room, you understand.'

I poured out two tumblers. We each took a drink and

Debbie screwed up her face. 'Wow, that certainly packs a punch. It's made my eyes water.'

'I could do with packing a punch right now. OK, all we need now is the borage.'

'We'll go down by the lake. You grab the glasses and we'll pick it on the way.'

Steve and Niall had disappeared. The air was warm as we walked down to the lake, the setting sun a deep, deep red.

I felt numb inside. Since the party I couldn't seem to stop drinking. I felt drunk after just one or two, but then I felt worse, not better. My tolerance to alcohol seemed to be low. My tolerance to everything seemed to be low. I felt as if I was operating outside my body, that all this was happening to a stranger.

'What a beautiful sky,' said Debbie. 'How would you describe that shade?'

'Blood red. Angry red.'

We settled down at a white plastic table by the lake. I added the borage flowers to the Pimm's and poured out two more glasses. I thought back to all the Sundays Niall and I had spent together in the early days. We had been young then, in love. What had happened? Where had all the feeling gone?

'What shall we drink to?' asked Debbie.

'Freedom.'

I took a big mouthful and closed my eyes. How was I going to tell my parents I was leaving Niall? How would I tell the children? I couldn't bear the thought of their crumpled little faces. Was I right to give up? I had never given up on anything in my life. But this wasn't a life. It wasn't good for the children. It wasn't good for me.

When I opened my eyes, Debbie's chair was empty. I closed my eyes again and dozed.

A shadow crossed in front of me. I opened my eyes again to see a woman walk past. She was taller than me, with dark-blonde hair cut in a bob. She was dressed in an olive-green raincoat, belted, with the collar turned up. I shivered and the hairs on my arms stood up. Was I seeing things? I closed my eyes once more and then half opened them. The same thing happened – the same woman. But as soon as I blinked, she was gone. I turned round and looked back to the house. No one in sight. What was going on? Was it the Pimm's? Was I that drunk? I topped up my glass and sat there glugging it.

Debbie returned with a bowl of pistachios. 'You OK? You're as white as a sheet.'

'I can't believe my own eyes. I know we've been drinking all afternoon but I've just had the strangest experience. A woman with dark-blonde bobbed hair, dressed in an olive-green raincoat just walked past me. Twice.'

Debbie stared at me. 'That's Anne,' she said quietly.

'What do you mean, Anne? Anne who? Where is she?'

'My friend Anne. Her husband murdered her when she tried to leave him. We often used to sit here and drink Pimm's. She loved Pimm's. We were sitting here the night before he stabbed her. Did she say anything to you?'

'No, nothing. She didn't even look at me. I must have dozed off and when I woke up she was here. She disappeared. I closed my eyes and when I opened them she did it again. This is weird!'

We sat in silence, the sun sinking lower, the sky like a blood-stained shroud.

I blinked. There were tears in my eyes. 'It's a sign,' I said. 'I think she appeared to tell me to have the strength to leave Niall. Only this afternoon I was wondering if I would have the courage. It's a sign. Do you really think that was Anne? Is that what she looked like?'

'Definitely. She loved it down here. Sometimes I would find her sitting here, when she was alive, looking out over the marsh.'

'And she died doing what she believed in, trusting her heart.' I drained my glass. It was becoming difficult to keep my eyes open.

CHAPTER TWENTY-SIX

EVEN OLD WINES DIE

There is nothing quite as seductive as the taste of the Pinot Noir grape. It's difficult to grow but a delight to drink. A bit like a man – hard to train but, hopefully, worth the wait. I was drinking Pinot Noir the night before Niall moved out.

After seemingly endless delays – the lease on his rented house wasn't right, the removal men were busy, the phone lines couldn't be changed in time, he had important meetings to attend – the removal van was scheduled to arrive one rainy midwinter Saturday morning.

I had spent the evening before in the pub, propping up the bar, drinking copious amounts of Edna Valley. I have no recollection of how much I drank or who I bored with my story. I do remember coming to on the hard, lumpy futon in the spare room, where I had been sleeping alone ever since the week after the champagne party. I found myself holding my breath. Would he really move out today, or would there be more excuses?

I got up, tiptoed down the stairs and peeped into the boys' room. They were all fast asleep. Number Three son was wedged sideways in his cot. No matter how many times I turned him over, he would flip back and lie on his front, knees tucked under him, nappy-clad bottom stuck in the air. I covered him up with his ABC duvet and stood looking at him for a while.

Outside the bedroom, I paused on the landing. Little over

a year ago I had crossed this landing from my office to my bedroom, just minutes before giving birth to him. Today, I could hear Niall's snoring from behind a firmly shut bedroom door.

I was halfway down the stairs when I sensed someone behind me. I turned to see Number Two son's pixie-like face grinning at me, his strawberry-blond hair static and sticking up at right angles as if he had back-combed it.

'You're up early, Mummy.'

'Yes. Lots to do. Daddy is moving to his new house today.'

'Oh. I'm hungry. Do we have any Sugar Puffs?'

'Look in the pantry,' I replied.

'I can't get in there, it's full of boxes. Is Daddy taking all the food?'

'Of course not.'

'Why does Daddy call the pantry a larder?' he asked innocently.

'I don't know. Look, here are the Sugar Puffs.'

We cleared a space on the kitchen table. He aimed the Sugar Puffs packet at his favourite Aladdin bowl, scattering cereal across the table. He stopped with the milk bottle in midair.

'Which house will my bowl be in?' he asked.

'You can keep it here if you like. I'm sure we can buy you another one for Daddy's house.'

'I doubt we'll find one the same. They're very rare, you know,' he replied, solemnly.

I turned away and stared at the cooker, avoiding his eyes. He took his bowl of Sugar Puffs off to eat in the playroom. On the cooker was a huge saucepan full to the brim with stock. The fat had risen to the surface and partially solidified. It looked like crazy paving. A lamb bone was just visible, surrounded by grey scum.

My stomach turned. Niall and his foul stockpots. But now there'd be no more mornings of having to come down to this. No more questions from guests as they came into the house: 'What *is* that smell?'

I picked up the pan and tipped the contents down the sink, watching the slimy liquid slither down the plughole. I knew this was sacrilege. Niall had sulked for weeks when our cleaning lady had mistakenly thrown away his precious stock. I washed the saucepan and fished the nasty debris from the sink, feeling queasy. I was drying the pan when I heard his familiar cough behind me. Guiltily, I placed it on the back of the cooker and busied myself clearing up the scattered Sugar Puffs. He went straight to the cooker.

'Where the hell has my stock gone?'

'Down the sink,' I replied. 'I thought you'd need the pan.'

'You stupid cunt! I was going to take it with me!'

I winced at his use of that word. I'd made the mistake of telling him that this one word was the worst possible insult for a woman. 'I can't see what your problem is,' he'd said. 'It's simply an Anglo-Saxon word. Look it up in the dictionary.'

A huge white van pulled up in front of the kitchen window. The cavalry had arrived. Good old Andy, the man with the van, always smiling and used to moving the great and good – and the not so good – of Berkshire. It was reassuring to see his good-humoured grin. 'What terrible weather,' he said when he came in.

I set about making tea, filling the kettle and placing it on the ring next to the empty stock pan.

Number One son peered round the door, took one look at the chaos and headed straight for the playroom, shutting the door behind him.

'Well,' said Andy, 'we may as well start down here.'

I escaped upstairs and watched from the boys' bedroom window as the packing cases were loaded into the back of the van, my vision distorted by the rain streaming down the windowpane. I turned round and caught sight of my reflection in the mirror on the far wall. I still had red horns above my mouth from last night's wine. Why had no one told me? I rubbed furiously at the corners of my mouth, smearing the stain into the grotesque shape of a clown's mouth.

Number Three son was stirring. I changed his nappy and put him back in his cot, handing him a book. He threw it back at me and bounced up and down. I lifted him up and lay down on the bed, cradling him. I wanted to close my eyes and drift off to sleep – to block out reality, go back to Pinot Noir wonderland – but, no, the chances were there'd be nothing left in the house if I did that.

My son started a loud, hungry cry. I'd have to face the kitchen again to get him some milk. I trudged down the steps with him in my arms. In the kitchen, Niall went to take him from me.

'I'm just going to give him some breakfast,' I said, shoving the baby into his high chair. The baby beamed and began banging a toy brick. I snatched a favourite cup from Niall as he went to take it. 'You're not taking that! That was a present from my mother.'

A toy brick came flying across the kitchen table, knocking the cup out of my hand on to the floor, smashing it. Niall smirked.

Andy reappeared. 'The van's virtually full,' he said. 'We'll get going.'

Number One son was standing by the door. 'Can we go with Daddy to see his new house? Please, Mummy?'

'I suppose so, if Daddy says it's OK.'

They got into the car, ready to follow the van. I closed the door before they'd left and climbed the stairs to our old bedroom, which was mine again now Niall had gone. The bed was unmade and there was a dirty shirt on the floor. A half-empty glass of red wine stood abandoned by the bed on top of a French cartoon comic, *Fluide Glaciale*. I pulled the sheet off the bed and lay down on the bare mattress, pulling the duvet over my head.

*

I opened my eyes, blinking with confusion. My cheek chafed on the bare, stained mattress. It was dark outside. It took me a minute to work out that it was five in the afternoon. I reached to switch on the light and almost knocked over the glass of red wine. I picked it up and drank it. It tasted oxidised.

I ran a bath, adding two capfuls of bubble bath, and climbed into the huge Victorian claw-footed tub. The house was silent. The door creaked and in stalked Lafite, the cat. He stretched, arched his back and lay lazily down next to the hot-water pipe, one eye half open. 'Surprised he hasn't taken you too,' I muttered.

Tired, I closed my eyes. I had expected to feel elated, but I felt flat, and strangely hollow. My eyes and throat were sore. My throat was often sore from early-morning retching.

I'll go over to my dad's, I thought. Mum's away and I can cook him supper. They lived in Devizes now, which wasn't too far to drive.

I looked at the picture over the bath – an illustration by Karen Ludlow I'd bought from the *Guardian*. It was called *This Year's Fashionable Accessory* and depicted women with babies made into handbags, headdresses and fastened like pets on leads. I thought of my three boys. Accessories to the crime of a broken home. I recalled Tina, the one girl in my class at junior school whose parents were divorced. Everyone had looked down on her. Now my house was a broken home. I gazed down at the floorboards, studying the one that was split, with the hole that all three boys loved to post things into – pennies, hairgrips, shampoo-bottle lids, bubblegum, pebbles. I had once caught Number Two son feeding tangerine segments into it.

'Bro-ken ho-mmme, bro-ken ho-mmme,' I repeated out loud. The cat looked at me. I shivered. The skin on my fingers was white and shrivelled. Time to move on. What should I wear? 'What *does* an about-to-be-single mother wear?' I asked Lafite.

It was pouring with rain as I stomped down the garden to the garage. I climbed into my MX5, switched on the headlights and the frog-eyes popped up. I jabbed a tape into the player. Kid Creole and the Coconuts came on – 'Annie, I'm Not Your Daddy'. I stopped the car at the end of the road. I couldn't see where I was going. I wiped the inside of the windscreen and realised with surprise that I had tears streaming down my face.

'This is ridiculous,' I said to the night. '*I'm* divorcing *him*!'

I unzipped the roof and folded it down. Devizes wasn't far. I already had mascara running down my face – I might as well go the whole hog. Pulling a baseball cap over my dripping hair, I screeched away, narrowly missing a car that seemed to appear from nowhere.

What was my dad going to say? He and Mum had been married for over forty years. As good Catholics, they didn't believe in divorce.

I had some fillet steak with me for supper and some boiled new potatoes I could fry. There would probably be some frozen peas in the house. My father could not cook at all; it would be good to make him a hot meal.

As I neared the Avebury roundabout I was dazzled momentarily by the lights of the Wagon and Horses. I toyed with the idea of stopping for a drink. No. I'd get something far tastier at my father's. I indicated for the Devizes exit, but at the last moment decided to carry on round the roundabout towards Avebury. As the stone circle came into sight, the full moon came out. Christ, the whole world would be mad. I slowed down as I neared the centre of Avebury. A leather-clad biker roared past, tooting his horn. I smiled and waved back. Perhaps life wasn't so bad.

Kid Creole and the Coconuts came to an abrupt stop and Classic FM automatically clicked in. Dvořák's 'Cello

Concerto' swelled from the speakers. This was the first piece Niall ever played to me, the first weekend we had spent together. I swallowed hard and swiftly switched off the radio, nearly yanking off the knob. I turned the car round and set off towards Devizes.

When I arrived, I turned into the gravel drive. Dad was standing at the door waiting for me, his beard looking whiter than I remembered it. I realised my legs were wet as I walked into the house.

'Hi,' I said, reaching over to kiss him.

'Yuck, wet, wet, wet. You're soaked. How come?'

'I drove here with the roof down. It's OK, I didn't get cold – I had the heater and the music on.'

'You nincompoop! You've got black all down your face.'

'It's only mascara,' I replied.

'Take your wet jacket off and come and sit down.'

In the kitchen, he looked at me. 'How did it go?'

'It went. He went. And the boys have gone to look at the new house. I need a drink.'

'OK, hold your horses,' he said, taking a bottle of Heidsieck Monopole champagne from the fridge. Ready on the table were two Georgian champagne glasses. 'Maybe not very appropriate, but I expect you could do with a glass of this.'

'More than just the one. Cheers. Not sure what we should drink to . . . Ooh, that's delicious. It tastes old, honeyed, like dried apricots.'

'You and your dried apricots,' he laughed. 'You'd better go and dry your hair. Do you want to go out for an Indian?'

'No, I've brought some food to cook, your favourite – fillet steak and fried potatoes. Any frozen peas?'

'I expect there are some in the freezer. I'd better find something decent to drink, then.'

'This will be the first meal I've cooked in years. You know how precious Niall was about cooking. And you know what, Dad? I can't think of anyone better to be cooking it for.' My eyes welled up again. 'Have you heard from Mum?'

'She called last night. She was in Hong Kong, calling from the Jockey Club, no less. She said the day's examining had gone well.'

I found the griddle and heated it up. A drip of water from my hair splashed on to the surface and sent a globule of fat spitting on to my hand, burning me.

'Shit, shit, shit. Sorry, Dad, it's really hot.'

'Run it under the cold tap straight away.'

'It's OK. How do you want your steak cooked?'

'*Bien cuit, madame.*'

'*D'accord.* Hey, Dad, I've got the leaky glass again. Thirsty work, cooking.'

Steak, potatoes and peas plated up, we sat down at the kitchen table.

'Here, try this,' he said, handing me a glass of red.

I studied the reddy-brown colour. What had he unearthed? No one in the family knew what he had in his seemingly bottomless cellar. Magician-like, he would produce bottles at family parties that none of us had ever seen .

'This smells amazing.'

'Might be a bit over the hill. Taste it.'

I took a taste. This was seriously old Burgundy, rich and sweet with a flavour of ripe red cherries and a hint of sweet pipe tobacco. I was transported back to my dad's study in Norwich, age five, watching him light his pipe.

'It's Echezeaux 1949, Bouchard Aîné, of course. Don't tell Mum we drank it. She'll be cross she missed out.'

'It's fantastic. What a treat. Where do you stash all these beauties?'

'That's my secret,' he replied. 'My steak is just right. *Très bien cuit, ma petite.*'

'Refreshing to know I can cook, after all.' I took a deep breath. 'Dad, I know Niall and I splitting up is really difficult for you and Mum, but—'

He held his hand up. 'Hush. Drink your wine. It's fading fast. Be quiet and just drink it.'

We chinked our glasses and solemnly drained them, sitting in silence, looking at each other.

'Even old wines die, Alice,' he added gently.

My shoulders started to shake. Tears splashed down into my glass.

CHAPTER TWENTY-SEVEN

LIFE IN THE FAST LANE

Newly separated, and after that wet drive to my dad's, I rekindled my love affair with my sports car, which I'd bought years earlier. No matter that it was a two-seater and I now had three children.

As a child, I grew up in Cringleford outside Norwich and lived one door away from Colin Chapman of Lotus Cars. On Sunday mornings one of my brothers and I used to go to the Lotus test track. We often watched Graham Hill and other drivers whizzing round in the latest Lotus prototypes. More exciting still was to be allowed to sit in the passenger seat for a lap or two. Speed and terror mixed with adrenaline – I was hooked as a little girl.

It had taken over twenty years to achieve my ambition and buy a sports car of my own, which I did with the advance for *The Hamlyn Atlas of Wine*. Back in August 1989, when I'd bought it, before the boys had been born, I hadn't been able to afford a Lotus, and although I had wanted to buy a British car, the new MGs had yet to be made, so I'd settled on a bright-blue Mazda MX5. My sports car was the only new car I'd ever owned and when I brought it home I'd thought I'd arrived.

The car became a feature in our lives. As soon as he could talk, Number One son christened her 'Little Blue Car', which quickly became shortened to 'LBC'. If, when putting

ALICE KING

the boys to bed at night, I asked them what treat they would like the next day, a favourite reply was, 'A ride in LBC with the lid off, Mummy.'

Now single again, and without my children half the time as Niall and I had agreed on joint custody, early-morning drives in LBC were the perfect remedy for sleepless nights and hangovers. A quick burn-up allowed me to start the day with a smile rather than self-pity.

It was on one such day that I was invited by Gérard Basset to Hotel du Vin in Tunbridge Wells. We had been having email discussions on the possibility of me tutoring some tasting dinners. Off I zoomed.

Gérard Basset is one of my favourite Masters of Wine. He is also one of the most talented blind tasters I have ever seen in action, but modest about his astounding ability. As I arrived, I was starting to congratulate him on the success of his hotels when he stopped me in mid-sentence.

'I've long been a fan of your writing and your books,' he told me.

Flattered, I didn't know what to say. I was moved by his kindness. Why couldn't I have fallen in love with a man like this?

We sat in the sunshine and spent the morning comparing our favourite producers, wines and grape varieties. To meet someone who shared my passion but in such a gentle, un-assuming, uncompetitive way touched me. But lunch was purgatory.

'What would you like to try – anything from the list?' he asked.

Here I was, looking at one of the best lists in the country, knowing that in an hour or so I had to drive home, because I had to pick up the boys from nursery at six o'clock.

We settled for a glass of non-vintage Pol Roger White Foil, a favourite of us both. I had described this in *Fabulous Fizz* as 'liquid sex in a glass'. We concurred on this spurious tasting note. On that day, drinking it on the sunlit terrace, the earth certainly moved for me.

We followed the Pol Roger with a glass of sensational white Burgundy, Montrachet La Garenne 1995, from one of our favourite producers, Etienne Sauzet. I savoured this beauty, revelling in its rich, buttery flavour. It was nectar and I had to be reminded to eat the salmon in front of me. I was far more interested in the wine. My mind and my body craved more.

Declining another glass, repeating that I had to drive, I felt close to tears. I must have looked bereft. Gérard signalled something to the waiter. Over coffee and a Montecristo No. 4 cigar, the waiter returned with an unopened bottle of the Montrachet.

'This is for you to enjoy with a friend when you get home,' said Gérard. I tried to decline, though not too hard. I allowed myself to be persuaded.

Driving down the M4, roof down, hair flying, I speculated as to when and with whom I would drink this Montrachet. I could still taste it. The motorway was busy. I was in the outside lane, barrelling past the Reading exit, when suddenly the engine died. I pushed my foot down on the accelerator – nothing. My life flashed in front of me. I hadn't written a will. Who would look after the boys? Why hadn't I brought my other car, the battered old Mercedes estate? If I was going to crash, that was the car to be in. Was I going to pay the ultimate price for being a poser in a soft-top? That would teach me. Except it wouldn't. I'd be dead.

I tried to indicate, but all the power had gone, including the electrics. I looked in the mirror. The motorway was full behind me. I couldn't come to a halt in the fast line – that would be fatal, and not just for me.

I took a deep breath and steered the rapidly slowing car across two lanes of traffic, coasting across the cross-hatching by the exit road, and came to a halt near the grass verge. I closed my eyes and waited for the sound of a crash. None came. There must be a God! I had hit no one and no one had hit me. Miraculously, a gap had opened as I free-wheeled off the motorway.

I got out of the car. I had no idea what to do next. I looked down at myself and realised I must look pretty odd standing next to the motorway, dressed in a long, black Moschino dress slit to the thigh. I opened the boot to retrieve my cardigan and cover myself up – well, at least the top half.

A car pulled up behind me. Out stepped a good-looking man with green eyes and wavy black hair. He was wearing overalls covered in splatters of paint and had a canvas work-bag over his shoulder.

'Are you all right?' he asked.

'I've broken down and don't know what to do!'

'Well, let's push your car off the road before anyone crashes into it.'

He lent me his mobile to ring the RAC. By this time I was shaking uncontrollably from head to foot. He agreed to wait with me until the RAC arrived. Luckily, they were quick. The fanbelt had gone – I would have to wait for a tow-truck to take me home.

'Will you stay with me?' I asked, pleading with my best little-girl-lost eyes. 'Just until the recovery truck gets here?'

'OK. But I better phone the missus to say I'm going to be late,' he replied.

We climbed back into LBC, which was by now in a lay-by. He told me about his day at work, I told him about mine. It was 5 p.m. but the sun was still hot. Once I had stopped shaking, I realised I was thirsty.

'Have you got anything to drink, like water, in your bag?' I asked.

'No. I've got a mug, but that's not much use, is it?'

I opened the boot to see if there was any water in there. I spotted the Montrachet. I picked up the lukewarm bottle.

162

'Do you like wine?' I said. 'This is one of the best white Burgundies in the world.'

He laughed. 'You're not going to drink that now, are you?'

'Why not? I haven't got to drive any more. It's gone five o'clock and we could be waiting for some time. What's more, I'm thirsty!'

I fished my corkscrew out of my handbag. I never travel without a corkscrew.

He looked on as I swilled out his dirty tea mug with wine and filled it up.

'Cheers!' I said. 'Thanks for stopping to help me.' I took a slurp from the mug. Even at this temperature, the wine tasted sensational. 'Try this – great wines have to be shared.' I slurped down the rest of the wine and refilled the mug for him. 'I thought I was a goner,' I said, feeling light-headed. 'Hey, have you got a light?'

He nodded and I retrieved the remains of the Monte-cristo. We sat there in silence for a while, passing the mug of Montrachet back and forth, surrounded by a cloud of cigar smoke and listening to the noise of the traffic passing by. I wondered what Gérard would think of me now. Not quite the setting for drinking this fine wine he had in mind.

'The trouble is,' said my new friend as the tow-truck pulled up, 'I don't think my missus is going to believe that I stopped to help someone, when I get home reeking of expensive wine and cigars.'

CHAPTER TWENTY-EIGHT

Princess on the Loose

One of the first things I did after the divorce was to buy a new bed. It was huge – six and a half foot square, the kind with two bases screwed together topped by a monster mattress. Such a bed required entirely new linen, of course, and I delighted in buying fine white Egyptian cotton sheets, duvet covers and square French pillows. It was cleansing to discard the washed-out, grey shrouds of my marriage.

When the boys were at home, a bed this size was perfect. They would clamber up in the morning, the eldest hauling up the youngest, and all three would fall asleep, one on either side of me and one across the bottom. The four of us had enough space to dance the fandango in our sleep.

But when the boys were with Niall, where they lived on alternate weeks, I felt hopelessly lost in it, as if its vast, virginal expanse was mocking me. After extolling the virtues of being able to sleep star-shaped, I soon found myself sleeping curled up in the foetal position, comatose and unmoving, on the right-hand side of the bed, able to slip out in the morning leaving no need to make it.

Alone in the bed on yet another evening, nothing but a bottle of Tasmanian Pinot Noir for company, I decided it was time to christen my new bed. It wasn't the sex I missed; it was cuddles I craved.

I'd been tempted to play away from home on many a drunken press trip, but I'd always managed to extricate myself at the last minute – sometimes literally – from any compromising situation.

For years I'd had a friend I knew fancied me. We had spent a lot of time together, drunk many a black velvet together, and just about managed to keep our relationship platonic. He was up for new bed-testing, accompanied by the perfect jug of black velvet. I opted for Murphy's over Guinness, as it's slightly sweeter. Generally I would blend it with a cheaper fizz like cava, though on this auspicious occasion a bottle of the full-bodied, creamy Charles Heidsieck definitely hit the spot.

Going to bed with him was an eye-opener, not least in the exciting and tender lovemaking. It made me realise how angry I'd been about the treatment I was subject to in my marriage. It was the first time for a long while I could make love without feeling anger towards the person I was in bed with. For years I had only ever made love drunk. True, I wasn't exactly sober this time, but I wasn't blind drunk either. It also felt good to be in bed with someone I knew genuinely cared for me, actually liked me.

But there was to be no happy ever after. My friend had other fish to fry. Still, having got the deed over and done with, I was keen to do more research and didn't obsess about him. I took a friend's saying – 'so many men, so little time' – a touch too literally. Having been practically a child bride, I felt I had much catching up to do.

Match-making friends were happy to try to oblige. One introduced me to the secretary of one of London's traditional gentlemen's clubs. We went out to Little Havana in London's Leicester Square. It's amazing how rum lubricates conversation and salsa dancing. Later, back at his flat, I remember laughing out loud when I saw that his several pairs of polished Church's shoes were kept in shape with old-fashioned wooden shoetrees.

I've always been untidy, so 'Shoetrees', as I christened

him, was good for me, with his prep-school, military-like air. He gently replenished some of the self-esteem that had been eroded in my marriage. In the six months we went out together, I loved having doors opened for me and being called 'gorgeous'.

Shoetrees was a good cook and loved fine wine; but – even more gratifying nourishment for my damaged ego – he was impressed by my knowledge. While fairly clued-up himself, he didn't attempt to compete. While I was with him, my propensity for compulsive, angry drinking seemed to mellow. I think it was his simple kindness that did it. I managed, just about, to remain compos mentis at his work functions – Henley, Ascot and the like. On the occasions we did have wild, drunken evenings with friends, I would be amazed that the lectures I was used to on the following morning never materialised.

When Niall remarried less than a year after the divorce, Shoetrees was there for me. He was kind and unassuming with the children. A semblance of calm returned to my topsy-turvy household. He maintained, however, a fairly distant, hands-off approach – novel for all-or-nothing me.

After I had a foolish, brief, drunken diversion with one of his friends, he declared his undying love for me. But in my heart of hearts, I knew he wasn't right. I was bored, missing the drama to which I was accustomed. After a tasting trip to Australia I came home, arranged to meet him, spent the afternoon drinking and met up with him on full drunken, fighting form. He saw red and that was the end of Shoetrees.

On my own again, I started going to the pub more often and drinking even more. I would go out 'for a glass' and stagger home several bottles later, bleary-eyed. One Saturday I went down to a local hotel on the pretext of watching the rugby. In truth, I was lonely and depressed. I looked around – smug, smiling couples everywhere. I frowned into my glass of Chilean Merlot. What was wrong with me? Why was I the ugly ducking sitting by myself in the Three Swans? Things would be so much better in my life if I had a man. Wouldn't they?

'You don't remember me, do you?' said a voice next to me at the bar. I had noticed him drink two pints of Stella in the ten minutes or so it had taken me to finish my large glass of red. 'I rescued your son's kite out of a tree on the common last summer, then fell out of the tree and broke my ankle.'

I turned to look at him. Younger than me, suntanned skin, dark, spiky hair and speckled green eyes. 'Best buy you a pint to thank you for your trouble, then,' I said.

We drank the afternoon away, returning to my garden at around eight. He was impressed by the grandeur of Avon House – most people were – and even more impressed when he spied the hundreds of bottles of wine racked up in the hall and the tasting room. We sat in the garden watching the evening primroses unravel, marvelling as they cast a fluorescent light in the dusk. I'm convinced they have strange properties.

I had never had a toy boy before. As we finished a magnum of champagne, going to bed with him seemed as natural as opening the next bottle.

He lasted five months, long enough to help me move house and make a dent in the wine cellar. He was great with the kids, often picking them up from nursery while I propped up the bar in the pub. I think that – for a while – I fell in love with him. But after kissing him so much, he seemed to turn back into a frog. Back to the lily pond he went.

Lying in my huge bed, alone again with nothing but a bottle of fizz for company, it came to me – I would have to kiss a lot of frogs before I found a prince. He was not to be the last.

CHAPTER TWENTY-NINE

NAIL BOMB

I had only popped into the supermarket for tampons, rushing for a train on my way to London. Then I saw them. For a second I froze like a rabbit in headlights. It was the boys – *my* boys, *my* children – with their new stepmother.

She was holding my youngest in her arms. In her *arms*. The other two boys were laughing and joking with their new stepbrother and sister, lobbing a monster pack of Walkers crisps into the trolley, as I rounded the end of the aisle.

I stood there in my black leather Versace minidress and knee-length black satin boots, my Lil-lets in my hand. They stopped dead.

'I'm off to a party in London,' I mumbled. 'I'm in a rush for the train. See you at the weekend, boys.' I turned and marched towards the cash desk.

'Ooh, Mummy, love the bows on the back of your boots – especially the yellow ones!' shouted Number Two son.

I carried on walking, took out a crumpled fiver from my purse, paid for my tampons and left without turning round. I marched towards the station, blinking back the tears that threatened to cascade down my face and put paid to the sparkly make-up on my cheeks.

I felt robbed, raped of my rights. I felt my stomach contract in the familiar spasm. At the station, the large glass of white wine I'd had an hour earlier came up, the acidity burning my throat as I vomited over the platform. My breath was smoke-like in the crisp winter air. A man in a pinstriped suit looked away, embarrassed. How could I go to a party feeling like this?

I boarded the train. As it moved off, I heard an approaching rattle of bottles. I looked up and saw a steward pushing a drinks trolley. I vaguely recognised her. She smiled at me. 'My, you're looking fine,' she said in her sing-song Jamaican accent. 'Any teas, coffees, drinks for the party girl today?'

'Ah, the cavalry. A large gin and tonic, please. I've just had a bit of a shock.'

'Ice and a slice?'

I unscrewed the Gordon's miniature and poured it into the plastic cup. Mother's ruin. 'Better leave me another one,' I said, fishing a tenner out of my bag.

'More tonic?'

'No, thanks, no need. I need it strong. I need a direct line to my heart.'

I gulped it back, the bitter juniper flavour coating my raw throat. I felt my stomach contract again but swallowed hard, crunching on a piece of ice. I gazed at the flocked seat facing me. The word 'bitch' was scrawled in felt pen on the plastic headrest. It swam, magnified in the tears in my eyes.

The train trundled on, jerking to left and right. Black and white movie stills flashed through my head. Their new stepmother – younger than me, a vague acquaintance, a striking Indian girl with long hair. Bumping into her in the pub. Commiserating with her about her toy-boy husband, who had run off with a younger American model. Laughing about our newfound singledom and getting drunk together. Returning to Avon House and drinking bottle after bottle of wine. Dancing to Tammy Wynette's 'D-I-V-O-R-C-E'. Lying on the floor together, weeping in front of the jukebox. Me handing out tissues, jokingly telling her to watch out – as a single local women, Niall was bound to come sniffing around. Me confiding the financial nitty-gritty of the divorce. Another storyboard memory – returning from holiday in Spain, picking up the boys from the nursery, Number Two son asking, 'Mummy, why was Daddy in bed with that Indian lady?'

I put my gin and tonic down, realising that I was crushing the empty plastic cup.

It was the ultimate betrayal. All right, I had wanted the divorce. But in my book there were certain places you didn't go – and that included bedding friends' ex-husbands. Up until that moment, though, I'd never actually considered her role as a stepmother, cuddling *my* babies.

Nothing can prepare you for the sight of an uninvited woman playing mother to your children. It is beyond jealousy. It punctures the soul with the intensity of a nail bomb. It makes your womb ache, your heart ache and reaches parts of your psyche that have no name or recognised form. It taps into the primeval urge that makes childbirth bearable and openly laughs at it, making a maternal mockery of its role. Logic plays no part – it is a feeling that all is not right with the universe, that someone has spilled the quantum soup.

I felt the rage rising in me as I neared London. I knew only one way to quell it. I left Paddington, exited into Spring Street and headed straight for the Jingle Boy, one of the Davy's chain of wine bars. I ordered a glass of champagne – Laurent Perrier Brut NV – and drank it in two gulps. The dry, apple-like fizz rasped the back of my throat.

'Leaky glass again. I guess I better have another one – and one of those Cohiba cigars,' I said to the barman.

'You celebrating something?'

'Nope, commiserating.'

I finished my glass and headed downstairs to the loo. I looked in the mirror and saw black smudges around my eyes where my eyeliner had run. I looked like a panda that had been in a train crash. Best repair my face. Shame I can't do the same for my heart, I thought, as I applied kohl.

Another two glasses later I realised I was running late and took a taxi to Jermyn Street. Bob was there, sitting waiting for me. I had met him at a Tondonia Rioja tasting shortly before Niall and I had split up. I had been amazed that he should find me interesting, attractive even. We were mates rather than lovers. He had just split up with his wife. We would compare notes and suggest coping strategies to each other. I would cry on his shoulder and we'd drink good wines together, both relieved that we shared many seemingly irrational emotions. It was gratifying to find I was not alone with those.

The evening's dinner and party was an attempt by Bordeaux producers to convince the wine press that affordable claret had a place in the market. But the wines on our table were mean, ungenerous, tart and austere.

'I don't want to drink this crap, do you?' I said to Bob. He had been attempting to shush me ever since I'd arrived. Fortunately, as I was late, we had been put on a separate table for two, so I didn't have to make small talk with colleagues. One walked past me and waved, heavily pregnant with her first child. Bet she wouldn't have to go through the gut-wrenching feeling of seeing another woman with her children, I thought bitterly.

'Come on, let's go. I don't want any pudding anyway, do you?' I said.

We took a taxi to his appartment in Farringdon, a stunning loft conversion in an old silk factory with twenty-foot windows. I would often stay there, regularly turning up the worse for wear, raging, late at night. But once inside Bob's flat, I felt calmer. He was kind to me, never shouted, and would always find me a bottle of something decent that I'd drink until I passed out. He would put me to bed or cover me up with a blanket. I could never explain to him how this unconditional tenderness stirred something inside me that made me cry late into the night.

'I'll get a bottle of the 1978 – perhaps that'll make you feel a bit better,' he said.

I gulped it back, the flavour of soft cherries and sweet vanilla ice cream mixing with the salt from my tears, numbing my throat and my thoughts.

'They are my boys, *my* boys. MY BOYS, goddammit!' were the last words I remember saying.

It was still dark when I left to catch the train home at seven the next morning. The air was cold. As I hailed a taxi, I noticed once again that my breath made vapour trails in the air. I was surprised I could breathe at all, surprised that life was still, somehow, simply carrying on around me.

Sitting on the train, my head throbbing, I opened my notebook and wrote:

> So there I was in Somerfield
> With a box of giant Lil-lets in hand
> When I came across my little boys –
> Who the hell had that planned?
>
> Has it ever occurred to her
> What that might do to my heart?
> Having to witness another woman
> Playing my own special part?
>
> It was tearing at my heartstrings
> I couldn't bear the sight
> Of my three stolen sons.
> I wanted to down bag and fight.
>
> Instead I focused on the party
> And I looked straight ahead,
> I talked and drank and laughed
> And wept later in my bed.

CHAPTER THIRTY

Pick Me Up

It was 4.30 a.m. and I had only the Groucho Club night receptionist for company. London was dead – no late-night partygoers, no cars, just the rain in the empty streets. I thought of my bed with its crisp, clean sheets and knew it was time to go home. I'd been here for days, setting out to go home at least once but only getting as far as a pub in Paddington.

The only way to get from Soho to Hungerford at this time was to take a taxi. The Groucho's taxi company, Dallas Cars, was used to me. I was loading my bags into the car when a man came walking down Dean Street.

'It's crap,' he said. 'Central London and nowhere to get a drink.'

'Yes,' I agreed. 'I guess a hotel would be the best place now. Even the Groucho bar closed two hours ago.'

'So where are you going?' he asked.

'Home. I've been here for days. It's always the same. I come for a day and end up staying for three. I've had enough of London.'

'Perhaps I should come with you.'

'Well, you can if you want, but it's seventy-five miles away.'

He climbed into the taxi. We sped away. In the streetlight I glanced across at him. He was beautiful with grey-green eyes. What is it about men with green eyes? I felt disorientated. Normally, Dallas Cars sent a Mercedes. Tonight they had sent a people carrier. It felt very empty. I glanced behind at the empty row of seats and wondered where everybody else was. My boys could fit in there easily. I supposed they were asleep at their father's now.

Best not to think about that. Too painful.

I was sitting directly behind the driver on the middle row of seats. My Soho hitchhiker was sitting at the other end, leaving a polite gap in between. I studied the velour back of the seat in front of me. It was difficult to focus after all that vanilla-flavoured vodka earlier. Whose idea had that been? Gingerly, I reached out my hand and stroked the fabric against the pile, creating a darker shade of grey.

I looked across at my passenger. 'You are delicious,' I said.

'Don't say that, it frightens me.'

I closed my eyes and went to sleep. It was daylight before we reached home.

As I opened the front door I could see the jukebox winking at me. I must have left it on.

'Is that really a Wurlitzer?' my companion asked. They were the first words he had spoken in over an hour.

'Yes. I bought it years ago.'

'Do you have to put money in?'

'No,' I replied, laughing. 'Not unless you have an old two-bob bit.'

He studied the records and pressed 101. Glenn Miller's 'In the Mood' filled the room, the richness of the sound permeating my skin.

'My mother learnt to dance to this,' I said. 'Would you care to dance?'

As we danced, we were dazzled by dawn sunlight reflecting off a copper-sheeted picture. The strobe effect made me dizzy, giddy with excitement. The music stopped and he followed me into the hall and down the steps to the brick-floored kitchen.

'Can I have a cup of tea?' he asked.

'Of course.' I made lapsang souchong and served it in my favourite green dragon Coalport china cups. He drank his quickly. I drank quickly too, burning my mouth, watching him. That would put paid to tasting for a while, I thought. But, then, I didn't have any tasting to do. I hadn't written anything for months. Where had all the work gone?

He was looking around the kitchen. 'Can we drink that?' he asked.

'What? Give me a clue – there are hundreds of bottles in here.'

'That bottle of champagne, there on top of the apothecary's chest.'

'Impressive. You're the first person I've met who knows what that piece of furniture is. I've been looking for an excuse to open that bottle of Veuve Clicquot La Grande Dame 1985 for some time. And you've just provided it.' I put the bottle in the freezer. 'Madame Clicquot would turn in her grave. She was an It-girl, you know, way ahead of her time.' I suddenly realised I didn't know his name. 'What's your name, Soho Hitchhiker?'

'Sean,' he replied.

'You look like a James to me.'

I climbed two floors up to my office, leaving him reading Kafka's *A Hunger Artist*. I was hungry myself, come to think about it. I couldn't remember the last time I'd eaten. There were twenty-seven messages on the answering machine. I felt my stomach tighten. It was bound to be trouble. I was always in trouble. Best not listen to them. Tomorrow would do . . . except it *was* tomorrow.

There was a miniature bottle of Kummel on top of a huge pile of unopened post on my desk. I unscrewed the top and the smooth, sweet aroma of caraway filled the room. Such a dinky bottle. I drank, feeling the spirit hit the back of my throat. My chest felt less tight and my heart rate seemed to slow as I swallowed.

I went back downstairs, took the champagne out of the freezer and opened it. 'Such a tone on that gentle hiss,' I said. 'Bit like the sound men make when they come, don't you think? This champagne is definitely as good as sex.'

He laughed. He was staring at me intently. He stuck out his tongue and started panting like a dog. 'Well, are you going to pour it or just hold the bottle?' he said. 'I'm very thirsty.'

I poured it out into Georgian champagne saucers. The tiny bubbles danced as they shot up the hollow stems. Looking down into my glass, I noticed the bubbles swirling together into a furious whirlpool. The perfect pick-me-up – especially with a Kummel chaser.

'These are fantastic glasses,' he said, as we clinked them together.

'Yes – apparently modelled on Marie Antoinette's left breast.'

'Well, she must have had small boobs,' he replied, laughing.

I sat down on my favourite cane chair draped with a real antique leopard skin.

'That leopard skin, is it real?'

'So many questions!' I laughed. 'I'm not sure I know what's real any more. Drink your champagne. This is seriously special stuff.'

'Can we drink it in bed?'

'Which of the spare beds do you want to drink it in?' I asked, looking at him with an amused grin.

'I'd rather drink it in yours, preferably with you in it as well.'

I laughed. 'Fair enough. Follow me.'

I led him up the stairs. I took off my clothes and dropped them as we climbed. I was wearing new yellow Lejaby lingerie I'd had to buy in London because I'd not taken enough underwear with me.

We climbed into bed. He leaned on one arm and gazed at me. He had sandy-coloured stubble poking through a sprinkling of freckles on the side of his face. His nose was slightly turned up.

'What exactly do you do?' I asked him.

'I pick up women like you in the middle of the night,' he said, refilling my glass.

When I awoke, he was gone. A champagne cork was placed dead centre in the middle of the pillow.

CHAPTER THIRTY-ONE

SUNDAY, BLOODY SUNDAY

My arrangement with Niall to have the children one week on, one week off suited me at first. In my head, I told myself it was like going on a press trip. I reasoned this would mean I wouldn't miss them too much. After all, travel was a normal part of my life. I was often away. But the reality hit me a few months in. A press trip revolves around being entertained and meeting interesting new people. Weekends home alone sat heavy on my heart.

To begin with, I convinced myself that I was a single thirty-eight-year-old with the world at my feet every other weekend. 'Fill your diary,' advised friends who longed for such freedom. But the novelty soon wore off and I grew to dread 'bloody Sundays', as my state of mind deteriorated and I failed to invite people to stay or organise places to be. I lacked the confidence to produce the elaborate meals I'd once presented as a matter of course. More than half of me – my boys – was absent every other weekend, and it hurt deep down in a place I didn't know how to reach.

Sunday soon became the day I would go to my local pub and pontificate about the components of the perfect bloody Mary (having had them for breakfast) to anyone who would listen. Inevitably this led to a session, usually followed by a few bottles of wine back at the house. I always shared them around – I didn't drink alone, did I? Other waifs and strays became my Sunday playmates. Sometimes we would cobble together some sort of Sunday lunch. Every script involved the wine flowing freely.

As my new Sunday pattern emerged, visiting friends and family was out of the question. One drink and I couldn't drive anyway. By late afternoon I would be ensconced in a mantra of 'Poor me, poor me – pour me another.' One Sunday I phoned the Samaritans. They listened patiently to my drunken ramblings.

How had it come to this? This hadn't been the life plan.

Monday morning. Dim flashbacks were playing in my head. I had been on the phone. Talking to . . . Who had it been? Ah, yes, the police. Oh, my God. The *police*? Judging by the empty bottle of Absolut by my bed, I hadn't been sober. What had happened? Why had I been talking to the police?

Memories started crowding back. I had dropped the boys off at their father's – the 'other house'. It had been full of large brown cardboard boxes. When I asked what they were, he told me they were to do with his new line of business.

I heard disquieting hints around town and asked a couple of mates to browse on his website. I wanted to know, even though I didn't want to face the reality. A glance at his website, Eros UK, left me feeling uneasy and queasy. And I am no prude. 'Eros Bodyglide lubricant – probably the longest-lasting condom-safe lube' was one product. OK, I thought, I can handle this. Rather a waste of Niall's fine brain, but, hey, nothing to do with me.

I continued looking down through the product range and an involuntary shudder went through me. Dildos, condoms, fetish toys, escorts, bondage tape, hair remover, plugs . . . Plugs? Oh, yes, of course.

All absolutely fine for consenting adults, the logical side of my brain said. But my drunk, illogical brain went into overdrive at the thought of all these things lurking in brown cardboard boxes in a house with children. It was just before

Christmas, when children are inquisitive. I had grotesque visions of my boys sneaking around opening vibrating boxes, confronted with giant dildos.

This new business was not one operated in private either. Ever the publicist, Niall was shouting it from the rooftops. It seemed the mothers in the school playground knew more about it than I did.

'I hope you don't think Niall's business is anything to do with me,' I told a neighbour of his.

'Oh, I use the bondage tape on my cat,' she laughed. 'It's a bit of fun, you know.'

I couldn't see the funny side. I ranted to some of the other mothers, who asked me what my problem was. Wasn't he simply selling a commodity?

I challenged them: 'How would you feel, honestly, if the father of your children ran such a business?' That shut them up.

I made sure Niall was aware of my distaste at his new line of work. 'It's none of your business,' he told me. 'Would you rather I sold illegal arms?'

Actually, I think I would have preferred that.

I knew he would never deliberately expose our children to this stuff, but reason can go out of the window when emotions kick in. It was after a session of beating myself up about my inability to change things for my children that I tried ringing Niall's mother – perhaps she could make him see sense.

'Do you know what your son is selling?' I slurred down the phone. 'Sex aids. And they are all in his house where the children might find them!'

'Don't be silly, ducky,' she replied. 'I've lots of croissants and prawn cocktails I could bring over,' she added, rather surreally.

I put the receiver down on the table and walked into the kitchen to open another bottle of wine. When I returned and picked up the receiver, she was still talking. I had watched with horror many times when Niall had hung up on her, but now I did the same.

Crying into my glass, I decided to phone the police. I drunkenly explained my concerns to whoever answered the phone. I tried to enunciate carefully, knowing I had poured the best part of two bottles of wine down my neck. They listened politely for some time, finally advising, 'Get yourself a good lawyer, love.'

I've no idea what happened, but the next time I saw the children they told me a door had been fitted and all 'Daddy's workboxes' had been locked up.

CHAPTER THIRTY-TWO

DOWNSIZING

In 2001 I had to sell Avon House. An income-tax demand for £46,000 was one thing; no income to pay it with was another. Where had all the work gone?

Ever since Tesco had declined to renew my consultancy contract, my income had nose-dived. All right, I had got horribly drunk at one corporate dinner. Embarrassing. Not a good plan. Actually, I couldn't really remember much about it, so didn't know how bad I'd been. Or perhaps it was simply that I had completed the job they wanted me to do – to help them become the biggest wine retailer in the UK. Maybe it was nothing to do with my behaviour at all. They hadn't replaced me with anyone, had they?

I could have remortgaged the house, but the thought of even higher monthly payments frightened me. I had already increased the existing mortgage to give Niall half the collateral in the house. That's what happened to you if you were a wife and mother who worked, I thought bitterly – you have to pay your partner off. I should have been the kind of wife who draped herself feebly across the chaise lounge, saying, 'Peel me a grape, darling.'

With the bills piling up, I'd taken in lodgers. I came back from one weekend away to find they had thrown a party. The kitchen had been half-heartedly cleaned up, but the bin was overflowing with squashed Carlsberg cans and soggy cigarette ends. It smelt just like the pub. There was another, worse, sewer-like smell hanging in the air. I followed my nose into the downstairs bathroom and looked around. I noticed a half-full bottle of Zinfandel Blush stood abandoned on the floor beside the shower. Christ, couldn't they drink something decent? Still, at least it wasn't one of my bottles.

Where was that smell coming from? I opened the glass shower door and the stench hit me. The shower tray was full of grey, sludgy water coated in scum. A long, black, fusewire-like pubic hair was stranded on the soap. I didn't like to look any closer to see what else was floating around. I slammed the shower door so hard it came off its hinges. The sewer must be blocked. The contents were coming up through the plughole. It had happened before – they had probably blocked the system throwing condoms down the loo.

That was the moment I decided I couldn't do this any more. I didn't need this huge house. It was falling apart and soaking up money. I decided there and then to sell it. If I was lucky, I might be able to buy something outright and have no mortgage.

I felt relieved to be moving out of Avon House at first, but something in me changed. The fight went out of me. It had been my house of dreams, where my third son was born, my daily reminder that I had achieved something in life and bought the largest house in the street. I felt as if I was leaving part of my soul there.

Even so, financially, I had no option. I sold Avon House and used the money to pay off the mortgage, my credit-card debts and the taxman. I had about enough left to buy a two- or three-bedroom house, but I hadn't found anywhere to buy yet. I put in offers on two places, but they fell through. I wasn't quite sure what to do next. As a stopgap, I went to live with my parents in Devizes.

'There is only one condition,' my mother said. 'I don't want you coming in rolling drunk.'

I looked at her coldly. 'Of course not.'

I would wait until she had gone to bed to creep in through the garden gate from the local pub.

In the end, I moved back to Hungerford and rented a tiny house – the Doll's House, I called it. I went from owning the biggest house in the street to renting the smallest. I stopped looking at houses to buy. They were all too expensive. And, anyway, if I took out a mortgage, how was I going to pay it?

My capital seemed to be disappearing fast and I was soon down to the end of it, with barely enough to put down a deposit on a house, let alone buy one outright. Where had all the money gone? I hadn't been that extravagant, had I? Well, all right, I had stayed up in London a few times, holing up in the Groucho, sometimes catching cabs home. Well, quite often, actually. But surely that was safer than risking the last train with all the drunks.

The boys always needed new things – clothes, books, bikes. It was 2003 now and they were getting so big. On the weeks they lived with me in the Doll's House, all three would be sardined into one little bedroom. I must have been crazy not to realise they would grow, need more space. I hadn't thought about that when I'd made my decision to sell Avon House. Still, no point thinking about that – it made my stomach feel tight.

Indeed, my stomach was hurting and my back ached continuously. I thought that perhaps I'd picked up some kind of bug somewhere, some sort of parasite. Every time I went to the loo, bright-green or yellow liquid poured out of me. Mum asked me if I thought it was to do with my drinking. She seemed hypersensitive about my drinking – what was wrong with her?

'Don't be stupid!' I snapped. I didn't drink *that* much. I'd always had a weak stomach.

To prove her wrong, I didn't have a drink for a whole day and a half. The condition continued unabated. So that proved it was nothing to do with the drinking, didn't it?

Not that I felt any better this morning. The sheets were covered in blood. Surely it wasn't normal to be having periods as heavy as this? Only one thing for it, one thing that could take away the dull ache in my back – neat vodka, straight from the freezer. A quick slug of Stolichnaya – buffalo-grass flavour was a favourite – seemed far more effective than painkillers. I prided myself on not taking drugs. They didn't agree with me.

I had to find a job. Perhaps it would make me feel better, less lethargic, less depressed. I leafed dispiritedly through the *Guardian*'s *Media Appointments* supplement. What kind of job could I apply for? It wasn't as if you saw many ads for wine writers. Or burned-out forty-two-year-old wine writers, more like, I thought.

I would have to rewrite my CV. Where was my laptop? I hadn't seen it for days. Maybe it was in the car. I looked out of the window. The car wasn't there. Oh, yes. I'd left it in the pub car park down the road last night. I'd only popped in for a quick one. But we had started playing spoof, and each time someone lost they had to buy a round. That would account for all the change that had fallen out of my jeans this morning.

The rain lashed against the Doll's House windows. I started counting the drops as I had done as a little girl. God, this was depressing. Stuck at home in the rain. I felt a tear trickle down my face, stopping on the top of my lip. I looked in the mirror. I looked pale and washed-out. There were the remains of a bruise on my cheekbone, gone yellow. God knows what I had bumped into. I couldn't remember doing it. I looked at my watch. Only ten thirty.

I walked into the tiny kitchen. Cocoa Pops were strewn like rabbit droppings all over the black and white tiled floor. The sink was full of dirty dishes.

What was that? An open bottle of unfamiliar-looking red

wine on the draining board. I hadn't bought it. Someone must have brought it round, but when? I didn't remember anyone coming over last night. I looked around to check how many dirty wineglasses there were, to give me a clue, but there was so much washing-up in the sink it was impossible to tell.

I opened the cupboard to look for a glass. It was empty. Goddammit, there is nothing in this house, I thought, slamming the cupboard door. I picked up the bottle and swigged at it. Ugh. God, this stuff was rough. Vin de Pays de l'Aude? More like Vin de Pays de Load of Rubbish. I found a plastic Bambi mug and sloshed the rest of the wine into it.

I could apply for a job tomorrow. There had been another job ad I had cut out, something for a PR company. Had I missed the closing date? I couldn't see the cutting anywhere. Well, I wasn't going to stay here all day and drink Vin de Pays de Load of Rubbish, I thought, taking another swig. It tasted even worse this time. The tannin made my tongue curl. I know, I thought. I'll finish this and then go down to the pub. Do the crossword. My friends Spike and Terry had been painstakingly patient in trying to teach me to do the cryptic one. Yes, that was a good idea, a good plan for the day. Finish this, get out of the house, have a bit of air. I'd definitely apply for that job tomorrow, once I found my laptop.

My black suede beaded Anna Trzebinski skirt was at the foot of the stairs. Strange place for it, I thought. Now, where were my black high-heeled Rodier ankle boots? They looked best with it.

I bent down to look under the sofa for the boots and felt the blood rush to my head. Whoa! I felt faint. I ought to have something to eat, really. I'd already been sick this morning. I was sick every morning. Weak stomach.

I put on my black trilby, grabbed my gold Moschino umbrella, left the house and walked down the road, the beads on my skirt jangling, past Avon House. Cardboard boxes were stacked in the window of my old office. There was a white plastic garden table in the bay window of my tasting room. It looked like a squat.

I arrived at the Three Swans just as the town hall clock struck 11 a.m., sat myself down at the bar and ordered a vodka and tonic.

Alice in bloody Wonderland, I thought.

CHAPTER THIRTY-THREE

Blow Job

Congealed claret-coloured blood is sticking to my inner thighs. A globule breaks free and trickles from my crotch to my calf. Browner, Chianti-like spots of it are spattered across the floor.

It's all coming back. I can barely breathe. Pictures flash through my head. Realisation dawns and bile surges from my stomach to my throat. My left hand is shaking. I stand up on trembling legs and hammer on the cell door.

I had dropped the boys at their father's. There was the usual acerbic exchange and I had driven off at speed, raging. I stopped at the Italian restaurant at the bottom of town. I asked if I could leave my car in the car park overnight – I prided myself on not drinking and driving – and ordered a bottle of Montepulciano.

Smiling couples were all around me. Why was I sitting here at the bar by myself? They were all judging me, I thought. I downed my fifth glass and glared at a woman who kept looking at me. Huh – one day you might be on your own, sweetie. I was tempted to stick my tongue out at her.

I couldn't face eating here. I ordered a takeaway pizza – American Hot, extra chillies. I was waiting for it when an acquaintance came in. I cringed to think about the drunken fling I'd had with him, and the humiliation I'd felt when he'd put the few belongings I had at his house – a few pairs of knickers, a bottle of Absolut citron vodka and two bottles of Wairau Rivers Sauvignon Blanc – into a black bin liner and left it outside his door to be picked up.

He came across to the bar and ordered another bottle of Montepulciano. Well, that was the least he could do, I thought angrily as I drank it down. I snarled at him. The bin-bag episode was unkind, I told him. He was an 'uneducated waste of space'. He left.

I picked up my pizza, asked for a cork for the bottle, stuffed it my handbag and zigzagged to the door. Outside, the cold air hit me.

I thought of my dark, empty cottage. Perhaps I should go after him. He wasn't that bad really, was he? I unlocked my car on the passenger side and put the pizza box on the seat. I clambered across to the driver's seat, snagging the gearstick on the way. Not far to go. I would be fine. I started the car and began pulling out of the car park. At the exit, I hesitated – should I turn left and go after him or turn right and go home? Perhaps I should toss a coin.

Suddenly, flashing blue lights were heading for me. A policeman knocked on my window. I couldn't find the switch to open it. He was mouthing something at me. Broken blood vessels criss-crossed his nose like angry threadworms and he had the beginnings of a sty under his left eye. Pig sty, I thought.

I located the electric-window switch, pressed it. Whoops, wrong window – that was the passenger side. This one.

'You're causing an obstruction, madam. Have you been drinking?'

'I am on private property,' I retorted. 'I hadn't decided which way to go. And, anyway' – pointing at the bottle in my handbag – 'I was taking the rest of the wine home to drink.'

'You are half on the road. Get out of the vehicle.'

'Hold your horses. I was just going to reverse. I've asked if I can leave my car here, anyway.'

A policewoman appeared from somewhere. Or was it the woman who had been staring at me in the restaurant earlier? She looked similar.

Suddenly – how did that happen? – I was in the back of a panda car, moving fast in the dark. We arrived at a police station, where two officers were standing behind a counter. Both had big, protruding beer bellies.

One of them removed the bottle of Montepulciano from my handbag, raised an eyebrow. The other tipped my handbag upside down. Out cascaded a litter of old tissues, train tickets, half-unwrapped tampons, sticky sweets, an old notebook, hairgrips and Threshers receipts. My purse was bulging with £50 notes. I began to mouth an old childhood game: 'I packed my bag and in it I put. . .' One of the policemen looked up. I realised I was talking out loud. He narrowed his eyes and appeared to wrinkle his nose. Was he trying to insinuate I smelt?

'Is this your bag?' he asked.

I considered a sarcastic reply but left it at a sulky nod. His colleague began laboriously listing the bag's contents in childlike writing.

'Take off your jewellery and your shoes.'

'My shoes?'

'Yes, your shoes.'

The list of my handbag's contents was handed to me to check and sign. It seemed interminably long. I'd better read this carefully in case they'd planted something on me, I thought. I started reading through it, slowly.

'Just sign it and get on with it.'

'I'm reading it,' I replied sulkily.

He snatched the list back and scrawled, 'Defendant refuses to sign.'

I was led to a room and asked to blow into a contraption

attached to a computer. My heart was beating fast and I began hyperventilating. At forty-two, this was my only brush with the law since getting lost in France aged eight. The French police were much kinder.

'Blow harder, it's not registering,' the officer barked.

My mind worked. Perhaps if I blew faintly, I would be OK. One of the policemen smiled encouragingly. I smiled back. Maybe they would realise it was all a silly mistake and let me off. He looked a bit like my dad. I blew twice more.

'You're not trying hard enough. Don't worry – we'll do you for failure to provide. You'll get eighteen months, anyway.'

They took me to a cell. I lay down on a sort of ledge. I looked around for a blanket, but the cell was bare. It was cold and I began to shiver. I could hear angry, drunken male voices from another cell. Then I passed out.

Nobody is coming. Blood is now running down both my legs. I look around for my handbag. It's not here of course. Oh, God. What time is it? I knock on the door of the cell again and again until my knuckles ache.

Finally, somebody comes. A young male officer.

'I need a tampon,' I say, pointing at the congealed blood on my ankles. He closes the door and returns minutes later, handing me a mini tampon, the kind I had for my first periods at twelve.

'I've had three children!' I snort, looking at it incredulously.

'Well, that's all we've got,' he replied, taking me to a lavatory with no door. On the way back to the cell, I persuade him to give me a pencil and a piece of paper. I promise not to write on the walls. With nothing else to do, I can at least try to write something, but no words come. I feel numb. I cannot believe I'm here. I'm sure this is a dream, that I will soon wake up from another drunken nightmare.

An hour later the blood is gushing down my legs again. I feel faint and scared, alone and shaky. I knock on the door over and over.

I hear jeering, singing: 'The more fuss you make, the longer it will take!'

I write this down on my piece of paper. I think of words that rhyme with '-ake' – fake, lake, wine lake, sake – yes, sake, for God's *sake* open the door and give me another tampon. Eventually the door is opened. It's the same young officer. He hands me two tampons and again accompanies me to the doorless lavatory.

I ask him what will happen. They are waiting for the duty officer, he says. I give him the name of my lawyer. I had given it to the two officers the night before but they'd claimed they couldn't find his number. This policeman finds the number straight away.

I speak to my lawyer. He says he doesn't deal with drink-driving but knows someone who does. He'll try to get in touch, otherwise there'll be a duty solicitor. 'You'll be fine,' he assures me.

I'm taken back to my cell. A woman comes in. She's about my age, with dark-blonde hair, and carries a clipboard. 'I am here to talk to anyone who thinks they have a problem with alcohol,' she says.

'What a relief,' I answer. 'I haven't got a problem with alcohol, but I've been in here for hours and would really like someone to talk to. I don't suppose you have any giant tampons on you, do you?'

She shakes her head. 'Well,' she says, 'if you haven't got an alcohol problem, I better go and speak to some of the others.'

'Yes. From the sound of things last night, some of the other people in here were really drunk. They may have a problem.'

She stares at me.

'I don't normally drink and drive,' I add. 'I'd had an argument. I was just unlucky, you know.'

'Do you ever drive in the morning after a session?' she asked.

'Of course I do – I have to take the kids to school. But I don't drink first thing in the morning.'

'You'd be surprised – you may well be over the limit in the mornings.'

Then it hits me. I am bound to lose my licence. How will I get the children to school? What will I tell Mum and Dad? Niall would be cock-a-hoop. How could I organise it so he didn't know? There must be a way – perhaps I can say I've developed epilepsy. Mind you, gossip is bound to get around. Maybe he will help out and take the children to school.

I sit in the cell for another hour or so. My shakes get worse. I still can't take it all in. I am brought a breakfast of soggy, microwaved hash browns and baked beans. Next, I am charged, fingerprinted, swabbed in the mouth for DNA, photographed. The flash almost blinds me. The police mugshot of Hugh Grant pops into my head, the one that was wired around the world after his debacle with a lady of the night. Blow job of a different kind.

This amuses me and I laugh as I am released from the police station and head straight for Café Rouge. I order a large glass of red. And another. My shaking stops. I am on my fourth when a friend arrives to pick me up.

I was a contrite girl in court, in my navy crêpe Armani trousersuit. I'd always associated it with the pinnacle of my success and done several deals in it. But as I stood n the dock, shame seeped into my soul. One inner voice told me I was bad, weak and reckless. Another whispered, 'You were just unlucky. How many times have you knowingly drunk and driven in your life? Less than a handful of times in twenty years. You're just unlucky.'

I received a year's ban to be reduced to nine months if I agreed to attend a drink-awareness course on Saturday mornings. There were fourteen of us on the 'naughty course', as I came to call it. We would carry on our research in the pub afterwards.

CHAPTER THIRTY-FOUR

DEATH OF A KING

My father died.

Mum said he'd been sitting in the garden while she was planting peas when she heard a thud. And that was it. A massive heart attack and . . . gone. She had been just about to make him a coffee, once she'd finished planting the peas.

I stood at the lectern in the church, looking down at my high-heeled pink and red suede boots, laced from ankle to toe. Dad loved them and used to call them my Moulin Rouge boots. 'You ought to be doing the cancan in those,' he had smiled.

I hadn't planned to wear them for the funeral, but in my hung-over rush to get to my mother's house, shouting at the boys to make sure they wore their best shirts, I had forgotten about my own clothes. Hence my unlikely mishmash of short, zip-up black Paul Costello dress, thick black tights and my outrageous Moulin Rouge boots. At least they had black laces.

I looked across at my dad's naval medals glinting in the sunlight on top of the pine coffin. How could he be dead? He who gave me beard rubs, who used to call me 'my Alice fair' and sing me to sleep with Irish lullabies; he who was always there for me and loved me unconditionally, even when I grew into a woman. He made me feel special. When he talked to me, it was always as if I was the only person in the world.

I took a deep breath and looked out over the congregation. The church was full. I focused on Number Two son's angelic face. I must get his hair cut, I thought.

I swallowed hard. Suddenly my throat felt dry. I had resisted the idea of slipping out of Mum's back gate to the local for a large vodka and tonic. Dad wouldn't have approved. He was always uncomfortable with any of us drinking spirits.

'A reading from the Prophet Isaiah,' I began. 'On this morning, the Lord of Hosts will prepare for all peoples a banquet of rich food and wine.' I paused and many of the congregation smiled. Dad loved good food and his passion for wine was matched only by my own. Our shared interest gave us a special bond. I knew he was proud of me and my books. 'The Lord will wipe away the tears from every cheek,' I went on. At this line I faltered. I will not cry, I told myself. I gulped and it echoed around the church like a desperate, strangled sob. My left hand started to shake. Somehow I managed the next few lines. The reading over, I teetered back to my pew and sat down. Number Two son squeezed my hand.

Pictures flashed up in my head. Daddy building me a sandcastle and giving me the flag to stick in the turret. Me running down a hill in the Brecon Beacons so fast that as he caught me we both fell over and tumbled further down the hill, crying with laughter. His beaming face beside me as I took him for his first drive in my new sports car, my beloved LBC.

Mum climbed to the lectern to give the eulogy. She is a magnificent speaker. Not for nothing did she teach speech and drama. I never knew my father had learnt to fly with the US Air Force. She spoke of how he studied hard to learn about wine and to speak French. The wine came more easily to him than the language, she observed wryly. I could hear him answering the phone at home in his appalling French: '*Ici Monsieur King de Londres.*' On one occasion, in spontaneous unison, all nine children had mimicked him.

'He was flamboyant, self-willed, outspoken, stubborn, irascible, quick to anger but always quick to beg forgiveness. Dominic King. A lovely man, a good man – we like to think a great man. God rest his soul.' Mum stepped down. There was a silence, then several people began to clap. Clapping in church!

We followed the coffin out into the churchyard as children from a neighbouring school ran out to play. As their squeals and laughter sounded in the background, the grandchildren threw handfuls of spring blossom and rose petals over the coffin.

I cadged a lift back to the house with an old friend of Dad's. I hadn't yet admitted to anyone I'd lost my licence. I needed to be back first to open the champagne. Dad had been quite insistent about that – had left instructions that we were to have a champagne party. Magnums, naturally.

I opened the door. The house was silent. I expected my father to walk round the corner, ask me where I'd been. Magnums of champagne on ice were floating in his naval rum barrel. Mum had bought it for him at an auction, delighted to have tracked down such a memento from the aircraft carrier he served on during the war. I read the polished brass plaque: 'The King, God bless him.' And he was my king, both in name and nature. I feel strangely comforted standing by his barrel.

I pulled out a magnum and tore off the gold foil. I could hear his voice, telling me at ten years old, 'Hold the cork and twist the bottle, not the cork – that's the trick.'

The cork popped and I poured out a glass with such haste that the bubbles fizzed furiously over the top. Tutting to myself – Dad would never have approved of that – I picked up the glass and drained the contents in two gulps, the bubbles pricking my dry throat. I poured the other twenty-three glasses with more care. I repeated the exercise with the second magnum, savouring this glass a little longer – three gulps rather than two.

The guests started to arrive. Since Dad's death all us children had been referring to this wake as 'the reception'. We had only ever organised weddings before. But the atmosphere was more in celebration than sorrow – Dad would have approved of that.

A friend came to sit beside me. 'So, how are you, Alice?'

I snort. 'Well, I'm not drunk, am I? Bet that surprised you, didn't it?'

She touched my arm. 'How are you really? On the inside?'

I paused before answering. 'Hollow, empty, numb. But OK hollow, OK empty, OK numb. I feel at peace with Dad. There was no unfinished business between us. And I haven't cried.'

'What is that pile of handkerchiefs doing over there?' my friend asked, pointing to the dresser.

I turned my head and looked at the stack of Dad's neatly ironed and folded hankies. Mum, walking past and overhearing, stopped and answered, 'There's one for each of the children to take home.'

Tears sprang from my eyes.

CHAPTER THIRTY-FIVE

COWBOY HAT

I opened the courtyard door and stepped gleefully out into the night rain. It was a light summer shower, just enough to coat the hydrangea leaves glistening in the moonlight. After three weeks in dusty, dry Arizona, where the daily temperature was 120 degrees Fahrenheit and there had been no rain for over a hundred days, rain was a novelty about which I had fantasised.

I did a little rain dance, clicking the heels of my new cowboy boots and laughing as I watched the beaded tassels on them bounce up and down. And that was not the only thing that was bouncing.

How ridiculous would I look if anyone could see me now? I thought – a forty-something woman naked but for her stretch marks, new suede cowboy boots and black cowboy hat, dancing in the rain around a pot of hydrangeas.

It was almost a full moon. Would that account for my madness? Was it jet lag and rain deprivation? Or had the number of salt-encrusted margaritas done their worst – or best – and destroyed whatever brain cells I had left?

I looked up at the sky. A single large raindrop landed on my eyelashes and in the split second before I blinked the mighty planet Mars magnified in size. There had to be some intergalactic significance that Mars was the closest to Earth it had been for millions of years. It must be some sort of sign. But a sign of what? I wondered, as I twirled faster in the rain. I could see why it was called the Red Planet, with its fiery, golden-crimson, almost artificial brightness. And if the god of war was named after it, perhaps it was time I went to war with some of my demons.

I knew I was drinking too much. In the weeks since my father's death, life had become surreal. Drinking was the only way to blot out the ache that took my breath away. The stronger the drink, the better. I had rocked myself to sleep for many nights, composing imaginary conversations with him. I was grateful that he had died before he found out about me losing my driving licence. I wondered what he would have thought about my demeaning night in the cells.

A few friends had dropped round on their way back from the pub that evening on the off-chance of a late drink. They always knew they were in luck when they saw the light on through the dimpled glass of the red door of the Doll's House. They had left as soon as the bottle of golden tequila was empty. I was alone again, an empty bottle for company. I had picked up a last glass of tequila that had somehow been forgotten, stripped to my cowboy boots and hat and come dancing in the rain.

'Captain of My Heart' was belting out of the jukebox. I went back inside, pirouetting on my stack heels to turn up the volume when the phone rang. In an exaggerated Arizona drawl I answered, 'Well, howdy!'

A surprised-sounding, slightly northern English accent replied, 'Good evening. You sound like you're having fun. What are you up to?'

Laughing, I thought how apt it was that this was a call from the god of war himself, a bloke I had met in the pub who loved to row with people, mostly in good spirit. 'Mr Confrontational Man' I had christened him. After years of such arguments during my marriage, I felt strangely comfortable with him.

'Dancing naked in the rain sporting my new cowboy

boots and a cowboy hat, drooling over Mars,' I answered, unable to keep the giggle out of my voice. There was a momentary silence.

'What, with nothing else on?'

I looked down. 'Nothing – except my stretch marks.'

'Well, why don't you come down here? I'd love to see your new boots.'

I hesitated. I was about to cite jet lag as an excuse when he added, 'I've got a bottle of Appleton golden rum. Come as you are.'

'See you in ten,' I replied, putting down the receiver. Reaching for my old pale-grey cashmere coat, I briefly considered going up the twisting stairs to put some clothes on. But those stairs were notoriously slippery. Best not to test my agility with new, rain-soaked leather soles.

The silk lining of my coat felt cool and curiously welcoming on my naked skin. I grabbed a large brown carrier bag marked 'Sedona Boots' and stepped out into the night. The puddles glistened in the streetlight as I clip-clopped along.

The town hall clock struck 1 a.m. Staring up at it, I recited, 'The clock struck one, the mouse ran down, hickory, dickory dock.' I smiled as I walked down the high street, passing a solitary late-night pub-goer. 'Hiya!' I waved. He looked the worse for wear and I chuckled into my collar, feeling decidedly wicked that he couldn't see the real naked me, concealed under my coat.

I stomped in every puddle on the way. By the time I arrived my coat was covered in teardrop-shaped splashes. I hammered on the door, calling, 'Howdy there, cowboy-boot delivery!'

He opened the door, handing me a tumbler full of golden rum. I took a gulp and my eyes watered as the fiery, caramel-like spirit hit the back of my throat. I opened my coat quickly, to prove I had brought my stretch marks with me, and closed it.

'I like the hat,' he said. 'And the boots aren't bad either.'

'Here, try yours on,' I said, handing him the carrier bag. 'Hope they fit. Black, size ten.'

He pulled them on and marched around the flat, a vision in black cowboy boots and a short towelling dressing gown, beaming like a schoolboy.

'So, how was Arizona?' he asked.

'My dad learnt to fly there during the w—'

Damn, damn, damn. Tears in my drink again.

CHAPTER THIRTY-SIX

LIVER TESTS

I had to pass a liver function test before I could reapply for my driving licence, which meant I had to give up drinking. I was not too daunted by that. I'd stopped drinking several times in the past – every year during the month of January and each time I wrote a wine book because I had to work at such a rate I couldn't afford a hangover. This always resulted in me writing quickly so I could get back on the sauce.

I realised, though, it had been a long time since I had stopped for more than a day. I was also shocked to realise I hadn't written a book for years. Where had the time gone? I calculated that I'd probably need to stop drinking for about three months. I put the drink down after a particularly heavy farewell weekend. I had flu symptoms for a week, with sweating and high temperatures, but strangely no runny nose. Could this be to do with drinking? It didn't seem like withdrawal to me – besides, I wasn't shaking, I smugly told friends.

The boys remarked on my bad temper. I was furious when I overhead Number One son telling his brothers, 'She's so stressy now she isn't drinking.'

I went to see a homeopath about my liver. 'Surely I can beat the system if you give me something to restore and speed up my liver's rejuvenation,' I said.

She told me I needed to look at my drinking long term.

'You don't understand,' I insisted. 'All I need is to get my driving licence back.'

Over some weeks, and despite not drinking, my liver functions tests were erratic. What was the point in stopping if the tests kept fluctuating?

I found myself tetchy and withdrawn, barely talking to anyone except to rant about my liver. My anger at the system grew. 'There are probably thousands of people walking about with odd liver function tests, but because they haven't lost their licences, they're OK to drive,' I whinged endlessly in the pub over my ginger ale. Ginger ale! My friends told me to stop ranting.

Angrily, I decided to go along for my official medical anyway, despite the fact that my tests still weren't normal. As soon as the blood test was over, I celebrated in the pub, relieved I didn't have to face a Christmas without booze. I couldn't understand it – I seemed to be getting helplessly drunk on very little, so drunk I couldn't remember anything after the third glass. 'It just shows you what happens if you don't keep practising,' I joked.

After a six-week wait for the results, my doctor called me in to see her. It was two o'clock in the afternoon and I'd already guzzled two large glasses of wine.

I had failed the medical.

I took the news very badly. I left the surgery in high dudgeon and moaned about it in the pub. I was angry at people I knew who drank more than me without apparent ill effect.

My doctor had suggested I go to see a liver specialist. I asked my sister Juliana to come with me.

'I'm pleased to report we can't see any evidence of cirrhosis on your scan,' the consultant told me.

My sister looked relieved.

'Look,' I said to him, 'I just need to know how long you think I will have to stop drinking to get my driving licence back. It's as simple as that. How long?'

'I'm afraid it's *not* as simple as that. Your driving licence is really neither here nor there. It's your health I am interested in. Livers are funny things. They can be fine one minute and then suddenly deteriorate. We need to look at your drinking. How much do you think you're drinking?'

It was if I hadn't heard his question. I shouted, 'And how am I supposed to get my children to school if my driving licence is "neither here nor there"? How long do I have to give up for – six months, seven, what? Just tell me!'

My sister was looking embarrassed.

'I cannot give you an exact answer,' came the specialist's cold reply.

I continued my rant outside in the car park. 'Calls himself a consultant! Why didn't he just answer my question? How bloody long do I need to stop drinking for? It's not rocket science, surely!'

CHAPTER THIRTY-SEVEN

STING IN THE TALE

I came to. Sweat was running down my body like rain down a windscreen. My heart was beating so fast it felt as if Duracell bunnies on speed were banging their drums in my chest. I ran my tongue around my mouth and realised I hadn't cleaned my teeth the night before. My throat was sore and it was difficult to swallow. The roof of my mouth felt like one of those insect strips that catch their prey in that gloopy syrup. Bile was rising in my stomach.

I could smell red wine. An upended glass was lying beside the bed, the wine soaked into the carpet like a child's drawing of a long, red tongue. I knew without looking at the clock that it would be 4.35 a.m. It was the same time every morning, and it was too early – too much of the day stretching ahead. I kept forgetting to ask my mother what time I had been born. Maybe that's why I always woke up so early.

This sweating was getting ridiculous. I moved my foot around, searching for a dry spot – the sheets and the duvet were as wet as if they had just been taken out of the washing machine. Perhaps I was having an early menopause, I thought. Or I was sickening for something – though come to think of it, these night sweats had been going on for a long time.

I tried closing my eyes, conjuring up my favourite visualisation of Dunn's Falls, the spectacular waterfall in Jamaica I'd seen on a press trip once. Maybe that would send me back to sleep. But I felt as if I'd been standing in the water-fall. I blinked my eyes open as a globule of sweat dripped off my forehead. Sighing, I raised my head slowly. I got out of bed, side-stepping the glass, and went into the kitchen.

There was broken glass on the floor. My favourite red stilettos were lying jack-knifed on their sides inside the front door. I put them on. I glanced at my bloodshot eyes in the hall mirror. They were a similar colour to my shoes.

I looked around for an idea of what had happened the night before, where I had been. The bin often provided clues. Ah, yes – takeaway cartons still coated with the remains of salt and chilli prawns and noodles, lying slimy and worm-like, gleaming in their protective monosodium glutamate. A visit to the Chinese takeaway van, then. How had I staggered there? Who had seen me? What time had it been?

The fear kicked in. My chest felt constricted. I made a dash for the sink and retched into it, again and again, watch-ing the yellow bile swirl down the plughole, taking with it a single helpless noodle.

Crossing to the freezer, I noticed it was 4.50 a.m. Bending down to pick up a discarded Rowntree's ice-lolly wrapper, I almost toppled over on my stilettos as the blood rushed to my head. I opened the freezer, retrieved the bottle of Absolut from the bottom drawer and held it up to the light. It was difficult to see through the frosted glass, but it looked as if there was about an inch or so in the bottom. Who had drunk all that? I had only bought it the day before. Who had been round the night before? There were no glasses on the table. I peered into the dishwasher – no, none there either.

The broken glass crunched underfoot. Looking down, I saw it was one of the boys' *Lion King* glasses. Opening the cupboard to find the dustpan, I was surprised to find six more Absolut empties lined up like bottles in a shooting range. I must tell my loyal cleaner, Stef, to throw them out. I'm sure this cupboard had been empty a few days ago.

Looking at the bottles, I felt a hot flush of shame. Discarded different wine bottles were easy to explain – they were for work, weren't they? – but six identical vodka bottles? Looking at the one in my shaking hand, I reasoned I may as well finish it, and poured it into a child's *Aladdin* glass on the table. One small one wouldn't do any harm. Perhaps it would help me go back to sleep. I noted how the oily vodka coated the sides of the glass. It was halfway to my lips when someone patted me on the back. Jumping, I turned to see Number Two son sleepily rubbing his eyes and smiling.

'Hee! Thought I'd surprise you, Mummy!'

'Well, don't!' I snapped. 'I nearly jumped out of my skin. Keep out of the way while I sweep this glass up. Anyway, what are you doing out of bed? It's only five o'clock.' I realised I was still clutching the Absolut bottle and placed it in the cupboard next to the other six, quickly slamming the door.

'I couldn't sleep,' he said. 'And I'm thirsty. I need water.'

I ran the tap and handed him a glass of water. 'Yes, I'm thirsty too,' I added more gently, as we drained our glasses together.

'You know what, Mummy?' he added. 'That's my glass you've got there.'

We walked out into the garden, where he climbed into the hammock and promptly fell asleep. I stood looking at him. Nothing seemed to rattle him. Despite the quicksand nature of his homelife, he retained his own pixie-like smile and his sense of humour. I gazed at the sprinkling of freckles across his nose and marvelled at how his hair glinted in the early-morning sunlight, like spun gold. He had an inner peace that I envied. Where had that come from?

The snowball tree was laden with flowers, and there were petals all over the lawn. It was going to be a scorcher. The birdsong seemed inordinately shrill. I went back to bed.

I awoke three hours later and started the familiar process

of piecing together the flashbacks from the night before. I recalled going to the Three Swans while waiting for the Chinese. I didn't think I'd been in the pub for long. Well, just a few drinks. I prided myself on only drinking single vodkas even though the house doubles were the same price. There was no way I'd drink that cheap stuff, anyway – Smirnoff was so much better. I vaguely recalled talking to a guy with blond dreadlocks who was drinking the cheap crap, which was why I'd started talking to him, explaining how much less pure it was and how deadly the resulting hangovers were. I remembered elaborating at some length about how Smirnoff Black Label was filtered through charcoal, which gave it a more creamy flavour, and was why those who knew about vodka drank it neat. Yes, that was it. Perhaps he had come back later for a drink. That explained it. *He* must have drunk the vodka.

My heart started racing. I couldn't remember him leaving. Where was my handbag – and all my credit cards?

Number Three son popped his head round the door. 'Mummy, I'm hungry. Can we have some croissants?'

'OK, I'll do you a deal. You find my handbag and I'll go and buy some croissants from Somerfield.'

'It's in the pantry,' he laughed. 'That's a funny place to put it!'

He returned with my leopard-skin bag over his shoulder. I checked my purse – all my credit cards seemed to be there, plus one crisp, red £50 note. I preferred fifties. I thought I'd had two – though it was possible I'd spent one in the Three Swans. Yes, that's right – I remembered handing one to the bad-tempered barmaid. I couldn't see the change anywhere.

Pulling on my Wrangler jeans and an old striped navy T-shirt, I looked around for some shoes. It was too far to stagger in my stilettos. My Reeboks were around somewhere. As I peered under the bed for them, I felt faint, light-headed.

The air was so close it felt like a storm was brewing. My skin was hot and clammy.

I looked in the mirror. My hair was unkempt, matted and curly, so I pulled on a linen hat. Rubbing the sleep dust from my eyes, I noticed my eyelashes were like hairy spider's legs, clogged with the remains of last night's mascara. More mascara was smeared under my eyes. I had a red horn of wine over the right side of my top lip. I rubbed it furiously. I hoped I hadn't walked round like that all yesterday – the last time I remembered drinking red wine was the glass, or two, I'd had at lunchtime. I put on my brown Ray-Bans.

'Can I come with you to the supermarket, Mummy?' asked Number Three son.

'No, you stay here and I'll be quick.'

'You always say that and then you're gone for ages!' he whinged.

'OK, OK, come with me, but hurry up.'

Once in Somerfield, he disappeared to find the croissants. 'I've just got to get a few other things,' I said to his retreating back. The store was air-conditioned and I felt cold and shivery.

May as well get another bottle of vodka while I'm here, I thought – it would save coming back later. I looked up and down the empty aisle and reached for the bottle. Why was the Absolut always on the top shelf? And why did they have security tags? Surely people didn't steal vodka?

On my way to the checkout, I looked at the bottle lying alone in the basket and hastily rounded the corner to add some Fairy Liquid, then covered the vodka up with some dishcloths. With three little boys around there was always a mess to clear up.

Why does everyone do their shopping at eight thirty in the morning? I thought, waiting impatiently at the checkout. I realised my left hand was shaking so, after wiping the sweat from my brow, I pushed it deep into my pocket.

Why did I always bump into people I knew? Number Two son's gymnastics teacher stood in the next queue.

Number Three son appeared beside me and put the croissants on the conveyor belt. The spotty youth on the cash desk seemed to be taking for ever. He rang a bell and held up the Absolut in his hand. Feeling my face colour, I watched the supervisor come to the checkout and, in slow motion, nod like a bloody nodding dog. I made a mental note to pick cashiers over eighteen who didn't need authorisation to sell alcohol for my next early-morning vodka run.

'We're having a party later,' I mumbled to him, hastily putting the bottle into a carrier bag.

'Are we?' asked Number Three son, too loudly. 'Who's coming?'

'Well, actually, we're going to one in the village,' I replied, already out of the shop and striding down the road so fast he had to run to keep up.

Once home, I disappeared into the pantry, opened the new bottle and filled my glass. After a few quick slugs I felt better. My anxiety lessened and I began to breathe more easily.

'That's still my glass, Mummy,' pointed out Number Two son, as he grabbed his croissant and danced out into the garden, humming.

By noon the heat was unbearable and my two younger sons were fighting.

'Let's go out for lunch,' I suggested.

'Only if you promise we don't have to stay too long,' negotiated Number One son, who had had his head stuck inside *The Lion, the Witch and the Wardrobe* all morning, barely speaking to anyone.

We trundled across the road to be greeted warmly in the Plume. 'Warm enough for you?' asked the barmaid.

'I'm boiling – and so-o-o thirsty!' I said, ordering three Cokes for the boys.

'What'll it be, then?' she asked.

'Oh, yes, I could do with a drink – er – a glass of white – the Sauvignon, please.'

'Large?' A conspiratorial wink.

The boys ate chicken goujons and chips. I wasn't hungry and was halfway through my second glass of wine when Number One son announced he was going home.

'Well, take the others and I'll be back soon,' I said, giving him money to buy ice creams from the teashop by the bridge. 'I know you're eleven now but still mind how you cross the road.'

After a third glass I reluctantly got up. Just as I was leaving, a friend arrived. 'Stay for another drink,' she urged. 'I haven't seen you in ages.'

'OK, just a quick one,' I replied.

'How have you been? You look a bit, um . . .' she hesitated '. . . well, frazzled.'

'Yeah, well, wouldn't you be if you had to put up with three fighting boys? Anyway, how was your holiday?'

I wasn't really listening as she began to tell me, sniffing my drink, then gulping it down when I realised it was two o'clock. 'Christ, I'd better be going – we've got to go to a party with the great and good.'

'Monsieur Le Chauffeur' – a friend who had borrowed my car since I'd lost my licence – was waiting outside the house. The arrangement suited him as he'd written off his own car and this way didn't need to stump up for a new one yet. It suited me as I had a way of getting the boys to school.

He looked hot. His sandy hair was sticking to his forehead, and there were imprints on his nose from his glasses. A lithe and fit dreamer, he had a passion for dancing – and the women he met at his nightly dance classes around the country. I was always envious I wasn't one of them.

'Ready in a minute,' I shouted.

'*D'accord*, Madame Le Roi,' came the weary reply.

Five minutes later the boys trooped out of the house, Number One still holding his book, Number Two with an armful of lilac from the garden, and Number Three clutching his football.

Halfway down the street Number Three piped up, 'Mummy, you've forgotten the vodka – you know, the bottle you bought this morning?'

'Oh, that wasn't for the party.'

'But you said it was. Why did you tell the boy at the supermarket it was for the party?' he persisted.

There was a silence in the car. Number Two son kicked him on the shin.

'So, where exactly is the party?' asked Monsieur Le Chauffeur.

'That big house to the left – the one with the wooden blinds, almost next to the butcher's.'

He dropped us off. The front door was open and we walked through the house to the garden. I couldn't help feeling envious. The hostess was moving to Bristol – to an even bigger and better house, I thought sulkily – and this was a farewell party. We each had a child in the same class, but our friendship had never been the same after a drunken weekend we'd spent together a few years ago with our husbands in Wales. I wasn't really sure what had happened, who had said or done what, but there had been an uncomfortable silence between us for a while.

Going into the garden, the boys ran off to be with their friends. Looking around for someone I knew, I saw a group of women sitting at a wooden table. They all looked the same – all blonde-haired, carefully made-up and in a seeming uniform of crisp, pressed white trousers or skirts and preppy shirts.

Scanning the length of the garden for some more lively

company, I was about to walk past when I noticed they were drinking rosé. I felt sure they had all stopped talking when I'd arrived. Christ, have I got my dress tucked into my knickers, or my boobs hanging out? I checked down at the flowery dress I had hastily changed into. Nope, all looked in order.

I sat at an empty seat. Wasn't anyone going to offer me a glass of wine?

'Is this a spare glass?' I asked, enunciating slowly. 'Mind if I have a glass of wine? I am so thirsty.' Someone passed the bottle down the table and I filled my glass. 'Cheers!' I said to the hostess. 'Happy moving.'

I looked around the table. I vaguely knew some of the women's faces from the school playground, not that I went there much. No doubt they had heard lots of bad press about me from the ex. I felt isolated.

'That's an unusual dress. Did you make it yourself?' asked the woman next to me. I looked down my nose at her own outfit, noting that her neatly ironed shirt looked as if it came from Primark.

'No, I didn't – actually, it's Moschino.'

'Oh. I thought you had crocheted it or something.'

'I think the technical term is "tatted",' I retorted. I noticed with alarm that my glass was already empty. 'Is there any more wine down that end of the table?'

Five minutes later the bottle in front of me was empty. I got up. What a boring bunch of women – Stepford wives! All perfect, with perfect lives, perfect husbands, perfect children. Which was all they were talking about. As I had no idea whose children were whose, it was difficult to concentrate. And, frankly, I wasn't interested. I wondered why I'd bothered coming. I could have stayed in the pub. No one seemed to be paying me any attention. I stood up.

I wandered out of the front door and on to the village high street. Number One son followed me. 'OK if I go up to my friend's, Mummy?'

'Which one?'

'You know, the one whose mum is an artist,' he replied.

'Good idea. I'll come with you – it's well dull here,' I announced, just as some other guests were arriving. My son cast me an embarrassed sideways glance.

We walked in silence together up the hill. He was still clutching his book.

I went into a garden following a sign that said, 'Open Studio'. The garden shimmered in the afternoon sun. Suddenly I felt really weary and almost tearful. I vaguely knew this woman, though I couldn't remember her name. Our sons played tennis together. She was one of the few mothers who spoke to me in the school playground.

'Hi,' she said. 'It's great to see you.'

'Were you not invited to the great and good party down the road, then?' I asked.

'No, seems not. Would you like a glass of wine?'

'Oh, yes – I'm really thirsty,' I replied, glancing around the studio. I wanted some new paintings, having banished several that reminded me of my ex to the garage.

'Hope you don't mind that it's nothing special – I know you're a bit of a connoisseur,' she apologised, handing me a large glass of white.

'Oh, don't worry, I'm just really thirsty.' The wine was cool and refreshing. Far nicer to be here among interesting, arty, creative people.

I wandered around, looking at the pictures. 'I really like the calligraphy one,' I said, stumbling over the word. 'Difficult word to say at this time of the afternoon, isn't it?'

It was a framed poem, 'Harlem' by Langston Hughes. Screwing up my eyes, I could just make out the first line: 'What happens to a dream deferred?' What had happened to all my dreams? They were more disintegrated than deferred.

'I'd like that one,' I said grandly. 'I haven't got my cheque-book with me, but I'll drop a cheque round tomorrow.'

'Are you sure? It's a hundred and fifty pounds.'

'Yes, yes. Look, I know it's a bit cheeky, but can I have another glass of wine? It's so hot.'

'It'll have to be red,' she replied.

'Oh, that's fine.'

'We're just about to eat. Would you like some spaghetti bolognaise with us?'

'Yes, please, I'm really hungry. And thirsty,' I added, laughing. 'Look, I think I've got the leaky glass again.'

I sat down with my hostess and her husband and devoured two plates of spaghetti without saying much, concentrating on trying to get the wayward pasta into my mouth. I tucked the paper napkin into the top of my dress to catch the splashes of sauce. I felt safe with these people. They didn't seem to be judging me.

'It's really nice to be here,' I said. 'I didn't feel very comfortable down the road – you know, all those people. And they seem so . . . well . . . up themselves, really.'

She just nodded.

Her husband disappeared to get another bottle. 'It's only bog-standard Rioja from Tesco,' he said when he returned.

'Don't worry, I probably chose it – I used to work for them, you know.' Was he looking at me strangely? Or was it the thick glasses he had on? I felt the familiar paranoia at the pit of my stomach and smiled weakly at him. 'Thanks,' I mumbled. 'As I said, you're really kind.'

My glass was empty again. How did this keep happening? I looked at my watch. Nearly six o'clock.

'Best get back to the party,' I said. 'Thanks for the food, and the wine. I'll see you tomorrow with a cheque. Love the picture.'

I walked back down the hill with Number One son and spotted my car. I tried to focus on it as Monsieur Le Chauffeur waved. I felt a bit woozy. Sweat was dripping down my face.

'You OK, Mummy?' asked Number One son.

'Yeah. It's just the heat,' I replied, steadying myself on a wall. I walked through the open front door of the party house and was about to go out to the garden when the hostess pounced on me.

'Where the hell do you think you've been?' she snarled. 'Your youngest son has been stung by a wasp and has been crying his eyes out. What kind of mother are you?'

My youngest son walked by. He looked fine, though his face was bit smeary.

'Well, he's not crying now, is he?' I said.

'That's because it happened about two hours ago and we've been looking for you ever since. We've called Niall to pick them up.'

I sighed and looked around for Number Two son. It seemed the same women were still sitting at the same table, their lipstick as perfect as ever. They were staring at me. Stuck-up cows. I bet *they*'re drunk by now. 'Tipsy', as they would probably put it.

I spotted Number Two son and managed to get all the boys in the car.

'Where did you go Mummy?' asked Number Three son. 'Four of my friends and me got stung and you weren't there. Look at my sting.'

I was examining it, leaning over him and trying to get his seat belt done up, when a taxi pulled up close by. Oh, Christ, I thought, here comes their father. The last thing I needed after this was a confrontation with him. I ducked down, hoping he wouldn't see me.

'Monsieur Le Chauffeur, home, and fast!'

'How was the party?' he asked.

'Oh, typical Stepford wives. Load of fuss about a wasp sting.'

CHAPTER THIRTY-EIGHT

VAMPIRE LIPS

It was January 2005, and I'd just been to see my therapist. I started seeing her five years earlier shortly after the divorce, to try to work through my feelings. I'd only had one large glass of Fetzer rosé. I had gone to the pub after my appointment to kill an hour while I waited for the train back to Hungerford. She had talked about responsibility – about me taking responsibility for my own life, about not operating from a place of blame, about taking a look at myself and not blaming everything and everyone else for my perceived misfortunes – for the mess I seemed to be in.

And it *was* a mess, of that there was no longer any doubt. I couldn't hide from that any longer, not even in a glass. I had fooled myself for long enough. What had I become?

After seeing my therapist, I had been standing at the bar in my leopard-skin coat and my pink trilby, just about to start on my second glass of rosé, when I had felt hot, my legs went weak, the pub went fuzzy . . . and the world went out.

I had come to on the floor with the publican looking at me in shocked concern. I had been able to taste blood in my mouth. Apparently, I had gone down like a felled tree.

I had told the paramedics I was fine. I was more embarrassed than anything else. I wasn't even drunk – not on one glass of rosé, surely? I had taken a taxi home and gone straight to my bedroom.

Now look at the state of me. I peer into my bedroom mirror.

My face is ashen, greyish-white, almost translucent. I rub some rouge into my cheekbones. They are prominent now. When I was eighteen, I used to use expensive green gunk, Ultima 2 from Revlon, to take the high colour out of my face. Now I am trying to put it back in.

My eyes are bloodshot, the mascara smudged. I've been crying. The man who arrived to fix my computer shortly after I returned home told me, 'Don't worry about the bill. I can see you've had a nasty fall.' I was so touched by his kindness it seemed to flick a switch in my soul and I burst into tears.

Not much I can do about the chip on my front tooth. My tongue searches it out every few seconds. There is something perversely comforting about this jagged edge. I've always been proud of my perfect teeth. Now they're not perfect any more. Still, if I keep my mouth shut and don't smile, this tiny chip won't show. I don't feel like smiling anyway. I comb my fringe straight to cover the scrape on my forehead. In this twilight, the graze looks like tiny red ants marching from my hairline to my eyebrow.

I tip the contents of my handbag on the floor. God, what a mess. I pick up a lipstick. Squinting, I look at the tiny gold print on the end – it makes me feel dizzy, sick. I must have banged my head when I fell. Elizabeth Arden's 'Captivate'. It's a deep-brown, dried-blood colour. How apt. That'll do to cover the bruise on my lip. With any luck, no one will notice in the pub's dingy light.

My left hand is shaking. It's never been the same since the time I broke my wrist falling off the loo, drunk. Perhaps I banged it again when I fell today. I stare at the hand and will it to stop shaking. It takes no notice. I transfer the lipstick to my right hand. If I paint my pinched, narrow lips a bit fuller, perhaps the bruise won't show. Someone once said I had a perfect Cupid's bow. Huh. What had Cupid ever done for me?

Five o'clock. I'd better get a move on, the pub is open and it's Friday. Or is it Thursday? I'm not sure. If I don't know what day it is, I must have bruised my brain. Actually, I feel faint again. When did I last eat something?

I start to shape my lips. I hate my face. I hate my lips. I hate my eyes. I hate me.

'I hate you,' I say to my reflection. 'I hate you, do you know that?'

My frown makes my head hurt. I've never been any good at putting lipstick on. They say you're supposed to use a brush, but that takes ages. I know what I'll do – I'll drink red wine, something really deep in colour like an Aussie Shiraz, and then the bruising won't show.

Angrily, I wipe the lipstick off the top of my lip with my thumb. It stings. 'Captivate'– what a name for a lipstick. Who could I captivate like this?

Cap-ti-vate. Rhymes with 'hate'. 'Hate, hate, Cap-ti-vate,' I say to my reflection. My voice is beginning to rise. There is a hysterical edge to it. I seem to hear it coming from a long way off, like a police siren in the distance.

'Blame, blame, that old game. Blame, blame, that old game,' I say, as soundbites of my therapist's words whirr around my head.

Using my little finger, I gingerly rub lipstick over my lower lip. My lips are numb. I have the strangest detached feeling, as if they belong to someone else.

I really am becoming hysterical now. I yell at myself in the mirror, 'I'm sick and tired of this!'

My mouth – black lipstick on the bottom lip, black bruising on the top – twists itself to form words with these lips that are not my lips. 'Responsibility,' it tells me. 'It's your responsibility.'

My eyes stare. Picking up my kohl pencil, I pull down my left eye. The pink of my eye is angry red. I rest my forehead against the cold glass of the mirror. Gilt bunches of grapes around the top of the frame mock me.

It's true. I am responsible for my life. No one else. I can't keep doing this to myself. I can't keep drinking.

No wonder I keep passing out.

No wonder I'm covered in bruises.

No wonder I'm alone.

No wonder I can't drive.

No wonder I've no money.

No wonder I've no work.

No wonder I no longer own a house.

No wonder I don't see my family.

No wonder the phone never rings.

No wonder my friends have given up on me.

No wonder my own children are scared of me.

No wonder I look such a mess.

No wonder I hate myself.

It is the drink: I have to stop drinking.

I drop the kohl pencil and watch it fall to the floor in slow motion. I walk across the room, fall face down on to my bed. The lipstick leaves a sinister vampire's smile on my pillow. I curl into the foetal position and rock.

'Sick and tired,' I whisper. 'Sick and tired. Sick and tired. Sick and tired of *being* sick and tired.'

PART THREE

*One Day
at a Time*

CHAPTER THIRTY-NINE

Shadow Angel

I knew what was happening. I'd had it before. Withdrawal.

I awoke at 4 a.m., fully clothed. The ghastly vampire's smile was still there in lipstick on my pillow. A full moon stared rudely straight through my bedroom window, bathing me with madness. I felt odd, disconnected.

I was hot. Sweat poured down my face. My fringe was wet, plastered to my forehead. A river of perspiration ran between my breasts. I wrestled off my cowboy boots. My skin was itching. I took off my trousers. I could feel a bumpy rash, like nettle rash, all over my thighs. I traced it round to my now-protruding hip bones, scratching. My arms were itching too and had the same uneven texture, like woodchip wallpaper.

I knew what to do. Vodka would fix this.

The screensaver on my mobile phone suddenly lit up, casting a shadow-shape through the lampshade beside my bed. The outline of an angel, wings raised in salutation, was projected on to the wall. The light faded and the angel disappeared. My heart thudding, I froze for a few seconds. Was I hallucinating?

I pressed my mobile's keypad and the angel appeared again. Oh, God. She must be my guardian angel – the Sourire de Reims, my smiling angel from all those years ago.

It's a sign. I can do this. I can sit it out.

*

225

The next few nights followed a similar jittery, restless pattern. I found I could conjure up the shadow angel at any time, and did. The boys were intrigued. I told them she was my guardian angel, that we all had one. On the second day my left hand started to shake. It was always worse at night and I slept fitfully, clutching a tennis ball.

Daylight brought new hope. I tried to keep myself occupied and – never one to watch TV – began picking up books around the house. Short stories and poems were all I could manage, my concentration span short. Nothing much happened. I stayed at home, out of the pub. I fed the children. I felt like a child myself, living in good-girl limbo.

Whenever I had stopped drinking in the past I would feel as if I was flat-lining, then eventually I would reward myself with the rollercoaster drama of drinking again. But not this time. Not a single sip of wine for me. I had the same conversation with the committee in my head time and time again. Only total abstinence would ensure the reissue of my driving licence. *That* would be my reward, I told myself repeatedly, to be able to be a proper mother and drive my children around, take them to football, cricket, swimming, ballet – invite their friends round to tea and be able to drive them home.

I asked Number Two son when his homework was due in. 'Why do you want to know all of a sudden?' he asked, surprised. 'You've never asked before.'

Lunchtimes and 6 p.m., drink-trigger times, were the worst. I took to pacing around the garden, then decided to take my morning bath at lunchtime and take the boys to feed the ducks on the canal at 5 p.m.

When I told them to get their coats on, they sighed. 'Are we going to the pub?' I shook my head. As we traipsed down to the canal, they darted knowing looks at each other. I sensed they were holding their breath as we walked past the three pubs en route. I was doing the same. I crossed the road, so we took the zigzag route to where we fed the ducks. 'I will, I will,

I *will* get my driving licence back' became my silent mantra.

I felt relieved and bereft at the same time, but once past the first week, it was a joy to fall asleep rather than pass out. Waking up in the morning being able to remember going to bed was a novelty.

I told myself that this self-imposed abstinence would not be for ever – six months, say, or however long it took for my liver function tests to return to normal. A nagging voice in my head said, 'What if they don't? What will you do then?' I ignored it.

I began to eat again, taking delight in my food, though a meal without a glass or six of wine was purgatory. Water didn't do it for me.

Time moved on and I stopped counting the days and started counting the weeks. It was extraordinary how quickly I felt physically better. I decided not to tell any of my family I had stopped drinking. They'd heard it all before.

By week four I felt more connected, slightly less shell-shocked. I started to think about making a concerted effort to find some work. I reckoned I had enough capital from the sale of Avon House to survive about another year, tops.

Then I received a phone call from Meridian Television. I had done a few local news items for them in the past, mainly publicising wine tastings I was holding or commenting on award-winning wines in the news. When the call came in, I held my breath, wondering how I could explain that I wasn't drinking at the moment.

Fortunately, the job didn't involve drinking alcohol. Was I up for doing a piece to camera involving a water tasting? Did I think I could tell the difference between bottled and tap water? This was to link in with a report from *Which?* on the cost of bottled water. The filming could be done in a nearby coffee shop.

I couldn't believe my luck. Was my smiling angel orchestrating this? I wondered.

CHAPTER FORTY

TEMPTATION

Week five without a drink and I was getting ready to do the water tasting. Clothes were strewn all over my bed. I hadn't realised how much weight I'd lost. Many of my TV-type dresses hung off me.

I'd felt so nervous when I woke up I'd had to run, retching, to the bathroom. It wasn't until later that I realised this was the first time I'd been sick in five weeks. Five whole weeks!

I settled on a pair of black crêpe flares and a purple cashmere jumper. Still two hours to go. I always used to get nervous appearing live on TV. Back then I had survived by obliterating the anticipated anxiety with a few drinks the night before, operating the following morning on a cocktail of the leftover alcohol in my bloodstream mixed with adrenaline. I could feel the Three Swans Hotel calling me from just fifty yards over the road. Surely one or two vodka and tonics – singles, of course – couldn't do any harm? Such a tiny amount wouldn't affect my liver function tests, would it? The voice in my head was getting louder. I was pacing around my office, flexing my fingers, when the doorbell rang. It was Sue, a friend I'd asked to come and hold my hand during the shoot. I hugged her.

'You OK?' she asked. 'You look a bit pale. What's wrong?'

'I'm scared, really scared. Why don't we just pop across to the Three Swans for a sharpener?'

'Don't be daft. You're not drinking. And you don't need one now – you've lasted all these weeks. You'll be fine,' she assured me. 'You're always really good at these kinds of things. You're looking good, too. Very slimline.'

'Oh, come on,' I protested. 'One won't do any harm.'

'Alice, you don't need it. And it won't do any good either.'

We sat in the kitchen and drank Earl Grey, trying to do *The Times* crossword – the quick one. Six across, five letters. 'V-o-d-k-a . . . There may well be some vodka in the freezer. Let's have a small one, shall we?'

'No, no, no, no and *no*!' she insisted. 'Let's go down to the coffee shop and see if we need to set anything up for the shoot.'

The filming went well. I duly tasted the waters, able easily to detect the difference between bottled and tap.

'We just need some final drop-in shots,' said the producer. 'Let's use your friend and find someone else – a man, preferably.'

'Yes, well, we're both looking for men, aren't we, Sue?' I joked.

'What about him?' she asked as a man, stocky with thinning dark-blond hair and startling blue eyes, walked into the coffee shop and smiled at me. 'Do you know him?' she asked.

'Actually, I do, vaguely. His name's Martin.'

We filmed Martin and Sue drinking a coffee and a bottle of water together, laughing and nodding in mock conversation for the camera. Satisfied, the camera crew packed up and left. Hugely relieved it was over, I sat down for a cup of coffee with a Perrier chaser.

'We ought to be celebrating with a glass of champagne,' I lamented to Sue.

'A nice strong double espresso, that's what you need. That'll do the trick,' suggested Martin.

I looked at him. 'You look really well, much better than

229

when I last saw you. Have you been on holiday?

'No, I haven't,' he replied. 'But I've stopped drinking.'

'Oh? And you used to drink shedloads, didn't you?'

'Yep, my drinking was totally out of control,' he replied. 'I used to drink during good times to celebrate and bad times to drown my sorrows and cheer myself up. I used to drink if the sun was shining or if it was raining – in fact, I used to just drink all the time and my life had become totally unmanageable.'

'You weren't that bad, were you?' asked Sue.

'Yes, I was – I was worse.'

'I've stopped drinking too,' I announced proudly. 'I haven't had a drink for five weeks now.'

He switched his gaze to me. 'Yes, I'd heard you drank a lot. So why have you stopped?'

'It's a long story. Basically, I lost my driving licence – not that I was in the habit of drink-driving, you understand – and I have to have a medical to get my licence back. I've already had one medical, but due to some kind of mix-up, even after four months of not having a single drop, my liver function tests were still over the top. But I am determined to get my licence back.'

'Alice,' he said, 'surely it's not your licence you need back – it's your life.'

'Yes!' Sue interjected. 'You're right. I keep trying to tell her this isn't about getting her driving licence back, it's about her health and sorting out the damage she might have done to her body.'

'Oh,' I gabbled, 'even the liver specialist thinks there might have been a mistake in my last blood test. So, anyway, Martin, if you're so clever, how did you stop?'

'I go to AA – you know, Alcoholics Anonymous.'

'Do you? Is it like the Masons? I've always wanted to know what goes on at those meetings – you know me, the nosy journalist.'

'Have you really? I'll take you to one if you want. There's one tomorrow.'

'Um, I might have the boys,' I stuttered. 'But by all means give me a ring. God, this coffee is so strong it's making my hands shake. I bet you used to get the shakes all the time.'

CHAPTER FORTY-ONE

First AA Meeting

I wasn't an alcoholic, of course, but I had reasoned that since I wasn't drinking anyway, I might as well go to Alcoholics Anonymous. You know, for support. My therapist agreed. Anyway, going to AA didn't make me an alcoholic, did it? Going to France didn't make me French.

Now we were whizzing along the country lanes in Martin's car, on our way to the meeting, and this was reality. I was nervous. I was thinking, What am I doing in a car with this man? I had no idea why I had expressed an interest in going to an AA meeting. It must have been a caffeine rush from the coffee, a moment of madness in my – let's face it – otherwise staid, self-imposed dry desert of a life.

As Martin slowed the car, I was overwhelmed by anxiety, creeping up into my chest from the pit of my stomach – that sense of being in trouble, the way I used to feel after a bout of heavy drinking. I immediately felt thirsty. A nice, calming vodka and tonic, that's what I needed – that would dissipate the feeling.

'So, what actually happens at these meetings?' I asked. 'They're not formal, are they? I'm not sure now why I'm coming. Perhaps I could wait for you in the pub. There must be one nearby.'

He laughed. 'No, this meeting is in the middle of nowhere. Don't worry, you'll be fine.'

'What if I see someone I know?'

'Then they'll be there for the same reason you are. So it's OK, really – you have no need to be scared.'

'Hey,' I protested, 'hold on a minute – don't lump me into the same category as all the other . . .' My voice tailed off as I looked at him, unsure of the terminology, thinking the word 'alkies' may be a little harsh. 'Anyway, I'm here because I am curious, not because I've got a problem. You do under-stand that, don't you?'

He didn't answer and just nodded knowingly, as an indul-gent parent would with a child who has been caught red-handed stealing biscuits and is still denying it.

I pulled my pink trilby down over my eyes. For once I didn't want to draw attention to myself. I was dressed sombrely in a black jumper and trousers, though the trilby and the leopard-skin coat I had grabbed as we left were hardly inconspicuous, it occurred to me. We got out of the car. I followed Martin, feeling sheepish. I was thirsty. God, this coat was a mistake.

There was a knot of people standing around outside what looked like a village hall. They didn't look like alcoholics to me – more like the sort of well-dressed, sober, respectable residents you would expect in a posh village like this. Two were around the same age as me, two looked older, and one guy with black spiky hair was in his early twenties. They were laughing, joking with each other. I was introduced to them, first names only. They all shook my hand and smiled at me. I felt as if I was at a drinks party with the vital ingredient missing. A large vodka and tonic – ice and fresh lime, yes – would be perfect right now, I thought, and would give me something to do with my hands.

As if he had read my thoughts, an older man, a retired military type with sparkling blue-grey eyes and silver hair, shook my hand and kept hold of it. 'First meeting?' he asked.

I nod.

'Well done you for coming along. I can assure you you'll never regret getting sober. It will change your life.'

'Actually, I'm sober already. I've just come along to see what happens at an AA meeting.'

'Well, you're very welcome. Try to listen out for the similarities rather than the differences in people's stories,' he suggested.

Stories? I think back to *Jackanory*.

'And don't worry if you don't feel like saying anything. Take time to reflect and listen.'

A picture of my father popped up in my head. He would regularly tell us to 'take time', whether time to think or, indeed, to laugh. What would he have thought of his daughter at an AA meeting? Suddenly I felt tearful, vulnerable and unsure of myself. Somebody handed me a cup of tea. He looked familiar, but I couldn't place his face.

Inside the hall, it was light and airy, open to the rafters. Chairs were set out in a circle round a small oak arts and crafts table. Two crimson roses drank deep in a vase in its centre. On the floor were white cards with slogans, like the flash cards I was taught to read with. These slogans were 'Keep it simple', 'First things first', 'One day at a time'.

The man who had given me the cup of tea started talking. I definitely knew that face from somewhere. He introduced himself: 'My name is Joseph and I'm an alcoholic.'

My mind went into overdrive. Did that mean he still drank? Had AA taught him to drink sensibly? Did I know his face from the pub? He introduced a man sitting to his right. 'I'd like to welcome Stewart, who has come from another group to share his experience with us.'

Stewart looked self-assured. 'I'd like to welcome Alice – I can remember my first meeting, when I came in, desperate, virtually on my knees,' he said.

Obviously he drank far more than I did, then. I wasn't that bad. The military man was looking at me from the other side of the circle. Christ, perhaps he could read my mind. 'Listen for the similarities, not the differences,' he had said.

Stewart began to tell his story. After a few minutes I found myself nodding in agreement. He described the exact emotions I had wrestled with all my life. How he had felt different as a boy, the odd one out. How he was successful in his job but felt like a small child underneath who would eventually, somehow, be found out. How he had always run away from his feelings – first literally, by running away from home at age six, and then as an adult by drowning them in drink. How he had started drinking to change the way he felt and to kill his fear. How once he started drinking he couldn't stop, often setting out to have just one or two and then not remembering coming home. How his life revolved around alcohol, how he used to surround himself with people who drank at least at much as him, ignored his family and spent huge swathes of time in the pub.

As he said all this, I felt my face colour.

He told how he had been a functioning alcoholic for years without realising it – how he used to think it totally normal, cool even, to get drunk every day, revelling in telling cronies his drunken stories. How, as his drinking progressed over the years, his circle of friends had shrunk. His wife left. He had become increasingly angry and bitter, not seeing his children. He had drunk all the more on the strength of it, in a vicious circle. How he had lost his driving licence, his job, and still didn't think he had a problem. On and on he went.

It was my story. Exactly.

My face flushed and my heart beat fast. I looked around the room. Everyone was listening intently. Was there some sort of scam going on here? Had Martin filled this guy in on the details of my life? It was uncanny. It was as if Stewart had been reading my journal. Not only were there alarming similarities in his actions, but his emotions mirrored my own. The similarities scared me.

He told a story about downing a bottle of Southern Comfort before a family party. I shifted uncomfortably, having flashbacks of the last drunken Christmas I had spent with my family and how upset my mother had been.

He described how much he had loathed and detested himself and how he, too, drank to obliterate those feelings. I felt a tear trickle down my cheek. I started to sniffle and a lady next to me handed me a tissue. I felt panic-stricken, as if something or someone was holding me under water. I found myself holding my breath, staring intently at the roses on the table, studying their petals. They were exactly the same colour as those I threw over my father's coffin as it was lowered into the ground.

Stewart explained how one morning, after waking up covered in blood with no memory of how he'd got home, he'd felt so desperate he knew he had to do something. That was when he had picked up the phone and called AA.

Then the tempo of his story changed. It became upbeat, full of hope and talk of recovery. He told how his life had been transformed since he'd stopped drinking and started coming to AA. How, slowly, by not drinking – one day at a time – he had begun to regain his self-esteem. His relationship with his children had improved, he'd found a new job, and friends had started calling again. It hadn't been easy at first, getting through days such as Christmas and his birthday without a drink, but if at any time he felt desperate for one, he simply picked up the phone to another AA member or went to a meeting.

I began to feel detached from my body. I gazed ever more intently at the roses, blinking my eyes. Was I really sitting in an AA meeting? How did I get here? What was I doing here? Snapshots of my own drunken behaviour from as long as twenty years ago flashed by in my mind like a slideshow.

I looked up as Stewart concluded: 'AA has given me the

tools to live a happy and fulfilling life, where I can hold my head up high. With the help of mates in AA and my higher power, I've not had a drink for over five years now, a day at a time.'

Five *years* without a drink? That's 5 times 365 days, not including leap years. Oh, come on now. That seemed beyond the realms of reality. Why give up for that length of time? To give up for ever seemed extreme. Whatever would I do with myself? Life would be so dull, flat-lining, being a good girl. Still, I reasoned, I probably wasn't as bad as him and would be able to start drinking again after I'd got my licence back.

What did he mean by 'It's the first drink that does the damage'? Surely he didn't get drunk after just one drink?

People in the circle started 'sharing' with Stewart, one at a time. No one interrupted each other. All recounted memories his story had evoked for them. They talked about what kind of week they'd, how they'd felt, what had been going on at home, at work and in their heads. Everybody simply listened to each other; no one commented; no one offered advice.

I was amazed – especially listening to the men talking about their emotions, about how things in their everyday lives had upset them, and the actions they had taken rather than reach for a drink.

I thought back over my life, realising that every time something had happened I hadn't felt comfortable with, my knee-jerk reaction had been to have a drink. In fact, that had been my knee-jerk reaction to any event – good, bad or indifferent. Was I really like these people? Surely I couldn't be an alcoholic, could I? Anybody would drink if they had my life, wouldn't they?

My mind went back over Stewart's story, how he had kidded himself for years that he didn't have a problem, how he had come up with innumerable weird and wonderful excuses as to why he drank. Had I done that?

All the signs in Stewart had been there for others to see,

but he had been blind to them, he had said. Was I like that? Surely it was just bad luck, losing all those work contracts? And losing my licence was definitely a case of wrong place, wrong time. Wasn't it?

The room went quiet for a moment. I spoke up: 'My name is Alice and I've come along to find out what AA is all about. I was interested to hear Stewart's story. I'll just leave it there for now.' I faltered, for once in my life at a loss for words. Was this a dream? A quiet, calm voice in my head said gently, firmly, 'This is not a dream. You are here. You are here because you need to be here.'

The meeting ended, and everyone stood up and held hands. What was going to happen now, ring-a-ring-a-roses? Someone pointed to a laminated prayer on the table: 'God grant me the serenity to accept the things I cannot change, courage to change the things I can and the wisdom to know the difference.' I recited it with the others.

I was quiet in the car on the way home, going over Stewart's words. I have the ability to remember people's words verbatim, a useful trick as a journalist.

Martin was talking to me: 'What did you think? Do you think you'll go again?'

'It was . . . interesting,' I replied, cagily. 'I have to admit, I was surprised. All the people look so, well, *normal*. I was expecting a load of down-and-out drunks, you know, tramp types. They were all so friendly. Several people gave me their telephone numbers. Is that usual?'

'Yes. Lots of us call each other most days. It's a great support network, especially if you're feeling down or if you feel like picking up a drink.'

'Well, I still don't think I'm an alcoholic. I know I'm a heavy drinker, but I think I've just been a bit unlucky.' He was silent, so I babbled on: 'Still, it's somewhere to go rather than the pub while I'm not drinking, and the people did seem really friendly.'

'There is another meeting tomorrow lunchtime. Why don't you come along?' he asked.

'I'll see. I may be busy. I'll call you.'

After Martin dropped me off, I realised where I'd seen Joseph before, the one who'd given me the cup of tea. He was a friend of a friend – he'd been round to my house once for a vodka tasting. Well, more of a session, actually. Yes, that was it. He'd been drunk when he arrived and his coat had been at mine for months after. Come to think of it, I must have been quite out of it myself. I couldn't recall the end of the evening.

Was that what Stewart had meant by 'blackouts'? They should have been a telltale sign that he had a problem, he'd said. I thought memory lapses were perfectly normal after a few drinks. If that was a blackout, I had been having them almost as far back as I could remember. There was that time, just before I got married, when Niall had exploded with rage, telling me I'd stolen a bottle of wine from a party. If it hadn't been for the bottle in my bag, I wouldn't have believed him.

I felt oddly tense as I opened my front door. I had the strangest feeling of something tugging at me, as if I was being pulled along by a speedboat but couldn't stand up on my waterskis.

I looked in the mirror. 'Am I an alcoholic?' I asked my reflection. The house was resolutely silent. The moon shone in, lighting up the gilt grapes on the top of the mirror.

CHAPTER FORTY-TWO

MAD HATTER'S

I felt lighter when I awoke the next morning, as if I was floating rather than drowning. I lay in bed, thinking about the
meeting and what I'd heard there. I felt something I hadn't
felt since . . . oh . . . since I couldn't remember when.

Hope.

I was convinced that somehow, everything would be OK if
I only believed that it could be. I had seen and heard hope in
the meeting, and it was contagious – I wanted what these
people had. There was some magic ingredient in their lives
that made their eyes shine.

I had been told, 'If you put half the effort into your recovery as you did into your drinking, you'll be OK. The advice
to any newcomer is to get to as many different meetings as
possible.'

Not normally one to take advice, for some reason I accepted this. I took Martin up on his offer of a lunchtime AA
meeting and found myself at what was nicknamed locally
the Mad Hatter's Tea Party.

I could see why they called it that. This was a much more
fluid, relaxed meeting with people popping in and out
depending on their lunch breaks. It was held in a small
church room around a table piled high with sandwiches and
homemade cakes.

Again I was amazed by the openness of the people there,
how friendly everyone was. I sat spellbound as these strangers

bared their souls. It was humbling, listening to them explain how they had reached their respective rock bottoms in drink – some more dramatic than others – and what had made them decide to stop drinking. I realised with a start that I had hit my own rock bottom when I had collapsed in the pub. Perhaps the bang on the head had knocked some sense into my pickled brain.

Suddenly, I no longer felt alone. I was among people who understood my compulsion to drink, better than I did, and didn't judge me.

I felt more at ease to ask questions in the relaxed atmosphere. I took a deep breath. 'My name is Alice and I might be an alcoholic,' I said. The room fell totally silent in that second. 'How do you know if you are an alcoholic?'

'No one comes here by accident,' came the reply. 'If your life has become unmanageable due to alcohol, there is a fair chance you may be an alcoholic.'

Was my life unmanageable?

Well, I got by, didn't I? Or did I?

Having had such a successful career, I now had no work and no house. I had few friends and a history of broken, messy relationships. I thought about the thousands of nights I couldn't remember going to bed, the dreadful hangovers, the shame I constantly lived with. I contemplated the deep unhappiness I felt, my overwhelming feeling of hopelessness, the hollow loneliness of my life and how time and time again I had sought solace in the bottle. I had no purpose. I had lost sight of who I was. My self-respect and self-esteem were on the floor. Were all these things really down to alcohol?

I didn't have a chance to ponder much further, as a woman, a similar age to my mother, with silvery hair and twinkling hazel eyes, started to speak. She told how drink had taken over her life, how she had often ignored her children in her never-ending quest for the next drink. Like

Stewart, she was telling a version of my story. 'I didn't realise I'd been ill, that alcoholism is a disease – a physical, mental and spiritual illness,' she said.

An illness? I thought I drank too much because I was greedy and weak-willed. Had I been ill?

She started to describe my own symptoms – constant nausea, diarrhoea, headaches, back pain and panic attacks. She thought she'd been going mad. She'd had no direction in life and loathed herself for her behaviour.

I stared at her. I took a gulp of tea. The bitter tannin hit the roof of my mouth as if saying, 'Sit up! Pay attention!'

'By finally accepting that I was an alcoholic after years of denial, and staying sober one day at a time, I have a totally different life today and a wonderful relationship with my children,' she ended.

I frowned in thought. What kind of relationship did I have with my children?

A sudden, vivid, monochrome image came into my mind. I was cradling a bundle wrapped in a shawl. But there was no baby's face peeking out – there was a bottle. In that second I realised with horror that I had been an absent mother, that alcohol had become my all-consuming baby.

It was true. I was not here by accident. I was in the right place, at the Mad Hatter's Tea Party. I was Alice, after all, who had found the bottle and taken the direction 'Drink me' too literally.

Something stirred and shifted in my heart. I felt as if something had tenderly wrapped me in a soft, pink, cash-mere blanket. Feeling safe, and held by some intangible force, I accepted it – I was an alcoholic.

CHAPTER FORTY-THREE

HIGH AS A KITE

Lid down ready for the road, gleaming blue in the June sunshine, my Little Blue Car is positively smiling. I know I am. I have my driving licence back after two years, four months and one week. It has been four months since my first AA meeting.

The squat leather gearstick feels good in my hand. Can I remember how to drive? I start her up and grin at Number Three son beside me. We listen to the car's throaty purr. We're off for a picnic – 'To celebrate that you can drive again, Mummy,' he says.

To me, this is a different kind of celebration – of freedom. I have regained my life.

'Will you start drinking again now you have your licence back?' a few doubters had asked.

One day at a time, the answer is a categorical 'No.' Why would I? Today I have the option to choose life over drinking. Without alcohol I am now free to have feelings and reactions, and to be the best me I can be. Life and health is coursing through my veins again.

Racing along the country lanes, I recall one of my father's pet sayings: 'Success is failure turned inside out.' Not for the first time I thank God I *did* lose my driving licence. I shudder to think where I would be now if I hadn't.

We meet up with an old friend, Jenny, one of the few friends honest enough to mourn the demise of her favourite drinking partner. We used to have a lot of fun together in my early days of drinking, when it still *was* fun. She is also a fantastic cook, so my son and I decide to let her supply the picnic.

And what a picnic it is. In a field of yellow cowslips is a fine spread – spicy chorizo sausages, potted shrimps and raspberry meringues with little flags with the words 'King of the Road'.

I watch my son's kite cavorting wildly in the sky. Jenny hands me a glass of ginger ale. As I take my first sip, I hear a familiar sound, the pop of a champagne cork.

'It's a bloody shame that you can't enjoy a weeny glass of this Pol Roger,' she says.

I look at her flute and watch the bubbles racing furiously upwards, glinting in the sun. 'It is not that I can't,' I say. 'It's that I choose not to.'

When I was in the grip of my compulsion, I had no choice. Once I had had one glass, I had to have another, and another, and another until I was drunk. My addiction had shackled me. Now that compulsion to drink, and keep on drinking, has miraculously been lifted right out of me.

I know what Stewart meant when he said, 'It's the first drink that does the damage.' Without the first there can't be a second, a third, or any more at all. I only ever have to decline one drink – the first.

'Even if I could have one, it would just be a flute full of consequences,' I add. 'You cannot imagine the relief I feel to be free from the guilt of drinking and then throwing up, the constant covering-up for my bad behaviour. I have the free-dom to choose to go wherever I like. Freedom from all that drunken mayhem. Freedom to eat these sausages without puking up.'

While my friend snoozes, glass in hand, I reflect on the seeming paradox that this newfound freedom has come about by an act of surrender – by admitting I was powerless over alcohol. The day I decided I couldn't drink was the day I started to get better. By admitting defeat, I won back my life. I am out of my alcoholic prison and – as long as I don't take that first drink, just that first one – I will remain a free woman. AA has given me my Get-Out-of-Jail-Free card. Without my now-regular meetings I wouldn't be here at all, let at alone driving.

'Look at this!' shrieks my son as his kite loops the loop. He runs along with it, whooping with joy.

I jump up and follow, running across the field, chortling, 'I'm free! I'm free!'

'You've been drinking, Mummy!' he jokes.

'No. But I'm as high as your kite!'

CHAPTER FORTY-FOUR

CRAYFISHING

My first summer of freedom rolled on in a passage of surprising days. A friend I had meet at AA invited the boys and me out for a day cruising on his narrowboat. I had heard about an alternative way to catch crabs, baiting net bags with fish fingers. I wondered if the method would work for the many freshwater crayfish in the local Kennet and Avon Canal.

We looked under the sink for the little net bags you put washing-powder tablets in. There was a nest of saved carrier bags and old dishcloths (do they breed under there?) but not a net bag in sight.

'We'll get one at Somerfield when we buy the picnic,' I said.

'We'll need three,' pointed out Number Two son.

'You can share one,' I said. 'My mum didn't buy nine of everything.'

He rolled his eyes. We ended up buying three.

Attaching string to each bag and baiting them with fish fingers, we set off in the boat along the canal, the boys laughing and trailing their baited bags in the wake, or launching them lasso-style at other boats and the bank. There was great excitement when we spied our first crayfish, trapped on the gates of a lock. Like many of the great things in life, it was just out of reach.

I lay on top of the boat watching the sunlight through the

trees. White water lilies as intricate as origami floated in the still water. I thought back twenty-three years to the first time I had been along this stretch of the canal, walking hand in hand with Niall. I was twenty-one then, blonde and beautiful and already in love as I teetered down the towpath in my stilettos after a good, long, liquid lunch.

A lot of wine had flowed under the bridge since then. Too much, for me. But here we were today, with the sun well over the metaphorical yardarm and not a drink in sight. In the old days I would by now have appeased my hangover with a bloody Mary, celebrated our departure with a glass or six of fizz and be well into the second bottle of white Burgundy.

I was brought back to the moment with a squeak and a splash. Number Two son had toppled overboard. By the time I had sat up, he was laughing, lying back in the water, floating.

'It's quite relaxing really, Mummy.' He grinned. Minutes later, after we had hauled him out, Number Three son fell in – or did he jump, so as not to be left out? Number One son, sensible elder brother that he is, threw him the lifebuoy, which caught him squarely on the nose. There wasn't too much blood.

Peace resumed, we tootled on down the canal. Four miles an hour is about the right speed. We moored up, clambered off and dropped our lines. In less than a minute, Number Three son squealed. His line was twitching. He pulled it up. Three crayfish were clinging to the net bag. Amazement all round.

Forty or so crayfish later, we selected those with the biggest claws, dropped them in boiling water and barbecued them. I made garlic mayonnaise and we feasted on these finger-licking freshwater beauties. Number One son suggested we set up a stall selling them, such was the interest from passers-by. The crayfish tasted delicious, especially the sweet meat in the claws. We washed them down with English

Cox's apple juice. The combination was sensational.

The sun began to drop in the sky, turning it crayfish orange. The boys took to the towpath and raced the boat home, where they put themselves to bed, too tired to shower at an unprecedented eight thirty.

What a perfect day. And I'd not even thought of a drink.

Next time, I mused while lying in the bath later, when I'm a bit slimmer, I'd like to lie on the boat in my leopard-print bikini.

I felt a surge of gratitude flow through me. Recovery was only ever one day at a time, I had learnt, but this had been a good day. Getting out of the bath, on an impulse, I knelt and gave thanks – to what, I'm not sure. Perhaps my smiling guardian angel, perhaps my childhood God, perhaps AA. But something, somewhere, some higher power, was keeping me sober.

CHAPTER FORTY-FIVE

NAKED AT THE BOOK CLUB

Only 8 p.m. In my newfound sobriety, the days were getting longer. No longer drunk, comatose or hung-over, I cooked the tea, helped the boys with their homework, played Scrabble with them, read a book, twiddled my thumbs. And *still* only 8 p.m. I decided I needed to get out more. The pub had obviously lost its allure. There's a limit to the pints of lime and soda a girl can drink. I decided to join the local book club.

I gazed at a table covered in bottles of wine. Someone asked me what I'd like to drink.

'Coke, please,' I mumbled, eyeing the bottle of creamy New Zealand Lindauer fizz.

'Coke?' echoed the voice, unbelievingly. 'I thought you were a bit of a wine buff.'

I opened my mouth but no words came out. I wondered blackly if the owner of the voice had ever had a bottle of New Zealand Lindauer fizz over her head. Buff that.

The hostess arrived at the table. 'Ah, there you are. Do you know the others?'

All around me playground mums nursed large glasses of wine, red, white and rosé. Inwardly, I groaned. Those Stepford wives again. I clutched my glass of Coke so hard I almost crushed it. I shifted uncomfortably from foot to foot and reconnected my handbag with my shoulder, except that my shoulders were so hunched they seemed attached to my ears. Exposed, I felt naked without my liquid armour. My brain was crying out for a drink.

A woman with blonde hair and a green jumper looked at me. In a strong Scottish accent, she said, 'I don't know you, but I know who you are.'

The words of song 145 on my jukebox popped into my head: 'Alice, who the fuck is Alice?' Invisible Woman would have suited me right then – Wonder Woman had long since departed. 'All alone with the playground witches,' whispered a voice in my head.

I made no reply and she knocked back her glass of red. I watched her swallow it in slow motion. I could virtually taste it – Wolf Blass Cabernet, a ripe, intense blackberry flavour with a hint of eucalyptus. I smiled at her. Perfect. She had red-wine horns around her mouth. I thought that was just me.

'Well, you know what playground gossip is like,' she added conspiratorially.

No, actually, I didn't. No one ever used to speak to me. God knows what she had heard about me. 'Confirm the playground gossip true and neck that bottle of fizz in five minutes flat,' urged a sly voice in my head.

The hostess saw my discomfort. 'Come and meet some of the others.'

I followed her round like a little lamb. I had to practise self-censorship, as every time I was introduced to someone my inclination was to say, 'Hi, my name's Alice and I'm an alcoholic,' like I was used to doing at meetings. That would have livened up the proceedings.

But really, I was furiously thinking, Who am I?

It's easier to work out who I'm not. I am no longer Alice the wine writer. Without that label I feel disorientated, unsure as to my status. Equally, I am no longer Alice the drunk. In the bad old days I would have arrived half cut, if I had arrived at all.

I am no longer Alice the wife, though listening to some of the book-club chat I think that can only be a positive thing. Looking on the bright side is a new experience for me. In the throes of my addiction I would opt for the negative stance in every situation. Unsurprisingly I attracted people of the same ilk, ensuring my downwards spiral into depression. Drowning my feelings with alcohol only served to accelerate the decline.

I was still unsure as to how to deal with Mrs Green Jumper, who was telling her neighbour she didn't enjoy the book we were here to discuss.

'So what didn't you like about it?' I asked gently, trying to tone down my old confrontational approach.

Her face contorted as she thought, slurping her wine. I recognised the look on her face – it was fear, the same emotion I'd felt arriving here tonight. She was worried about what I would think about her comments. It was a relief to know that fear was not exclusive to me, any more than red-wine horns.

'I can't explain,' she said. 'You're the journalist.'

'Oh, don't worry,' I replied, laughing. 'I'm nothing but an ex-drunk.'

CHAPTER FORTY-SIX

WRITING FOR THE GOOD OF MY SOUL

I suppose I should not have been suprised to meet another journalist, Pete, at an AA meeting. Us journalists are credited with being a hard-drinking bunch. Slight and eager, Pete looked more the starving Parisian poet than the archetypal florid hack.

'All my life I've written about drinking,' I complained to him. 'What am I going to write about now?'

He shrugged. 'Write about not drinking.'

I had made the capital from the sale of Avon House last four years, but it was running out fast and I was in a quandary as to how to make a living. Looking for work as a wine journalist didn't make sense if I planned to stay sober. True, you can taste wine without drinking it, but the whole lifestyle, the lunches, the dinners and the press trips would make total abstinence problematical. I had to find some other way to support the boys and myself.

Pete suggested I write a newspaper column describing the progress of my recovery. I was still less than a year sober and I was learning new things every day, whereas he'd been sober for some years.

I wasn't sure.

'I can write about wine standing on my head . . . but baring my soul and writing about my emotions? I've no idea how to do that. Anyway, if it is such a good idea, why don't you do it?'

'I'm too far away from the early days of my recovery. It's all raw for you. Give it a go,' he replied. 'What have you got to lose? Besides, you need the money.'

I sat down at my computer with butterflies in my stomach. I hadn't written for years, beyond a few poems and short stories. My confidence was at rock bottom, but it felt positive and exciting to be taxing my brain again.

I reminded myself of an old school report my mother used to quote: 'Words cannot express the verbal and written abilities which are Alice's outstanding features.' (That same report had added: 'Alice would do a lot better if only she believed in herself.')

But there it was, the blank screen. Where to start? It was one thing to write about wine, my passion for twenty-five years, quite another to write about something that had happened to me only relatively recently and that I still didn't fully understand.

I made a beginning, but I found it difficult to come to terms with the words on the screen describing my own behaviour. Had that really been me? How could I have ignored my problem for so long?

Talking about my illness in the safety and anonymity of the AA rooms among like-minded people was easy. Writing it down made it real – and much more serious. I had greater difficulty typing the words 'I am an alcoholic' than I did speaking them.

I wrote three sample columns and gave them to Pete to look over. He was gentle with me but harsh with my copy. I decided to aim for the top and a day or two later, terrified, I picked up the phone and rang an old friend at *The Times*. We arranged to have lunch.

I was nervous as I sat waiting in the vodka bar where she had suggested we meet. Gazing at the line of flavoured vodkas, I weighed up the possibility of a swift one – vanilla was a favourite. It would put me at my ease. But it was only the old 'just the one' lie in action. The irony of it: to be drunk on vodka at an appointment to try to sell a column about my recovery from alcoholism. That's the insanity of the disease. I was relieved when she walked into the bar.

I hadn't seen her for a few years, not since I'd got horrendously drunk at her fortieth-birthday party. After ten minutes or so of chat about our children, I told her I had accepted I was an alcoholic, stopped drinking and changed my life. I started to apologise for my behaviour at her party when, smiling, she interjected, 'Is this step nine?' A friend of hers was also in recovery and she was familiar with the twelve-step programme.

A conversation I had dreaded for days was over in seconds, and it had been so simple! It was a good lesson on the futility of projection and worry. I was so relieved by the geniality of her approach I nearly burst into tears. Kindness still touches me like that.

Lunch over, she took my articles away. She couldn't promise anything but would show them to other section editors at *The Times*. Securing a column was difficult, she warned.

It was one of those drab autumn days when the only certainty was more rain. I had taken the boys to see *Chicken Run*. Back home, I listened to my voicemail. Could I ring Sandra Parsons, editor of *The Times*'s T2 section? I closed the door of my office and took a deep breath.

Ten minutes later I walked out smiling.

'Boys, let's have a celebration tea. I can't believe it – it's so exciting – I'm going to write a column for *The Times*!' I exclaimed.

I rang my mother. 'It mightn't be the ideal way to see your daughter in *The Times*, Mum, I know, but I'm really chuffed – and scared.'

'I'm so proud of you,' she said. 'And your father would have been too.'

I cooked the boys their favourite tea of toad in the hole and we drank ginger ale from the hollow-stemmed Georgian champagne glasses I reserve for special occasions. The rain had stopped and winter's early dark had fallen. Number Two son called me out into the garden. 'Look, Mummy, look at the stars twinkling at us.' We chinked our glasses and stared upwards. The stars really are brighter in sobriety.

My first weekly column, 'Sobering Up', was published. The editor emailed me to say how much she liked it. Several hundred readers emailed me, many to say how they identified with my story.

I had a one-line email from Number Two son, then at boarding school: 'Mummy i am so proud of u.' I pinned it up in my office. I felt sated, contented to the core – a feeling I was unfamiliar with.

A friend and I decided to go out and celebrate. On a bright, chilly November day, eight months after my first AA meeting, I took LBC out of the garage and put the roof down. We drove to a roadside breakfast van on the A4.

Never had bacon and egg doorstep sandwiches with white bread tasted so good. We toasted the winter sun with mugs of builder's tea, the steam rising in upward spiral wisps that caught the wind.

Sue Peart, editor of the *Mail on Sunday*'s *You* magazine, had been avidly following my column. She thought my story would resonate with her readers and invited me to write a feature. I did so.

The first email arrived at 7.02 a.m. on the Sunday the article appeared: 'My name is Sally. I have read your article and just realised I am an alcoholic. I identified with so much you described – the downward spiral of my life, my loss of friends, job and self-respect. I am desperate. My life is in chaos. However hard I try, I cannot stop drinking. Am I a bad person? I think my husband might leave me and I am afraid he may take the children. I am ashamed. I don't know what to do. Please help.'

Sally's email set the tone for close on a thousand more that flooded in over the next few days. Many people were desperate in their loneliness, suicidal in their hopelessness. Others sought advice in dealing with friends or loved ones with a problem. 'I am tired of keeping secrets about my father's drinking, sick of not being able to bring friends round to the house,' said Jill. 'Where can I find help or support?'

All were pleading for advice. I realised I had touched a nerve. One in six Britons is thought to have some sort of problem with alcohol, either through their own drinking or someone else's. With the help of others in AA and Al-Anon (for relatives and friends of alcoholics), I replied to each and every email.

Many asked, 'Am I an alcoholic?'

'Only you can decide,' was my reply. 'But if you think you have a problem, you probably do. The question would simply not arise otherwise. If your life has become unmanageable because of alcohol, you are probably one of us.'

Another often-asked question was, 'How does AA work?'

This set me thinking. The short answer is, I have no idea. AA offers the support of like-minded people who don't judge, having been there themselves, and offers alcoholics a tried-and-tested methodology of changing their behaviour by following its famous and much imitated twelve-step programme. All I know for sure is that is *does* work, for me. The compulsion to drink disappeared. I don't know how that happened, exactly – and frankly, I don't give a damn!

People were concerned that they couldn't go to AA while still drinking. This is not the case. All you need is the desire to stop drinking. Action and acceptance – living in the solution and not the problem – is the key to continuing recovery.

It felt good to be able to put something back into a world I had taken so much from. Helping other people also helped to keep me sober, grounding me and serving as a reminder that I could have all my misery back, with interest, any time I chose.

No, thanks.

CHAPTER FORTY-SEVEN

One Step at a Time

I was invited to a ball at London's Dorchester Hotel. How could I refuse? I could no longer afford designer ball gowns so I headed for TK Maxx to find something to wear. I was delighted with my £29.99 full-length black velvet dress with diamanté shoestring straps and a plunging neckline. My cleavage was possibly the only part of me that had remained constant through drunkenness to sobriety.

I preened in front of the mirror at home, seeking advice from Number Two son, my in-house fashion consultant, as to which shoes I should wear. 'Definitely the strappy black Gina ones,' he counselled, having given my suggested shiny red stilettos the thumbs down.

Number Three son pressed 307 on the jukebox – 'This will get you in the mood, Mummy.'

'Dancing in the Street', the Mick Jagger and David Bowie cover, pumped out into the room. I sang along with the words: 'It doesn't matter what you wear as long as you are there!' but stopped in mid-song.

Oh, my God! How on earth was I going to dance without a drink or six inside me? Indeed, how would I get through an entire evening with people drinking all around me? This ball would be the first big social event I'd been to in eleven months of sobriety. I'd been worrying about Christmas looming. This would be a dry run for the festive season, I told myself.

I arrived at the Dorchester. Reluctantly parting company with my favourite red velvet Yves St Laurent jacket, I felt exposed and clung on to my brocade clutch bag as if it housed the Crown Jewels. My date for the night, an old friend, smiled encouragingly, even though I was gripping his arm tight enough to stop the circulation.

A waiter came forward with a tray of champagne glasses. The glasses were whispering to me, 'Just one, just one.' I selected a glass of fizzy water and, putting on my professional head, observed the 'bead'. The bubbles were considerably larger in the water than in the fizz. I noted how much more sluggishly they rose up the glass. Anything to quieten that sneaky siren's song.

I was introduced to a group of people. Most of them would have had a sharpener or two at home before coming out, I thought wistfully. I hoped the knot in my stomach wasn't evident through my dress. I looked up to the ceiling, at a loss for words. I had been to more Krug parties at the Dorchester than I could remember – indeed, I couldn't remember several of them at all – but never before had I noticed the spectacular moulded ceiling.

We sat at our table. I was separated from my date and placed next to a charity auctioneer. He was rotund, jovial and most concerned about my empty glass. 'What, you never drink?' he asked.

I opened my mouth and it gushed out, 'I am an alcoholic. I used to be a wine writer and now I'm writing a column about sobriety for *The Times*.'

He raised his eyebrows, smiled. 'How interesting. I used to – well, still do, really – have a similar problem with food.'

I eyed his glass of claret, rich, red and mellow, its cigar-box aroma wafting up my nostrils. I looked away. Glancing around the table, I noticed how slowly people were drinking. The man opposite me had had the same glass of white wine in front of him for over half an hour. The life expectancy of drinks in front of me was measured in seconds.

The time came for the auctioneer to sing for his supper. He managed to bid the room up into paying £21,000 for the pleasure of having Albert Roux cook a dinner party in the winner's home. Two couples were bidding so Roux offered, generously, to do it twice. I could live on £21,000 for a year! Watching the auction, I forgot about my wineless glass and enjoyed the banter around the table.

Auction over, the music started. I was relieved when my date, who was itching to dance and unable to persuade me, disappeared to dance with a woman at the next table. I sat back and watched, happy for once to be a wallflower – albeit a dehydrated one. No one on the dance floor seemed drunk.

I looked away as I saw my date heading in my direction, but he pulled me on to the dance floor. My mind raced back. Had I ever danced sober in my life? No, was the quick conclusion. The last time I could vaguely remember dancing was rum-drunk in a favourite Jamaican restaurant, the Hi Lo in Oxford, with a group of guys who claimed to be Bob Marley's Wailers. 'Imagine you are a worm that has been cut in half,' one had told me, pulling me up on to the table. 'Each part of your body needs to writhe separately. Come on – wriggle!'

But right then at the Dorchester, I felt more like a worm that wanted to slither into the earth. I faltered, Bambi-like, and tried to smile, though I was conscious that my *Come Dancing* grin looked sprayed on.

The music stopped and I went to make a quick exit, but my partner grabbed me again. Sweet's 'Ballroom Blitz' started up. 'Blitz, Blitz, Ballroom Blitz!' I mouthed manically. Then I changed the words: 'Dance, dance, I *can* dance!' I continued through gritted teeth. Halfway through the song, I looked around. A few people seemed even gawkier than me – and they'd had a drink. My face relaxed into a real smile. It was a relief not to be the drunken centre of attention. I began to enjoy myself. The next record – 'Le Freak' – brought back memories of being fourteen and drunk on vodka and lime at the Young Farmers' Dance. It seemed like another century. Actually, it was.

I grabbed a surprised auctioneer and we boogied. Leaving the Dorchester with my date, literally dancing in the street back to the car, I realised that rarely was anything as bad as fear made it. I could dance sober, one foot in front of the other, one step at a time.

CHAPTER FORTY-EIGHT

First Christmas

Laden with bottles of vintage champagne, I piled the boys into the car and headed for my mother's house for the 2005 Christmas family party. The boys were excited. They loved meeting up with their eighteen cousins almost as much as they loved the presents.

For myself, I was terrified. The year before saw me arrive drunk, ignoring the family's fine wines to disappear to the pub for large vodkas and drunken rubbish-talk with the locals. I had ignored my mother and my brothers and sisters, who were all trying to come to terms with Christmas without our father, in favour of my constant comforter, the bottle. They had faced their pain. I had tried to obliterate mine.

An uncomfortable memory surfaced – my eldest sister losing her temper and shrieking, 'Stop ruining your life and your children's! Just stop!' I couldn't recall my indignant, slurred reply. Just as well.

There was a large pop from the back of the car. 'Look out!' yelled Number One son. 'Everybody duck – exploding champagne corks!' The boys jabbered on excitedly in the back.

As my anxiety had increased, so had my speed. I eased my foot off the accelerator – I had to slow down, think about my behaviour. No point trying to hide it away in the bottle banks of my mind and pretending it didn't happen. My mother had had to deal with my drunken phone calls and

262

my selfish, spoilt-brat behaviour. My brothers and sisters had been subject to my drunken prima donna antics at family parties going back years. My behaviour had caused a rift between my eldest brother and myself, and I had missed the closeness we had shared through my teens to my early thirties.

My sister Juliana had been saint-like in her patience with me, while I had ranted and raved. She'd invited the boys and me on several family holidays. My other brothers and sisters had remained in touch, albeit at a distance, and when I had spoken to them it had always been about me, me, me. I had no clue what was going on in their lives. Counting up, I realised with a shock that there were five whose houses I had never visited.

Although I had stopped drinking, I knew it was unreasonable to expect my siblings to greet me with open arms. The tornado may have stopped blowing, but the devastation remained. Making amends to my family was going to take time.

'Are you looking forward to seeing your brothers and sisters, Mummy?' piped up Number Two son. 'You look really worried – you keep frowning.'

'Yes,' I said. 'I'm worried about my drunken behaviour last year.'

'Don't worry,' he replied. 'They'll forgive you. They're your family, after all.'

What a child – eleven going on eighty. I hoped he was right.

We arrived and marched in with the bottles. 'I come bearing gifts,' I joked to my mother.

'How wonderful,' she replied, hugging me. 'We were getting low on champagne. Weren't you tempted to drink them?'

'I was the other day. Not today,' I replied.

My siblings came out in ones and twos. They all greeted me warmly, as did their partners. I served the champagne. My left hand was shaking.

'So, which one is best?' asked one brother.

'Oh, all of these are good. I only brought the best ones. Here, try this – Billecart-Salmon Rosé 1996. Summer pudding in a glass – delicious.'

Juliana handed me a glass of pomegranate juice. 'Not quite the same, I know,' she said.

We chinked glasses.

'Thanks,' I replied. 'For everything.'

Lunch was served. Everyone sampled the champagnes, expressing appreciation. No one was in the least bit drunk. I sat and watched them enjoy the Krug Clos du Mesnil 1995, one of the most complex, multi-layered champagnes I had ever tasted, with its unusual creamy, floral flavour. It is produced in tiny quantities – unlike the forgiveness and love my family appeared to possess.

I started to apologise to my eldest sister for the previous year. 'Don't worry,' she said. 'You've been ill. You look so well now. It's just wonderful to see you getting better.'

I blinked back tears and took a gulp of pomegranate juice. It went down the wrong way and I started to choke. 'Drinking too fast again!' laughed my brother.

We started giving out the presents, youngest cousin first. It felt good watching all the happy, excited faces and I felt blessed to be part of such a large family. I no longer felt different or alone. I started to relax, grateful that they weren't judging me, glad not to be the embarrassing, intoxicated centre of attention. The children attacked their presents with glee, tearing the paper off with delighted shrieks. After two hours I retired to the kitchen for a cup of tea. Number Two son followed me in.

'What was your best present, Mummy?' he asked.

'Good question. I'm not sure.'

'What about being sober? That's like a different present, isn't it?'

I looked at him in amazement. 'Good thinking,' I replied.

'Yes . . . the gift of sobriety. You're right. What a funny boy you are!'

He winked at me and left, tossing his new juggling balls to his cousins.

I sat down and savoured the delicate aroma of my Twinings Rose Pouchong tea. What had sobriety meant to me in the last year?

I looked up the word in my mother's dictionary – 'Absence of drunkenness,' it read. I could improve on that – absence of guilt, shame, remorse, hangovers and retching. My gain was colossal. I had recovered my self-respect. I had banished the self-pity I used to drown with drink. I was more at ease in my own skin and slowly rebuilding relation-ships with friends and family. I was touched by my brothers' and sisters' forgiveness and continually delighted in the ever-deepening closeness of my relationship with my sons. I even had my sense of humour back. All this in less than a year.

My mother came into the kitchen. 'You know, Dad would be really proud of you,' she said.

'Mummy,' I replied, with a tear in my eye, 'thanks. Thanks for not giving up on me. I bet you wanted to kill me this time last year.'

'No,' she replied softly. 'We could see you were killing yourself.'

CHAPTER FORTY-NINE

First Anniversary

I woke up and saw it was still dark, the stars shining. An old crescent moon was sinking into the west. It was a special day – my first anniversary – a whole year without a drink.

There had been a time when I couldn't have imagined a day without a drink, let alone 365 of them. It hadn't been easy. When I first stopped drinking I didn't think I would ever enjoy myself again. I lay in bed and, as on every other day of my recovery, thanked God I didn't have a hangover. I felt grateful and pleased with myself, eager to celebrate my anniversary when the dawn came.

I got out of bed and looked in the mirror. Things have definitely changed on the outside; I look totally different for a start. My skin has returned to its natural glow and I've put some weight on. When I was drinking I was a curious colour, a sort of translucent greyish-white. Actually, I rarely looked in the mirror – I couldn't face it – such was my self-hatred. But it is what has changed on the inside that really counts.

Though there was something still niggling in the back of my mind. Did I really have cause to celebrate? When I first went to AA, they told me I'd been ill – that I had an illness, a disease, a kind of allergy that once activated, resulted in me not being able to stop drinking, and, while drunk, saying and doing things I would never have considered when sober. There was a part of my brain that didn't fully accept this explanation. 'Weak-willed, degenerate and bad' were some of the things I'd been called. Was that closer to the truth?

I went into my office and switched on the computer. I Googled 'alcoholism' and found myself at the World Health Organization's definition: 'A disease marked by loss of control over drinking, caused by a pre-existing biological abnormality, and having a predictable, progressive course.'

'A pre-existing biological abnormality'? Well, that made sense. Maybe I would still have been an alcoholic if I'd become a fashion writer. Just a better-dressed one. The American Society of Addictive Medicine talked of a 'primary, chronic disease with genetic, psychosocial and environmental factors'.

There was an email from Bill, the scientist friend to whom I had mentioned my misgivings. 'This is a simplified explanation,' he wrote. 'Alcoholism *is* an illness. Pleasure centres in the brain are stimulated by chemicals such as endorphins plus alcohol, cigarettes, drugs and many other things. This causes the brain to release chemicals which then affect the brain's pleasure centres.' It was a relief to know that it wasn't simply a matter of being greedy.

'In consequence,' he continued, 'some people just can't handle alcohol and drugs in the same way. Those suffering from alcohol abuse can often not control the need to take alcohol because of the demands of their brain – you imbibe and the brain rewards the body, saying, "Thank you." This is how habit forms on many levels and is linked to your brain's own individual pleasure centres. Brains do not forget – so it will always be waiting for you!'

I twirled round in my chair. Two well-respected bodies and one scientist defined alcoholism as a disease. So it *was* a disease – 'a primary, chronic disease' – that was not my fault, but it was my responsibility. It was up to me whether or not I activated it by taking a drink.

I smiled and realised I had even more cause to celebrate. Unlike many other killer diseases, I could keep mine at bay by simply not drinking one day at a time, no drugs or nasty treatments necessary. I could now give myself permission to party.

I decided to bake a cake. My mother had recently reminded me of when I had won the cookery prize at school, age fourteen, for a spectacular chocolate confection. I baked the cake and climbed back into bed – without the cake, that is. A strange thing to do at 5 a.m. – but healthier than drinking vodka, I told myself. I dozed off and awoke again with the sun streaming into my bedroom.

Like an excited child, I found it difficult to concentrate on work as the morning wore on, watching the clock, willing it to be four o'clock, when the boys came home. I had invited four friends to celebrate and one arrived at three thirty with a huge present. I unwrapped it to find a hand-painted *Alice in Wonderland* tea set, complete with plates saying, 'Eat me,' and a milk jug saying, 'Drink me.'

The boys got home at the same time as my other friends arrived, two of them also recovering alcoholics. I almost cried when I read the cards. 'We are so proud of you.' I read those words over and over again. Where would I be without my friends and family? Drunk, likely. Or dead.

We sat round the table for cups of Earl Grey tea and huge slices of chocolate cake.

'This is just like our Mad Hatter's AA meeting,' remarked one friend. Number Two son disappeared, to return moments later with my purple velvet top hat. He plonked it on my head.

At that moment the doorbell rang. Hat still on, I answered the door to find the milkman.

'It's my, erm, birthday,' I explained, debating for a second whether to go into detail. He handed me his bill as squeals of laughter filtered through from the kitchen.

'Sounds like you're having a right old boozy time of it,' he said, winking at me. He knew me of old.

'No – just high on life, honest!' I giggled while paying him.

I wandered into the sitting room, where my guests now were.

'Mummy, can I put the Wurlitzer on?' asked Number Three son. 'Then it will be a real party.'

The jukebox lit up and cranked into action. Number Three son was grinning and frantically pressing buttons. Andy Fairweather-Lowe blasted out: 'Wide-eyed and legless, I've gone and done it again.'

Thank God I hadn't. I laughed. Cause indeed for celebration.

CHAPTER FIFTY

CROSS WORDS

Valentine's Day came and went. No cards. I was not without male admirers, though the men I knew were friends rather than lovers. I'd had my fingers burned early in recovery by having a brief fling with a friend in AA. The advice is not to start any new relationships in the first year of recovery. Looking back, I can see why. I had simply replaced my compulsion to drink with my need for attention and approval.

Picking men up drunk was one thing, but chatting up a man sober was much more challenging. I also had no desire to hang around the pub looking for a mate. As the months went by, I found myself spending more time with Pete, the journalist who had encouraged me to write my column for *The Times*. When I met him, I was raw, still shell-shocked and massively lacking in self-confidence. I looked up to his four years of sobriety – I couldn't imagine going that amount of time without a drink.

We started going to the theatre together. One of the most memorable plays we saw was a magnificent performance by Martin Shaw in *A Man for All Seasons* at Bath's Theatre Royal. Was that what I needed, a man for all seasons? Was I ready for a 'proper' relationship, whatever that meant? In truth, any thought of a relationship scared me. The thought of failure was too daunting.

But it was a delight to find someone with whom I could

share my love of words. Our text messages became fast and furious and increasingly flirtatious. We would spend hours bantering on the phone about books, authors and poets. I had much to catch up on, having roughly had a twenty-year literary sabbatical while drinking. As he jokingly put it – at least I took him to be joking, though just as with my brothers I was never quite sure – 'I was reading Dante while you were reading wine lists.' Touché.

We took to doing the crossword together and ended up doing it in bed, playfully squabbling over it. No champagne, just raspberries and honey.

Sober sex doesn't happen by accident. Pete and I had discussed whether we should go to bed together. Would it ruin our friendship? Well, at least for a few minutes! Making love by design rather than drunken accident made it all the more tender, special and thrilling for me. And I certainly saw stars – the glow stars on my bedroom ceiling, that is.

But as the months passed, it appeared that I wanted more from this relationship than he did. He was working full-time, so much busier than I was, and I didn't feel sated. For all-or-nothing Alice, feeling like a part-time girlfriend didn't go down well and I began to feel undervalued, unimportant.

The competitiveness and quips between us that had once been so much fun started to take on an edge and it became obvious that we weren't making each other happy. One day Pete bumped into Niall by accident and commented how alike they looked. I had never noticed any similarity, but this started me thinking. Were they alike, in looks or character? And then one day, at the end of summer, after yet another row he walked out of my life. The texts stopped.

I felt gutted, but I understood that I couldn't change him; I could only change myself. I had to accept that I wanted more of a full-time relationship, or certainly more than he appeared to be offering, and that we were not good together. We seemed to be bringing out the worst in each other rather than the best, firing up each other's insecurities instead of soothing them.

I reasoned that if I could give up the bottle, I could give him up; indeed, it appeared we had given up – and given up on – each other. But logic and emotion are two different things. It was hard. I prayed a lot. I cried and raged and talked and talked to my girlfriends. I went to lots of AA meetings.

And I didn't drink.

As time went by, I began to feel better. I realised I had been needy, perhaps stiflingly so. As much as I hated to admit it, that old adage about learning to love yourself before trying to love someone else was true. It dawned on me that much as I might like a man around, I didn't *need* a man to validate me. My heart was mending, slowly.

Anger. A dangerous place for a recovering alcoholic. We can drink on anger, and – most dangerous of all – anger over the most ridiculously trivial things.

Number Two son needed new tennis shoes. So all three boys and I drove the ten miles to our nearest shopping centre hoping to find a bargain. We chose a pair and waited twenty minutes to be served. The shop assistant went off and returned after a further fifteen minutes, saying, 'We ain't got 'em in a size four. Seven is the smallest. So I've brought those instead.'

Number One son giggled, but noticing my face contorting into a sneer, he prudently grabbed my elbow and steered me away.

Number Two son, oblivious to my smouldering rage, said, 'What about these Lacoste ones? I love the crocodile.'

'You must be joking,' I snapped. 'Have you seen the price tag? They're nearly fifty pounds!'

Number One son intervened again: 'He's a spoilt brat, Mummy, and you always give in to him. Let's go to a different shop.'

We traipsed to another store. Garish signs greeted us promising 'massive reductions on Reeboks'. We went in. I found a half-price pair in size four and triumphantly presented them to Number Two son.

'Reeboks are for girls,' he sniffed.

I was overcome with rage, threw the trainers down in a tantrum and marched off across the shop to find an assistant. We waited ten minutes to be served and, exasperated, I beckoned to the boys to leave. As we walked out, Number Two son pounced on a pair of size fours lurking by the exit.

'These fit perfectly,' he said timidly. 'And they're only ten pounds.'

Number One son was about to question the coolness of the brand, Le Coq Sportif, but sensibly kept his mouth shut. Just in time, as I was ready to explode again.

I drove home. A driver cut me up at a roundabout and I tooted my horn, raised my fist and screamed, 'Road hog!' at him.

'Mummy,' said Number Three son, who had been quiet until now, 'is that road rage?'

I spluttered and muttered, 'I'll show you road rage.'

The three nodded knowingly at each other, plugged in their earphones and turned on their iPods.

When I arrived home, I couldn't park outside my house, the way blocked by a large van. 'National Blood Service', it said on the side. 'Please give blood.'

Give blood? Draw blood, more like – I could have scratched the driver's eyes out, the way I felt. I parked down the road and stomped home, chuntering, 'God give me patience! Don't these people realise I'm trying to stay sober?'

It had been a long time since I had lost my temper, and the rush of adrenaline in me pressed the 'alcoholic' button. Suddenly I had a raging thirst. I deserved a drink after a morning like this, didn't I? A bottle of chilled rosé . . . or a nice, cool beer would do the trick. I sat there, obsessing about a drink, fighting it. My mobile went – a friend from AA.

'Hungry?' he ventured.

'No, angry,' I replied.

We went out to lunch across the road at the Three Swans. I attacked a deliciously bloody fillet steak, smothered in fiery English mustard. Nothing like a bleeding piece of meat to dissipate rage. I recounted my morning's antics.

After only a few minutes we were both giggling about it. My anger – and thirst – abated. All I'd needed was to share my feelings, get them in context. In the past, I would have acted on my seething rage and would have tried to quell it with a drink – and another and another – invariably ranting and raving about other people's appallingly selfish behaviour, totally oblivious to my own.

My bad behaviour aside, nobody died and nobody got drunk. It was close, mind.

CHAPTER FIFTY-ONE

SOBER SURFING

It was autumn half-term 2006 and Numbers One and Two sons had two weeks holiday rather than the standard one. Two weeks? How would I keep two active boys busy without spending a fortune I didn't have? I was pondering my dilemma when a friend piped up, 'I have a cottage at Appledore in north Devon you can have. Take them surfing. They'll love it.' I hugged him tight.

So there I was, standing on the pebbled shore on a sunny but blustery November day, looking out to sea, watching the white horses break. The tide was a long way out and I could just see the outlines of my boys bobbing about on their boards.

It was extraordinary how proficient they had become in just a few days, both of them managing to stand up during their first lesson, learning how to turn, to catch the swell at the right moment. Each evening they returned to the cottage, sun-kissed and exhilarated, full of surfer-dude talk until they crashed out, early, utterly exhausted.

Justin, one of their surfing instructors, saw me watching. 'Aren't you going to join us?' he asked. 'It's fantastic surf out there today.'

'It hadn't occurred to me,' I replied. 'Anyway, isn't it freezing? I'm not as hardy as the boys.'

'Funnily enough, we've got a wetsuit in just your size.

Come on, surprise them. I'll find you the suit and a board and we'll get going.'

'But I've never surfed before!' I protested.

'Neither had your sons until a few days ago.'

Before I knew what was happening I was trussed up in a wetsuit and striding down the beach, board under my arm, quite the surf chick. There was no time for fear, but as we struggled across the pebbles, it occurred to me how much I had changed. When I was drinking, I wouldn't have considered surfing. I probably wouldn't even have been here to watch them; I'd have been holed up in some dark, dingy pub.

Justin showed me how to do a 'pop-up' – the intricate movement from belly-down to feet – and the interim move from belly to kneeling. 'Kneel as if you were saying your prayers, only lean forward and hold on.' Once I was in the water, I could see that prayers may well be a necessity.

He held my board while I struggled on. I was pleasantly surprised that the water in my wetsuit was not that cold. 'It's had all summer to warm up – that's why this is the best time of year to surf,' he said. As my board wobbled from side to side, he shouted over the crashing of the waves, 'You need to keep your weight centred. Surfing is all about balance!'

Quite, I thought, my mouth full of my first taste of seawater for years. I had been searching for balance all my life. Having been self-obsessed and self-centred for so many years, I'd gone totally the other way when I'd first sobered up. Much to my friends' amazement, I became so compliant and selfless I was in danger of becoming a doormat – equally unhealthy.

I was glad of the leash round my ankle, otherwise I would have lost my board in the crashing waves, so much bigger now I was here out among them.

'Watch out for the white water – if you're not paying attention, it can catch up with you and knock you off balance,' called Justin. A wave crashed over my board as I got to my knees and I slid off, head first, into the water.

'Spectacular wipe-out!' laughed Justin. 'Keep your feet inside the rails.'

'I specialise in going off the rails,' I yelled back. 'What are the rails?'

'The edges of the board. Keep your weight centred – that's the trick.'

A wave picked me up and I beamed at the exhilaration of riding it, albeit on my knees. As I stabilised myself on the board, my sons spotted me.

'Mummy, is that really you?' bellowed Number One son, his expression incredulous. 'Mummy, on a surfboard!' he shrieks across to his brother, riding a huge wave and spectacularly surfing along the 'tube', catching the white water as it broke.

Justin did a headstand on his board while riding a wave. Number Two son, a gymnast, followed suit. I marvelled that both my boys should exhibit such remarkable balance – in all areas of their lives – given what I'd put them through.

Come to think of it, I used to be a bit of a gymnast myself, legendary for my headstands – I recalled with a shudder that drunken day by the whirly pool, when I'd showed off my aptitude. For today, I thought I'd quit while I was ahead. I felt a real sense of achievement for having taken part – on the crest of a wave!

CHAPTER FIFTY-TWO

SERENITY SANTA

It was midnight on Christmas Eve. My second sober Christmas. I crept along the corridor to see if the boys were asleep. Peering through the frosted glass on their bedroom door I heard Number Three son giggling, 'Eek, look, there's a shape at the window.'

'Sure,' replied Number One son, sarcastically, 'and I suppose it has a hooded red cloak on too.'

Good idea, I thought, and began to rummage through the airing cupboard. Somewhere there was a Father Christmas outfit that used to clothe the mannequin in the hall at Avon House. Ah, found it, behind the mislaid crumpled damask napkins that had given up waiting to be ironed. I put it on, admired my reflection in the hall mirror and took deep breaths to stifle my giggles. As I looked into the mirror, I was temporarily dazzled by the twinkling lights from my alternative Christmas tree. I was proud of it. It was quite arty for me. It was a branch, part of a fallen tree rescued from Savernake Forest. Well, stolen, actually. I had dragged it along a muddy path and bundled it into the back of the ancient Merc and triumphantly driven it home with the boot open. I had rigged it up next to the jukebox, where it twisted up at a right angle along the ceiling and divided into three spindly branches. Suspended by fishing wire from the light fixture, Number Two and I had decorated it. We had opted for the minimalist approach of white fairy lights that faded on and off, clear glass baubles and shiny deep-red apples and pears coated in sugar-like glitter.

As I stood at the door, I felt as if I was looking into an enchanted forest. The magic of reality dazzled me. All my years of striving to manufacture and inhabit a fantasy world, driven by more and more alcohol- and adrenaline-filled highs, had blinded me to the beauty of normality.

I was struck by what this bit of dead tree signified for me: a new life, split branches depicting the three paths I could take. At any time I had a choice. One was drunkenness and despair; the second involved staying sober and not changing my behaviour; and the third, the right-hand branch, saw me changing my behaviour and improving the quality of my sobriety. I knew I was on the right path.

More stifled shrieks from the bedroom reminded me there was work to be done. I made a few Santa-like appearances past their bedroom door and retreated into the kitchen to finish the last of the wrapping and the stocking stuffing.

The kitchen was heavy with the aroma of cloves and cinnamon from the mulled fruit punch I'd made earlier. I smiled as I poured myself a glass. Earlier, after the carol concert, several friends had dropped by. They had commented on feeling tipsy after a few glasses of my winter concoction and were surprised to learn there was no alcohol in it, just cranberry and blackcurrant juice, slices of clementines, an orange stuck with cloves, a cinnamon stick, a pinch of ginger and a judicious dollop of runny honey.

A few drunken revellers meandered past the kitchen window, zigzagging across the road. One, complete with festive reindeer horns, missed the pavement completely and veered into the wall. He waved as he noticed me peering through the steamed-up windowpane.

'Happy Christmas,' he hiccupped, as he ricocheted off a parked car and disappeared down the street. Everything was quiet, save the rhythmical snoring of Number One son.

I lugged the three bulging red velvet stockings into the sitting room and over to the fireplace. On top of a large handmade wooden number 11 London bus stood a bottle of ginger ale, a single hollow-stemmed Georgian champagne glass, some chocolate coins and a few jellybeans. There was also a neatly written note. Holding it up to the flickering fire, I read, 'To Santa, here is your ginger ale (as you are a recovering alcoholic) and some lovely chocolates and sweets.'

Not for the first time that evening my eyes filled with tears. What a magical note, full of childlike, matter-of-fact acceptance. I climbed into bed in my Santa outfit and fell asleep.

CHAPTER FIFTY-THREE

FORGIVENESS

I am drunk. I alight from the train at Hungerford Station and reel home, my heels echoing in the clear midnight air. Avon House is lit up – there is a party in full swing. I pick my way through the bodies and the bottles down to the basement. Niall is sitting in half-darkness in the children's playroom, a giant claret glass in his hand.

'What are you doing here?' I ask.

'I've decided to move back into the basement,' he replies.

'You can't just do that,' I protest.

'This can be my bedroom.'

I think for a few seconds and then accept it. 'We'll have to find our old red bed. It may be in the garage.'

He stands up and we embrace. In that instant, I forgive him – and myself.

He follows me up two flights of stairs to my office. Guests, including several old boyfriends, move to one side to allow us through. I open the door. Two workmen, grey with plaster dust, are re-wiring my office, gouging the walls with drills, making new channels for the cable. We stand in silence and watch them. My whole body, from my hair to my heels, reverberates with the drilling. The workmen pack up and leave, closing the door behind them.

'We made a mess of things, didn't we, Queenie?' Niall says.

'Yes, we both made mistakes, amazingly big mistakes,' I reply.

We smile at each other and chink our glasses.

I open my eyes. I feel as if I have been running up a steep hill and have now reached a plateau and slowed to a steady pace. The clock tells me it's 6.50 a.m. and the dawn is silent. It is a full five minutes until I realise I've been dreaming.

Forgiveness tastes good. It seems fitting that today I have been sober exactly two years.

CHAPTER FIFTY-FOUR

SAS

The rain was dripping down the window. I lay in bed trying not to be awake. I knew I should be writing, but I wasn't. Thoughts were spinning round my head like a manic washing machine – worries, fears, anxieties that made my heart beat faster, made me sweat, made me *thirsty*.

For the first time in months the thought of a drink came into my mind. I wanted something to take the edge off everything. I thought of the euphoria I would feel after the first drink, the numbness before I blacked out. I wanted to silence the committee meeting in my head. I didn't want to think; I didn't want to feel.

The night before, my debit card had been declined at the Co-op. For just £3.32. I had to abandon my two naan breads and *crème fraîche*, hurtle home and scrabble through old handbags for loose change. Obviously I was up to my overdraft limit. And I was two years sober! This sort of thing was not meant to happen!

I was alone in the house. Even if the boys were there, what could they do? I thought of tossing a coin as to whether I should have a drink. There was at least one bottle of champagne in the pantry. The temperature of the fizz would be just right. I could almost feel the dancing bubbles on my tongue, pricking the back of my throat.

I knew there was no problem in the world that drinking would not make worse, but the coaxing voice in my head was getting louder. The compulsion – the *need* – to drink had long gone. Only occasionally, the desire to drink came back. There is a difference. There was nothing I could do about compulsion, but desire left me with a choice. I could give in to it or not.

Reluctantly I got out of bed. This would not do, duvet-diving at 9 a.m., obsessing about a drink. I needed to take action. I thought back to the AA advice: 'Don't pick up a drink, pick up the phone.' I rang my keep-fit buddies, Sue and Sue, 'Big' and 'Little'. We called ourselves the SAS – for Sue, Alice and Sue.

'Fancy a walk?' I asked.

'Sounds good to me,' said Little Sue. 'The rain has just stopped. See you in ten. Wrap up warm – there's a hell of a wind.'

I put the phone down and dressed quickly. I realised I was hungry and headed to the pantry for cereal. Where was it? Oh, yes, on top of the wine rack. I grabbed the gluten-free Vita Pro and looked at the packet. 'Protein-rich soya, rice and corn cereal flakes with honey and cinnamon.' Sounded good. A flash of gold caught my eye. I looked down and gazed just for a second at the shiny foil. Two bottles of fizz, Jacquart and Veuve Clicquot, both vintage. I closed the pantry door quickly and opened the fridge for milk. No whispering bottles in there, thank God.

The doorbell rang and I stepped outside to join my friends. It was one of those early spring days when we had already had all four seasons – wind, hail, rain, thunder, lightning and now blue sky. It was cold and we walked fast out along the road and past the marsh.

I walked with my eyes wide open, striding ahead, pounding the road.

'Hold on a minute,' said a breathless Little Sue. 'What's eating you? You're going like the clappers. I can't keep up!'

'I'm thirsty.'

'Don't worry, I've got some water in my backpack,' she replied.

I grimaced as we stopped, caught our breath and took swigs from the plastic bottle.

'I didn't really mean thirsty for water – I meant thirsty for a *drink*.'

Little Sue looked at me, her carefully plucked eyebrows almost disappearing under her black headband. 'Alice, it's only nine in the morning! Christ, do you still think about booze? How long is it now?'

We set off up a steep hill. It was as much as I could do to keep going. I felt sick. To take my mind off the hill, I did a calculation in my head. It was two years plus a month and a bit, I reckoned. Twice 365 plus 30-something.

At the top of the hill, as my breathing slowed, I opened my mouth and replied, 'Seven hundred and sixty days.'

The two Sues whistled. We marched on, arms pushing backwards and forwards, robot-like, fists clenched, bottoms wiggling – three women on a mission.

Resting for a moment, I looked around. My SAS sisters and I had become quite knowledgeable about the magnificent array of wildlife and flowers and shrubs around us. I could now tell my columbine from my chickweed. As the spring sun broke through, a herd of deer cavorted across a field in front of us.

Setting off again, my sensitive nose began twitching, detecting the unmistakeable, pungent aroma of foxes. Wild pale-yellow primroses peeked out between the horse chestnuts just beginning to sprout their sticky buds. An early gatekeeper butterfly settled on a cobweb that glistened with dew. Suddenly I realised all thoughts of alcohol had disappeared. The desire had vanished.

At the end of our circular march, we stopped at a café and sat outside in the pale sun drinking decaf coffee. I retrieved my childhood *Observer's Book of Wild Flowers* from Little

Sue's backpack and looked up the Latin names for old man's beard (*Clematis vitalba*) and cow parsley (*Aethusa cynapium*). We planned our next day's assignment – to find some *Salix aurita*, or pussy willow.

We were all three laughing, trying to pronounce the Latin names. It was clear none of us had done Latin at school. Little Sue, who worked in my local pub and saw me at my drinking worst, chuckled, 'I'd never have believed it a few years ago if someone had told me I'd see you planning an expedition to find pussy willow. Vodka, yes. But pussy willow?'

Later, as I strode home, I felt happy, joyful, heady and high – just as I used to after that first magical taste of champagne. If I'd had a glass that morning, it would have led to a bender. Thank goodness I had picked up the phone, not a drink.

CHAPTER FIFTY-FIVE

FAULTY WIRING

The irony of it. I am off to my local bookshop to sign copies of the updated edition of *Fabulous Fizz* and I can't touch a drop. The fridge is full of the stuff, chilling for the signing. Quick. Put the kettle on.

The doorbell rings. It's my old friend, Monsieur le Chauffeur, now Monsieur le Former Chauffeur.

'I arrived early for the book signing so I thought I'd drop in for a cup of tea,' he says.

I hug him, rather too tightly. 'Thank God you did. I could hear the fizz in my fridge calling to me. I was sorely tempted to open a bottle to calm my nerves.'

We sit down with a soothing cup of Earl Grey. He picks up the *Guardian* and starts reading. Looking over the top of the paper, he says casually, 'Tell me, do you think controlled drinking ever works?'

'It didn't for me, and I tried every trick in the book – not drinking in January, not drinking while I wrote a book, not drinking during the week, not drinking at the weekend, not drinking spirits, not drinking before six o'clock, not drinking when I had the children.

'Controlled drinking to an alcoholic is an oxymoron. It doesn't work. Oh, I had delusions of control, but they were short-lived. When I returned to my drinking, I always ended up drinking more and faster every time. My brain tells me that just one glass of champagne would be fine. And it

287

would be, if it was just one. But when did I ever have *one* glass of anything?' I realise I am ranting but can't stop.

'The "I've had enough" wiring in my brain is faulty – and, here's the rub, it always will be. I can't ever have a drink, not on high days or holidays or even book-signing days like today.'

I have his full attention now. 'Hmm. Have some more tea,' he says.

But he has opened the floodgates. Nerves make me gabble.

'I know that as long as I don't take the first drink, just the first one, I will be fine. A few AA friends who had given up for years found themselves right back where they started when they succumbed to the "just one drink" scenario. It's every alcoholic's obsession, you know, that one day we'll be able to drink like normal people.'

'Do we know any normal people?' he jokes, as I pause for breath.

'Normal people, as in non-alcoholics, don't feel the need to control their drinking. It doesn't cross their minds. Only people like me, with a drinking problem, feel the need to control it.'

Exhausted I stop and step down from my soapbox. He helps me pack the champagne into cases and we wander down the road to the shop. Almost immediately a customer approaches and buys a copy of my book. I hand her a glass of champagne and sign it to her mother for Christmas.

'What champagne will you be drinking this Christmas?' she asks.

'Well, my family love champagne, and if there is any left over from this signing, I'll probably take them some of this,' I reply, pointing to the bottles of Nicolas Feuillatte Grand Cru 1996 we had brought down.

Several more people arrive, including AA friends, who chortle at my situation. The other customers drink fizz. We indulge in flutes of ginger beer mixed with ginger ale and a squeeze of fresh lime.

Relieved it's all over, I walk home. Number Two son is standing on the doorstep. 'Did you have a good book signing, Mummy?'

'Really good, thanks. We sold fifty copies and I didn't have a drink.'

CHAPTER FIFTY-SIX

HANGOVER FROM HELL

I have the hangover from hell. It is 3 a.m. and I wake up, heart hammering, covered in sweat. My head is foggy and groggy, and my eyes feel swollen. My throat feels dry, and the mouldy-cardboard taste in my mouth makes me retch. But these days there is no permanent ice bucket by my bed – the only type of sick bucket for a wine writer.

I think back to the previous night. What on earth had I been doing? What a relief it is to be able to remember. I had spent the day with Pete at the arboretum at Westonbirt, marvelling at the magnolias, intoxicated by their milky vanilla scent, picking up stray pink petals and stroking them, soft as a baby's ear. The sun had been shining and I felt good. I hadn't clapped eyes on or heard from Pete in seven months, until I had bumped into him at an AA meeting.

As we walked through the trees, the conversation started gingerly, with me trying desperately to zip my mouth and let him talk about how he'd been. After half an hour or so we had resumed our normal banter of playfully interrupting each other, talking about the books we had read and how quickly or slowly our respective writing was going. We compared notes on our recovery, discussing the good days and the bad, and exchanged notes on who was still around in AA – those that had gone out drinking again and vanished or died.

We agreed we'd missed our banter. Hungry from the walking and the talking, we stopped at the Snooty Fox in Tetbury. I had cod with thick chips and mushy peas, washed down with lashings of Fentiman's ginger beer. We joked about how the evening would have been if we'd been drinking – the magnums of champagne and bottles of port lined up at the bar wouldn't have stood a chance. And no doubt we would have ended the evening climbing the stairs to the four-poster bed.

Instead, well fed, we'd laughed and chatted, grateful that not drinking didn't detract from our enjoyment. I decided to have a cigar, the Snooty Fox being the kind of hotel to stock decent brands. The first puff was delicious and I enjoyed blowing out the smoke and watching it swirl across the bar.

Our conversation suddenly somersaulted, touching on a hurtful incident around our parting. I decided I needed and deserved another cigar. At the bar, the hotel manager and a regular were playing spoof. 'Care to join us?' they asked.

'I love spoof,' I said. 'How many coins? I'll have to be quick – I'm here with someone.'

'Just take him his cigar,' replied the landlord.

'Can't,' I replied. 'It's mine.'

We played three games. The adrenaline surge when I won surprised me. I decided to have a third cigar and returned to Pete, boasting of my success. He stood up, ready to go, but I didn't want the evening to end and had ordered another cafetière of coffee.

'More, more, more!' he laughed.

'Yep! Two addicts together – what could be *more* normal?'

We drove home almost in silence, and he dropped me off. I thought to invite him in but decided against it. To have become lovers in the first place, when we had been such good friends, had probably been a mistake, I reluctantly told myself.

Hence this humdinger of a hangover – of the emotional, coffee and cigar variety. At this moment in time, it feels as toxic as any alcoholic combination. I gingerly get out of bed and think about the day ahead. I have to attend the funeral of a friend in AA at nine thirty, and at noon a crowd of boys will be arriving for Number Three's tenth-birthday party. I have a cake to make, games to get ready and – oh, no – dozens of balloons to blow up.

It occurs to me that I will always need to keep an eye on my addictive behaviour, to face the insatiable 'more, more, more' part of my character and learn to feel satisfied. I have to steer away from quick fixes. I resolve to give up men – and cigars – and concentrate on my writing. Well, for the time being anyway.

CHAPTER FIFTY-SEVEN

SNOWDROPS

I am standing in a sea of snowdrops, spread out before me like a white, shimmering mirage between the trees and the river, as far as the eye can see. I've been to see my therapist and am in a contemplative mood.

When I was drinking, I would head to the pub straight after every therapy session. The bottle of rosé never used to touch the sides. Anything to avoid having to feel, to contemplate my part in whatever we had discussed. Half cut, I was never capable of processing my feelings or resolving any of the issues we discussed.

Now I no longer have booze, therapy sessions are becoming more challenging – and a great deal more painful. I'm shocked to feel stomach-churning emotions washing over my senses daily. I used to become angry after the first few drinks, exuding an aggressive, bitter sarcasm. I now realise that the anger masked deeper emotions such as grief, loss, guilt, jealousy and rejection.

Today I feel sad. I'm starting the grieving process for the loss of my dreams of marriage and happy ever after. It is spring 2007, eight years since my divorce, and this is the first time I've let myself feel the loss.

In the early days of my marriage I was madly in love. I was amazed to have found someone with whom I could have so much fun, someone who was amusing, with whom I could laugh and cry, someone who would support me in my work, make be feel visible and valued. It's easy to forget all the positive things about a marriage when it ends in unhappiness and hatred. Ours had turned into a deluge of drunken rows, the clashes of inflated egos and debilitating competitiveness. In drink – and I was always 'in drink' – it became convenient for me endlessly to dredge up the bad times and ignore the good. Now my newly active psyche can be indiscriminate in its memory selection, especially after therapy. Sobriety has opened my eyes and given me the chance to look at the past in a more balanced fashion.

Standing among the snowdrops, I realise that my marriage was more like a viniferous conjurer's trick, an illusion, clouded by a haze of fine wine. The man I married had not lived up to my childlike – and thus unrealistic – expectations. Drinking had stunted my emotional development. Despite growing older in years, I had lacked the emotional maturity to sustain a relationship.

I'm crying and the blanket of snowdrops is blurred around the edges. The scene in front of me looks more like a lake of snowdrops floating in champagne. It occurs to me that I'm not out of the woods in terms of recovery from alcoholism. I also need to acknowledge the demise of my relationship with fine wine, especially champagne, the real love of my life. I think of my father, who taught me how to appreciate it. I know he would be proud to see me facing my drink problem. I can see his smiling face and cheeky bearded grin as he salutes me, glass raised.

I realise with a start that my foot is sinking into the muddy path. This walk was a spur-of-the-moment decision and my high-heeled lace-ups are struggling to cope. I have visions of being sucked into a bog. Death by snowdrops? I move to firmer ground.

I find a church, sit down. The old, musty smell envelops me. I feel safe, held, cherished, and no longer alone. Sun streams through the windows and dances on the carved eagle on the lectern.

And I realise that it really is OK to experience all of these feelings. As I embrace them, I feel better, stronger, more powerful, like the eagle. I don't need to run away from emotions any longer, like I'd done when a little girl in France. I know these gut-wrenching feelings will pass – indeed, in only the last few hours, my grief has begun to change shape into acceptance. Magically, I feel full of hope, content to be sitting in a sun-filled church surrounded by snowdrops.

As I'm leaving, I glance at a leaflet in the church porch. I learn that snowdrops were used by the ancient Greeks as an antidote to poisonous drugs. I know I'm in the perfect place today.

CHAPTER FIFTY-EIGHT

READING THE LEAVES

'Floral, like a summer's day,' I jotted down in my notebook. I sniffed again. What was that elusive aroma? I took another slurp and let the liquid roll around my tongue. Suddenly the memory came back. Yes, definitely roses – like Turkish delight, I decided, as I spat into the sink and watched the copper-coloured liquid disappear down the plughole.

On to the next one. Concentrate. Deeper, more orangey-brown in colour. Was that a hint of nuts? But what kind? Hazelnuts? No, not hazelnuts. Not bitter enough for walnuts. Something softer, creamier, like macadamia nuts – but not quite. I closed my eyes. Chestnuts! That was it – toasted chestnuts. As a little girl, I used to eat them with salt on.

Only six more to go. To think I used to taste a hundred wines most days. I need not have worried that my taste buds would be out of practice. Although I'd been slow to start this morning, after the first few all the adjectives came flooding back, sometimes in a strange order, admittedly, but it was reassuring to know that I'd not lost my skill. It felt good to be tasting again.

I stopped and put the kettle on. How lucky I was, I reflected, looking out of the window, that I had a talent I could still use. In sobriety my taste buds were sharper than ever. No more furry tongues, thank God.

It must have been divine intervention that had made me

wake up one morning and decide to write to a tea company offering to write their tasting notes. To my surprise, they'd agreed with alacrity. So now, instead of starting the day with vodka, I start with a cup of tea. This then, legitimately, leads to another and another – until it is time to boil the kettle again.

I couldn't have predicted this twist of fortune from the tea leaves.

CHAPTER FIFTY-NINE

THREE FOR A GIRL

I am walking through a field of clover. It's summer 2007 and the early-morning dew is soaking through my new walking shoes, which are making a satisfying squelching sound in the wet earth. To my left, the ruins of Pembrokeshire's Carew Castle rise out of the mist. I'm convinced I can see ghostly figures manning the turrets, pale faces at the windows.

I blink, and as I open my eyes again a sharp ray of sunshine peeps through the clouds and dazzles me, casting silent, hopeful new daylight across the fields. A solitary fisherman stands on the causeway, casting his line into the swirling estuary.

I climb a stile into a leafy lane, the hedges brimming with pink and white dog roses. A scent hits me. Fox? No, it's a different kind of pungency, similarly earthy but fresher, sweeter. It reminds me of something, but what? Garlic mushrooms pop into my head. That's it. It's wild garlic, growing in abundance on the banks.

Crossing another stile, I enter a newly planted field of corn. Rows of sprouting shoots stand in formation like miniature ballerinas in green leafy costumes, swaying daintily in the breeze. I pause to watch a tiny spider breakfast on what looks like a bluebottle four times its size. The web, glistening with dew, reminds me of the Spirograph patterns I used to draw as a little girl.

Two and half years ago I wouldn't have woken up bright-eyed and bushy-tailed like this. I would have come to nursing a horrendous hangover, got the daily retching over with and be planning my first drink to numb my shame-soaked thoughts.

I'm on the way to the village shop to buy a newspaper. In my drinking days I hardly read at all, aside from the occasional wine book or Sunday supplement, bloody Mary in hand on my perch in the pub. I wasn't interested in what was going on in the world around me at any level – in nature, politics or other people's lives. As far as I was concerned, I was the centre of the universe. I worked on a need-to-know basis. Unless something directly affected me or my next drink I wasn't interested.

Thank God I'm not still stumbling down that old path. My eyes are open and I'm grateful someone showed me a different way. Now I can take simple pleasures in something as banal as going for a walk and marvelling at the beauty around me. It doesn't come much more beautiful or uncontrived than this, a castle set against rolling green fields and an effortlessly natural powder-puff sky.

Taking a different route back to the holiday cottage, I cross a field of lambs. They stand in a line, defiantly baa-ing at me. I open my mouth and baa back. After a few minutes I cannot baa any more for laughing, the tears tumbling down my cheeks. I scour the field for a black sheep, but there isn't one. I'm glad I'm no longer the black sheep today.

The next field is full of Jersey cows with Maybelline-long eyelashes. They would look good in mascara. They are friskier than the lambs, hoofing it down the field after me. Fear creeps in – are they bulls? – and I quicken my pace. Glancing behind, I realise they're close. I can see the milk whites of their eyes. I am convinced one has steam puffing out of its nostrils. Fight or flight?

I recall a farm holiday in Wales as a child, and being

frightened of the cows. 'Stand your ground and look them straight in the eye, they'll soon back off,' laughed the farmer.

Taking his advice forty years later, I whirl round to face the Jerseys – and christen my new shoe in a fresh, organic cowpat. No matter. I didn't get sober to be intimidated by a bunch of cows, I tell myself, standing fast. Face the fear and do it anyway. One beast bucks and hoofs backwards. Like line dancers, the others follow suit. I heave a sigh of relief and walk backwards for the stile, pirouetting at the last minute and stumbling over it.

I sit at my desk in the cottage looking out over the garden, the castle in the background, the sweet aroma of cowpat rising from my shoes. On the lawn there are three magpies. 'One for sorrow, two for joy, three for a girl,' runs the song in my head.

I always thought I would have four children. I have my three boys – is this a sign, 'three for a girl'? Probably not. At forty-six, the chances of having a daughter are pretty slim.

Then it comes to me. The girl is me – the happy little girl in me who was lost, drowned in alcohol, little Alice who was terrified every time big, angry Alice neglected her and staggered off on yet another bender.

I feel blessed to have rediscovered me.

ACKNOWLEDGEMENTS

Many people helped in the creation of this book. Thanks to Gill Morgan of *The Times* and Sue Peart of *You* magazine, who both suggested I write it; my agent, Ben Mason, of Sheil Land Associates, who sold it; Ian Marshall of Orion, who bought it; Steve Wyatt, who knocked the copy into shape; Jenny Ford, who helped and fed me; Pam Garraway, who tamed the computer when it went wild; Chris Razey, who tirelessly encouraged me; therapists Jacqui Smith and Tove Frisvold, who kept me sane; Sue Court and Sue Arkell, who kept me fit; Amanda Searle, who photographed me; my sister Juliana, who made me laugh when I cried; and my AA friends, who kept me sober.

Other people who deserve special mention are James Barnett, Big Chris, Bo and Charles, Marie Claire Brind, Hilary, Mikey Chinner, Klem Cowan, Jeremy, Paddy Lennon, Nigel Perrin, Reading Jim, Anna Valentine and Penny Wark.

Finally, thanks to my mother, who never stopped believing in me, and my three sons, who helped me retain a sense of humour.

USEFUL CONTACTS:

AA Helpline 0845 769 7555
  www.alcoholics-anonymous.org.uk
Al-Anon Helpline 0207 403 0888
  www.al-anonuk.org.uk
www.highsobriety.co.uk